THE CAVE:

PREPARATION

FOR TRANSFORMATION

BY JOSEPH SHREWSBURY

Printed in the United States of America

First Printing, 2015

ISBN 978-0-9963096-0-8

Two Caves Publishing

13228 Ferguson Forest Dr.

Charlotte, NC 28273

DEDICATION

This book is dedicated to everyone who visited the cave with me,

who asked the questions,

and who shared their stories.

You are the first of many.

ACKNOWLEDGEMENTS

I want to thank Sarah Godwin for the countless hours spent reading, providing feedback, and reading again, in order to keep the characters believable and the story consistent, and for her exhaustive note-taking in the cave.

I also want to thank my wife, Nancy, for allowing me to hide out in the evenings to work on the book and for always encouraging me to keep going. Your patience during the process deserves its own chapter.

Finally, I want to thank all of the people who hung out with me to discuss ideas, conduct experiments, and inspire stories. Since you are all prophetic, you know who you are.

TABLE OF CONTENTS

FOREWORD

This story began in early 2012 after a conversation with the Lord. The Lord reminded me about the years of King Ahab in 1 Kings 18 when Obadiah hid one hundred prophets in two caves. Obadiah was an administrator to the king. He worked as a businessperson in the government, but he was called to release a powerful prophetic force into the world.

The Lord told me that He is raising up hundreds of prophets who will serve in business, government, education, the media, and the arts, releasing their prophetic insight and wisdom into the places they work. He told me that now is the time to train the prophets and get them ready to be released from their caves—these prophets will build up the land, move in power, and speak words that will transform the world.

With that small revelation, a few friends and I began a journey that changed our lives. This book is a result of that journey. Together, we discovered many of the pitfalls of moving in power. We found that the foundation for building a strong and lasting prophetic community is to develop Christian maturity—the fruit of the Spirit.

We also discovered that speaking words alone was not enough. There is a requirement to step into what is being shown and to take action. It is the action that shows the degree to which one believes a prophecy. We found ourselves being tested in the fruit of the Spirit as, at the same time, we were being required to demonstrate our faith.

As you read, you will get a glimpse of the first steps to becoming a prophetic voice like the "Sons of Issachar" prophets spoken of in 1 Chronicles 12. They were men who knew the times and who knew what to do. They were practical prophets. They were able to access wisdom from God and were then able to translate it into actions that brought about the intent of the Lord. They were recognized by those around them as being beacons of hope in times of trouble. They were watchmen, intercessors, and warriors.

This experiment that began in 2012 has now become a complete course for those who are called to exhibit transformational power in their business, job, school, or family. The pages you are about to read are an outline of that course and a taste of many of the principles that we have uncovered.

Joe Shrewsbury, 2015

If you are interested in participating in the next course, please send an inquiry to JoeShre@obadiahfellowship.com

8 THE CAVE

INTRODUCTION: "ONE OF MANY"

THE DISCOVERY

The entrance to the cave was well hidden. It was obscured by a couple of magnolia trees, and was as far away from the main community as you could get and still be considered a part of the community. Hardly anyone ever stumbled upon the cave, so only those who were invited crossed the dark threshold of the entrance. It was here that I first met the teacher.

I had heard the call, faintly at first. I don't exactly recall, but it seems that the first time was in a dream. I didn't dream much at the time, so it was not clear if I had actually heard it or if I had just eaten some spicy food before bed. But before long I began hearing it while I was awake. Not only would I hear the faint whisper of my name followed by the words, "You are one of the many," but I began to get flashes of visions. There were trees and clear blue skies. As the visions grew clearer I saw myself walking along a row of dogwoods and then stumbling down a steep ridge, I would find myself in a hidden dip in the terrain. This is where the magnolias stood guard over the entrance.

I had never thought of myself as a prophet. I still don't, really. I am not really comfortable using that word when talking about myself. In fact, I'm not comfortable even talking about myself. I guess it is my personality. I prefer to remain hidden in crowds. At church I teach Sunday school for young adults, but I've never really sought out duties beyond that. At work I like to do a good job to be recognized by my employer, but I stay "under the radar", as they say. I don't crave overt recognition from my peers as long as I know I am appreciated for my good work. So hearing that I was "one of the many" piqued my curiosity. I knew I recognized the voice, but I had no understanding of what He was trying to tell me.

It was a little over a month before I finally found the place. I was taking a route home from work that was not familiar to me. The traffic report said there was major road construction on my normal route, so I decided to try what I thought was a shortcut. I was traveling along a two-lane highway when I noticed, off to the right side of the road, a long row of dogwood trees. The similarity to the visions was so strong that I knew it couldn't be a coincidence. I parked my car at the side of the road and began walking just inside the tree line. After traveling a couple hundred yards I noticed a dip to one side of the trail. I decided to venture down, and I nearly lost my footing on the way, catching myself on a sturdy magnolia tree.

Then I saw it. At first I thought it was a shadow, but it was at the wrong angle to the light. It was the entrance—the door to a future I never imagined I could experience. From the midst of the darkness of the entrance to the cave I heard a voice—a different voice—say to me, "You are one of the many." Then he stepped out of the shadow and I saw a man of medium height and build, with a scruffy beard and hair that was slightly more gray than brown. He had bright blue eyes and a smile that would disarm a storm trooper. He spoke again to me. "Hello, Jason. I've been waiting for you. My name is Obadiah. Follow me." With that, he turned and disappeared into the darkness of the cave.

THE CALL

I am not the type of person that will typically follow a stranger into a dark entrance to a dark cave in a remote area of town. I don't know anyone who is that type of person. It was insanity. Yet I found myself walking straight to where he had disappeared. I felt a strong urge to turn and run, as any normal person would do, and yet I could not get my feet to cooperate. They kept moving me closer, step by step, into the apparent oblivion that was before me. Suddenly, just as the darkness was so thick that I could see almost nothing, I stepped through some sort of transition and there was blinding light everywhere.

It took a few moments for my eyes to adjust, but when they did I saw Obadiah standing there in front of me again—blue eyes blazing in the light. He offered me a seat and I sat down. I realized that I was not in a cave as I expected, but in a large room. I glanced around the room, still getting used to the bright light, and I noticed the furniture scattered throughout. There were easy chairs, sofas, and cushions all around the walls. On one end, there was a large whiteboard, complete with new markers and an eraser. In a corner was a coffeemaker and a large garbage can. There wasn't much else in the room and it was clear that its purpose was for meeting with groups of people and for conversation. It wasn't quite a classroom, but it wasn't a lounging area either. It seemed designed to build relationships while learning.

I heard Obadiah walking across the room and I turned to see him moving to the corner. "I'll get you a cup of coffee," he said. "You like cream and sweetener, don't you?" I was stunned that he seemed to know so much about me. Normally, my first thought would have been that I had just followed someone who had been stalking me into a secluded cave where my body would never be found. But, for some reason, I had no fear. In fact, I was feeling peace at a deeper level than I could recall ever feeling. I replied, "Thank you. Coffee would be great about now." I paused and then added, "Do you mind if I ask you what is going on? I don't feel any fear nor do I sense any danger. Yet what I have experienced the last few minutes is confusing at best and unsettling at worst."

Obadiah remained quiet while he prepared my coffee and I knew it would not be appropriate to speak again until he answered. As he brought my cup to me he replied, "Today is the day that you receive your calling to become one of the many."

"I love a good mystery as much as the next guy," I said, "but I have no idea what you are talking about and I feel like I am not going to get many clues. Who are the many? What are the many? Help me to understand."

Obadiah sat in a comfortable chair across from me. "We are in historical times. You know from your experience in church that we are in the time of the Great Harvest, or we will be very soon. This harvest will come, but it will be during a time of darkness. We are about to enter into the times of Isaiah 60 and Joel 2. These times will require an army. The army will appear to be normal people living normal lives, but the Lord is raising up an army of prophets to release His Word into the darkness. There are many in this army. You are one of them."

"Prophets?" I asked. "Are you trying to tell me I am a prophet? I don't know about that. I will speak encouraging words to people now and then, but I am not anything like a prophet. I don't have the beard or the hair, and I don't handle rejection well. I may not be the person you were expecting."

"You're exactly who I was expecting." He replied. "In fact, you are a little late getting here. He started calling you over a month ago, and even showed you exactly how to get here. What took you so long to answer?"

I knew by the grin on his face that he was poking fun. I generally don't like to be teased, but this was different. I could sense that he had a genuine concern for my well-being, and that he was simply breaking some of the tension that had been building. I laughed out loud. "It wasn't my slowness that is the problem. You put this place so far out that it just took a long time to get here." I could see he was pleased with the banter and I slipped into a sense of ease talking with him.

He continued, "You are one of the prophets in this army of many. There are many roles and many posts to be filled. Your assignment is in the place where you already live. Your job, your home and family, and the people you typically come in contact with while going about your business. For now, that will be your scope of authority. Later..." He paused, and I could tell he was deciding if he wanted to share more.

"For now, that part of the future is not important. The task at hand now is to get you and the others ready. There will be a harvest in the midst of the darkness, but there will be intense warfare and resistance to deal with. Very few are ready. We must teach you and we must do it quickly." He had a look of determined urgency on his face. "Time is short, so let me tell you what we would like to offer to you."

I leaned forward. I could feel that the next few words could shape the rest of my life. I listened and was captivated by his proposition.

"The group training begins on Saturday morning. Your calendar is free for the next twelve weeks. This training will prepare you to become one who walks in the office of prophet as a part of a five-fold apostolic team. You don't need to worry about not fully understanding what that means now. It will be made clear later. Your part now is to decide if you want to become a prophet.

"There is much to learn in a short time. The result is that you will be a leader like the sons of (Issachar)—men who knew the times and knew what to do. They were mighty men of valor and were recognized by all who knew them to be extraordinarily wise and relevant.

✓ "You will be given an impartation of hope in the darkness. *is narrow and few will go*

But the road will not be easy. There will be many lessons to learn, and some of the lessons will require you to overcome strongholds from within and resistance from without. You have what it takes. We have seen it within you. Yet it is your choice to make."

I sat back and took a deep breath. This was a lot to take in. Issachar? Darkness? Harvest? Less than a half hour ago I was just trying to find a quicker way home and now I found myself having to decide about my part in the workings of God. The adrenaline was flowing so fast now that the coffee was of little consequence. I put the cup down and asked the most important question I would ever ask.

"If I decide to become one of these sons of Issachar things, how do I start?"

Obadiah smiled at me and simply said, "I will see you here at 8:00 am on Saturday."

18   THE CAVE

CHAPTER ONE: THE CAVE

GATHERING

I pulled into the clearing at about 7:45. I had driven this route home from work every day since the first encounter with Obadiah, and I found out there was a clearing hidden near some mulberry trees that provided room for about a dozen vehicles. From the road it looked like a break in the middle of the woods, but once I pulled into it I found that it had been covered with parking gravel at some time. Someone clearly intended for people to be able to park here.

As I pulled in this morning, there were two cars already parked there. Apparently, I wasn't the only one who had been scouting the area. I left my car and started back to the road where I originally noticed the dogwoods and started the short walk to the cave. The weather was a little chilly, but the skies were clear. It promised to be a very good day. As I walked past the magnolias into the cave entrance, I again experienced the same total darkness for a few steps until I was met with blinding light. Then I was in the room again.

While my eyes were adjusting, I heard voices talking. I recognized that Obadiah was asking what someone liked in their coffee. But there were three additional voices as well. My eyes began to clear—it seemed to be a little quicker this time—I saw two men and a woman standing near the coffeemaker with Obadiah. He had his back to me, but he called out, "Welcome, Jason. I'm glad you chose to come."

"I didn't realize you were giving me a choice," I laughed.

"We all have a choice in everything we do. Sometimes we merely opt for the default choice when we don't engage our mind and emotions in the process."

He doesn't waste any time, I thought. Or mince words, either.

By this time the others had turned to look at me. We all sized each other up and then decided a smile would be appropriate. I had a feeling I was going to get to know these people more than I usually care to. The woman was standing with her shoulder touching one of the men, and I guessed that they were married. She was slightly taller than medium height, but she didn't really look too tall either. Her hair was dark and about shoulder length, and her brown eyes were trying to conceal a quick wit and sense of humor. Her husband was about a foot taller than her, and I caught myself thinking the two of them could give birth to a very good basketball team. Realizing they probably hear that way too often, I dismissed the thought. He also had dark hair, almost jet black. He wore stylish glasses and somehow I perceived that he was a successful businessman. It may have been the clean casual way he was dressed and the way he stood, as if he was about to propose an idea.

"Hello. My name is Jason. How are you?"

The man spoke. "Hello, Jason, I am Mike and this is my wife, Catherine. I am doing well. It is great to meet you. We've been waiting a few weeks to get started, and it is exciting to start meeting the rest of the group."

"A few weeks? I hope I wasn't the last one that everyone was waiting for." I realized I had ignored the sound and visions for nearly three weeks. I suddenly felt a little embarrassed.

As if reading my thoughts, Catherine quickly piped in, "We don't know who the last person was, nor does it matter. It gave us some time to get childcare arranged. Friday night is now the official 'go to grandma's house' night. As long as we are out of here by noon, this will work out nicely."

I glanced over to the other man and he immediately smiled and said, "Hi. I'm Andre. It's good to have you on board."

"Hi, Andre. It's good to be a part, I think." I wasn't sure what to make of Andre. He seemed friendly enough and yet there was a hint of hesitancy in his stance that made me feel like he didn't really want to be there. He was slightly taller than average but not as tall as Mike, and he had a little darker complexion than the rest of the group that revealed his melting pot heritage.

Just then we heard footsteps at the door and another woman walked in, blinking and covering her eyes.

"Ow!" she exclaimed. "Why does the light do that? How can it be so dark and then suddenly so bright?" I had never thought about it, but now that she mentioned it, that was a good question. "Is that coffee I smell? Where is it?" She looked around as her eyes adjusted. "Oh. There it is." She made her way toward us. "Hello, everyone. I'm Maria. Where're the coffee cups?"

Maria was a younger woman of medium height, and seemed to have some Hispanic features in her face. Her manner didn't seem bossy. She was more like a party waiting to happen. I could tell that she never met someone who wasn't immediately a friend, and her demeanor inspired joy in everyone around her.

Then two more people came into the room. There was an older man—perhaps in his late 60's—who was about average in height, had a slight build and gray hair. We found out his name was Jerry. The other person, Hayley, was a woman who was shorter than average, had bright red hair, and seemed to quietly take everything in.

Obadiah offered coffee to all the rest of us, and we sat down with drinks in hand and waited for him to speak. Mike and Catherine sat together on a loveseat. Jerry and Hayley sat on opposite ends of an oversize sofa next to the loveseat. Andre sat in an easy chair closest to the door. Maria and I sat in easy chairs between the sofa and the door, and across from Obadiah and the whiteboard. Maria pulled over an ottoman and rested her feet. Obadiah began to speak.

"I'm glad you all made it. There are a few empty chairs for those who were invited and chose not to be a part. Everyone has a path to travel and a time to travel it. Given what we are preparing for, it is important that everyone has the choice to participate or not.

"I want to provide a few ground rules and then give some background information. First, this is an interactive time of practical learning based on sharing each other's insights and experience. That means that you will be expected to participate in discussions. However, I know that some of you will find sharing very easy to do, and others are going to be more reserved. That is okay, as long as you participate where you can.

"Second, you don't share what happens here outside of the room. There will be times of sharing experiences where many of you will open up with very personal thoughts and emotions. When that happens, the group must agree to cover each other with confidentiality. If you are not able to do that, then you are not ready for this calling.

"Finally, be honest and open about yourself. As you will soon see, everyone in here has a strong prophetic gift, so you aren't fooling anyone. Don't be worried about anyone breaching your trust, because we agreed in the second ground rule that everything remains in the room. If you don't think you can abide by these ground rules, then you are free to leave now and no one will think the worse of you."

We all sat and nonchalantly glanced around to see if anyone would leave. Everyone sat motionless. Obadiah continued.

"Does anyone have any questions so far?"

I spoke up, "When I first met you, you said, 'We must teach you and we must do it quickly.' Now I'm here and there is only you. Who is the 'we' you were speaking of?"

Obadiah smiled with a twinkle in his eyes. "That will be made clear later. Patience, as you will learn later, is a key to your future."

"Are there any other questions?" Obadiah turned toward Hayley and looked at her. "The question you have will help everyone if you ask it."

My immediate thought was, "That is creepy...or really cool. Probably some of both."

Hayley blushed and asked, "You said everyone in the room has a strong prophetic gift. When you and I spoke at our first meeting you talked about prophets. Is there a difference?"

Obadiah was right. That question was exactly what I would like to know. This is going to be an interesting twelve weeks.

PROPHETS

Obadiah smiled at Hayley and began speaking.

"That is a great place to start. You are all believers and you are all very familiar with the Bible. You already have some ideas about prophets. I'm guessing that most of you immediately think of bearded men in robes with angry faces and fingers pointing."

I remembered my comment at our first meeting about not having the beard or the hair and I blushed a little. I didn't know if that was a good-natured jab at me, or if we really all thought the same.

"We are going to get to know each other over the next few weeks, so now is a good time to start. Why don't we take a few minutes and let you discover what you already know? All of you are Christians and have experience with scripture. Split up into groups of two or three and see if you can think of some difference between prophetic gifting and being a prophet."

Everyone sat motionless for a moment, then Mike and Catherine glanced at each other and smiled because, as husband and wife, they knew that they already knew each other and didn't need an introduction. Maria immediately turned to her left and introduced herself to Hayley. Jerry was on the other end of the sofa and was right next to Catherine, so he asked if he could join them. That left me working with Andre to my right.

We all chatted softly, as if we were in the waiting room for a doctor for some reason. Every few minutes there would be a loud outburst of laughter from Maria and I got the sense she and Hayley weren't spending all of their time talking about prophets.

Andre and I scooted our chairs closer to each other so we could talk. He was still smiling and said, "Well, it looks like we're going to be doing all the work ourselves."

"I don't know." I said, "I think he is probably just trying to get us more involved in what is being taught. My wife is a school teacher and she says that engaging the students in the learning is a good practice to enhance the learning."

"That's what I mean."

I wasn't sure what he meant. "So, what do you already know about prophecy?"

"I know there were forty-eight prophets in the Bible, and seven prophetesses. I assume they all were prophetically gifted."

"But weren't there other references to prophets? Are those forty-eight just the ones that were quoted in the Bible?"

"I've never really researched it or thought about it. I never actually even counted them. I just looked that up on the Internet." I noticed he had some sort of tablet device with him.

"I wonder what it means to be prophetically gifted. Does that mean that some people are not prophetically gifted? How do you tell the difference?"

Just then there was loud sustained laughter from Maria and even Hayley was laughing. We all turned to look.

Obadiah seemed to enjoy that Maria was having fun. "Maria, why don't you share a little about what you and Hayley are finding so entertaining?"

Maria laughed again and then explained. "I've discovered that Hayley enjoys puns." Everyone laughed. "We were talking about prophets and prophetic gifting. It occurred to us that a prophet must be prophetically gifted. Somehow we started talking about prophets who used their prophetic gift for personal gain. That's when Hayley said that a prophetic gift can make someone a profit. P-r-o-f-i-t. Get it?"

There was a mixture of groans and laughter throughout the room. Obadiah seemed to genuinely enjoy that Maria and Hayley were having fun, and not taking things as seriously as the rest of us.

"Did anyone else come up with something as inspiring as that?" Obadiah asked.

Jerry spoke up, "I don't think anything can quite equal the level of insightfulness as that piece of wisdom, but we talked about prophets in the Bible. We don't remember exactly how many there were..."

"Forty-eight," Andre chimed in.

"Okay," Jerry said. "When we considered the forty-eight prophets in the Bible, we noticed that they all seemed to be called for a very specific time and purpose. That reminded us of what you told us in our personal encounters about the times we are in and how that is requiring prophets to be raised up. After that, the discussion went back to the idea of men with beards, living in the wilderness, and the other weird things from the Bible. We really hope that is not going to be part of our curriculum."

I joined in. "We didn't get much further than that either. When I came here, I thought I understood the basic teachings about prophets and prophecy, but I see now that I have just accepted it as a part of the Bible without really even trying to consider the implications. I'm not even certain I could define prophecy." I looked at Obadiah. "Will you help us get started? Are prophets and prophecy only important at specific times, or are they a part of the daily life in God's kingdom?"

Obadiah shifted in his seat to get more comfortable. "That is the question we will be seeking to answer throughout this entire course. Let me start with some foundational ideas."

✳ "At the most basic level, prophecy is seeing into the supernatural world of the spirit and communicating it into the natural. A prophet would be someone who does this. However, in the church we have further broken this down into stages. Some of this breakdown is biblically based, and some of it is practical observation, and some of it is simply tradition based on wrong interpretation. We know there are many who are called prophets that are not biblical prophets because they leave hurt and destruction in their wake. They claim to speak for God, yet the words they say do not reflect the nature of God and His love.

"In the New Testament we are told by Paul in Ephesians that everyone in the church may prophesy, and that we may do so for the purposes of building each other up, encouraging each other, and bringing comfort to each other. Because it is prophecy, this encouragement and comfort doesn't just come from kind words and a hug. It is based on some sort of revelation received through the spirit. That is what makes it prophecy, according to our definition.

"We also see in the book of Acts that there were some who were called prophets or prophetesses. They were recognized by their Christian brothers and sisters as having a greater level of gifting than other believers, and they had a track record of accuracy that built credibility. Therefore we know there are two ends of the spectrum."

"But, New Testament prophecy and Old Testament prophecy are different," said Mike.

Obadiah looked his way. "Are they? How so?"

Mike responded, "All New Testament prophecy was for building up, encouragement, and comfort. Old Testament prophets always spoke judgments to the people. The Old Testament prophets were directional, condemning, harsh, and a little scary. There wasn't any encouragement. They had to do weird things like walk around with no clothes, lay on one side for a year and then on the other side for a year. You just don't see that in the New Testament. You also notice in the Old Testament that there were just a handful of people who were prophets, but the New Testament enables every believer to be prophetic."

"That is an accurate depiction of the perception of most of the church today. I'm sorry I have to tell you that I disagree with most of that. It is true that the Old Testament prophets did weird things. But I don't believe their prophecies were not encouraging. Think about it this way. If the people to whom the prophets prophesied had listened to them and done what they said to do, then the destruction would not have happened. That is very encouraging. The only reason it did not encourage them is because they chose not to make a change.

"You also see prophetic acts in the New Testament. There is the example of Agabus tying Paul's hands and prophesying that Paul would be taken to Rome. That was a prophetic act. There were others, but I'm not going to tell all of them to you. There are some things you have to find yourself. In fact, this is a great time to look for some. Why don't you talk in groups of two or three and see what you can find. Try to pair up with someone different this time. Let's take about a half hour and then compare notes."

Since Maria was immediately to my left I turned to her and said, "You're someone different. Why don't you join with Andre and me?" She laughed and scooted her chair over close to us. Mike and Catherine decided to split up, so Catherine moved to sit next to Haley and Jerry moved over to the loveseat with Mike.

This time it didn't feel quite so much like a doctor's office. We all found ourselves talking in normal voices, but not so loud that we couldn't hear our groups. This time people were opening their Bibles or turning on their tablets with electronic Bibles. It suddenly began to feel more natural and we looked for examples in the New Testament like miners hunting for gold. Beyond that, I began to realize that I liked the people in the group. They had all made a positive first impression on me.

The time passed quickly and finally Obadiah called us back to attention and asked us what we found. Most of the answers described something that Jesus did as a prophetic act or a fulfillment of a prophecy. But some of the examples demonstrated some very creative thinking.

Catherine spoke for the first time. "I have one that may sound odd. I'm an artist and I look at things differently. But when I started looking for prophetic acts I had this thought that maybe the acts were not specific to prophets. So I just started to look for anything that demonstrated a spiritual truth. I saw in Acts 1 that the believers went to the upper room where they were staying and they spent all their time in prayer. After a time of this, the Holy

Spirit came and touched them with wind and fire. I thought this was a prophetic picture of how we can receive power. We go to a higher place in the spirit and devote ourselves to communication with God."

Obadiah's eyes lit up and he encouraged Catherine. "That is an interesting approach to recognizing prophetic acts. You are well on the way to grasping many of the deeper things we will be covering. I encourage all of you to challenge yourself to think differently. Many things can be prophetic acts, even those that are not intended to be so. There are prophetic messages everywhere. As you begin to access the eyes that see into the spirit, you will find a wealth of revelation that you have been ignoring."

"So, is this only available to us who live in the New Covenant church?" Jerry asked.

Obadiah answered, "The Father created everything at the beginning and established how the natural and spiritual interact at that time. You are asking if the prophetic is more widely available today than in the Old Testament days.

"When I look at the Old and New Testament, I see the same thing happening in both places. I also see lots of prophets in the Old Testament. For example, Samuel prophesied to Saul that he was to go to a certain place. On the way there he would run into a band of prophets coming down the hill and he would prophesy. If you look at the picture, you basically have dozens, if not hundreds, of prophets returning from a prophetic conference. When Saul met them, the spirit overtook him and the spirit came upon him and he also began to prophesy. We also know that at the time of Elijah, there were one hundred prophets hidden in caves. This was after Jezebel wiped out hundreds or thousands of prophets. There have always been prophets, and every community should generally have at least one person who functions in that space.

"I can't prove this to you scripturally, but there are certainly clues like the ones I have just mentioned. When you look at the culture at the time that the Old Testament was being lived and written, you will see that there was not any sense of surprise at seeing prophets. Consider this. Is it likely that prophets were so abundant that every village had one or two prophets that people had come to recognize and depend upon? You can almost picture a villager that discovers his ox is sick. He turns to his son and tells him to go get the prophet to come and pray for the health of his ox. The prophet was the person that the village looked to for spiritual guidance and wisdom."

Mike asked, "Do you think this still holds true today?"

"I feel confident that the principle holds true today," Obadiah replied. "But many towns, especially the large ones and the so-called civilized ones have chosen to rely on false prophets and those who are not prophets at all."

Maria piped in, "May I ask a very important question?"

Obadiah turned and smiled. "Of course you can"

"I had a large coffee on the way here this morning and another cup after I got here. I really need to find a ladies room. Can we take a break?"

The room erupted with laughter. Obadiah pointed across the room and said, "Go through that door and you will find an alcove with restrooms on either side."

Suddenly it struck me. I couldn't believe I hadn't noticed before. This room was not at all like a cave. It had four walls and a smooth floor. There were recessed lights in the ceiling. Andre had Internet access. Now I just discovered it has toilets with hot and cold running water. While everyone was getting up to stretch and refill their coffee, I met Obadiah at the side of the room and asked, "Where are we, really?"

"We are in the training room."

A little perturbed by what might have been a wisecrack, I ventured on. "I mean where did this room come from? I entered an opening of a cave, and this room does not appear to be a cave."

"You entered through a dark opening. You assume it was a cave."

"It looked like it was covered by a hillside. Usually dark openings in the sides of hills are either caves or graves."

"You are still thinking in terms of the natural world governed by Newtonian physics. You will need to learn to broaden your understanding of creation. The places you will need to go and the things you will need to do can't be bound by such tangible thinking. This type of thinking will limit your ability to perform miracles."

Obadiah sat down in his large leather chair. By this time we had captured the attention of the rest of the group who were quietly finding their seats. Obadiah addressed the group. "Are any of you familiar with the principles of quantum physics?"

Maria quipped, "I've watched most of the Star Trek series and all of Stargate, so I guess I know more than most people."

A lesser man would have rolled his eyes, but Obadiah kept a straight face and simply said, "There is a lot to learn, yet." I sat back in my chair and waited for him to continue.

"Before God created the universe He was all there was. So where did He put creation?"

Everyone paused a moment trying to figure out if this was a trick question. "Inside of Himself?" Jerry ventured.

"Very good, Jerry. And what did He create it from?"

There were many guesses.

"His will!"

"His spoken words!"

"He created the stuff to make it from!"

Obadiah drew everyone back to order. "We read in 1 John 1:5 that God is Light. One of the definitions of His Glory is an empowered light. In the realm of quantum physics, string theory asserts that everything in the universe is made up of tiny particles of extra-dimensional fields of light energy. These are subatomic particles, meaning that they are smaller than atoms. We recall from our elementary science classes that atoms are made up of protons, electrons, and sometimes neutrons. The subatomic particles are what protons, neutrons, and electrons are made of. These subatomic particles have odd names like quarks, leptons, and so on. Each of these have unique characteristics and are held together by forces, one of which is gravity.

"Could it be possible that the quantum physicists are beginning to identify aspects of the fabric of creation that were made from the Light of God Himself? If so, then understanding some very basic physics principles can give us a great understanding of the supernatural world in which we are participants. I won't go into a lot of detail. You should actually research this for yourself. But let me give you a little bit of information so that I can answer Jason's original question."

Andre spoke up. "So scientists are starting to realize there is a spiritual and natural reality? What does that have to do with Jason's question?"

"Do you recall John's statement in Revelation 1:10 that he was 'in the Spirit'? Have you ever considered what that means? Most of us picture him sitting on a stone next to the beach singing hymns and studying the Bible, perhaps praying and interceding for the believers. That is our traditional understanding of 'in the Spirit'. However, he immediately says he heard a loud voice behind him. Like the sound of a trumpet. He doesn't talk about any sort of transition taking place that took him up to heaven until chapter 4 when he saw a door standing open. In that case, he specifically says this was 'after these things', meaning it was not at the same time. The same previous voice invited him up to heaven and again he said he was 'immediately in the Spirit'. This had to be a separate occasion because there would be no need to become in the Spirit if he was already there. John clearly went back and forth between two different places, and from chapter 1 it appears that he could go there whenever he desired.

"There is a scientific explanation for this in quantum physics. Do you realize that quantum particles exist as more than one state at the same time? There was a well-known experiment that proved quantum material exists both as waves, which can be likened to the spirit, and as particles, or physical matter, at the same time. The thing that determines if the quantum particles are waves of energy, which we can call spirit, or particles, which we can call natural, is if the particles are observed. It sort of brings new meaning to the concept of being under the watchful eye of God. He isn't watching us to make certain we don't sin. He is watching us to make certain we don't dematerialize.

"An offshoot of this same experiment shows us that there is no way to predict the exact location of any quantum particle at any given time. It is called the uncertainty principle. The material from which all things are created can be anywhere in the universe at any given time, unless there is an observer watching it. If we choose not to observe ourselves in the natural, then we can instantly be in that place with God. In practice, we can be in the natural, in the Spirit, or both places at the same time.

Michael looked confused. "You are telling us this because...?"

"First, and foremost, because you are all going to be people who see into the spirit. You are going to be people who really learn what it means to be in two places at once—the spirit and the natural. You will be working miracles, and delivering people from their pasts. It is essential for you to know that all of creation is waiting for you to release them into the celebration they are supposed to enjoy.

"Second, Jason asked where this room really is. I can tell you that if you want this room to be inside the cave, then that is where it is. But we can be in the cave and somewhere else at the same time, or in the cave, or somewhere else. The room exists somewhere. I am not really certain where we are at any given point in time. However, I know there is some kind of transition place at that doorway that takes me to the outside of the cave. You can call it a portal if that helps you. I simply call it the doorway."

I thought for a few moments. "So you are telling me that while we are observing each other in this room, we are not in the cave? Is that why we travel through the blackness?"

"Not exactly. I am telling you that you are in the cave and you are in this room at the same time. You are in both places.

Haven't you ever wondered how you can be God's hands and feet on earth and at the same time be seated with him in the heavenlies? You are in two different places at the same time."

"I think I have it, now," I said, though I was not really certain.

"Good. Let's wrap up for this week. Your assignment for the week is to consider what the primary tool is for the prophet. You have been a great group, if not a little too quiet. Same time, same place, next week.

Everyone began cleaning their coffee cups and restoring the room to orderliness. I finished my part before the others and decided to leave. Even though the time seemed short, there was a lot to consider. I shouted a goodbye as I stepped through the doorway. This time I may have imagined that I felt a tingle and wondered if I was being dematerialized and rematerialize

CHAPTER TWO:
TOOLS OF THE PROPHET

ALIGNMENT

It had been an eventful week. Without expecting it, I started to notice that I somehow seemed to know things in advance. It wasn't a result of a visit from God or from angels. It was far fainter than that. Many times I would see something happen and remember seeing it before. It wasn't quite déjà vu, because I would generally remember seeing it a few seconds before it happened. I first noticed it the day after leaving the "cave". I was in a restaurant when I looked over and thought I saw a glass falling from a table; then I realized nothing had happened. As soon as I turned my head away, I heard a loud crash and looked back to see a broken glass just where I had seen it fall before. At first I thought this was really cool. Then it struck me that I didn't have enough time to prevent it from happening and I wondered what good is a prophetic gift to see the future if you only get two seconds' notice.

As the week continued, I began to notice the prophetic beginning to open up for me. Not only would I see things just before they happened, but I would find myself knowing about personal situations of other people without them telling me. This was actually a bit scary for me. Some of what I suddenly knew was very heavy and I didn't know what I was supposed to do with the knowledge. Should I say something? Should I treat them differently? Ultimately, I decided to just begin praying for them and their secret messes. I don't know if it helped them, but it certainly allowed me to live in peace. I wondered if that was what Paul meant by bearing each other's burdens, or if the peace I achieved is what many Christians mean when they say they prayed until the burden lifted. Regardless, I found myself spending more time in conversation with God, or at least to the extent that I knew how to converse with Him. Most of this was answered in my next visit to the cave.

This week I drove through slightly muddy ruts to get to the parking area. It had been raining for nearly two days and it was still coming down hard. The walk along the dogwoods seemed shorter today. It may have been because I was trying to observe some quantum leap that would jump me into the opening of the cave. But since I still wasn't certain what to make of last week's lesson on quantum physics, it is a safe bet that the trip seemed shorter because I was running. Either way, I was glad to reach the magnolias and step into the darkness of the opening.

"Watch your step!" Andre called out as I stepped into the light. There was a puddle of water in front of the doorway. "Everyone has been shaking their umbrellas dry right in front of the door when they come in."

I stepped over the water and hung my raincoat on the coat rack near the umbrella stand. I puzzled for a few moments over the fact that the water made it through the portal. As I went to get a cup of coffee I looked around and saw that everyone was here except Mike and Catherine.

"Good morning, Maria. How are you?"

"I am fine, Jason. How about you?"

"I'm doing quite well, though I've had enough rain."

The casual conversation continued among the group for another ten minutes when Catherine and Mike came through the door out of breath. "We are so sorry for being late. Josh woke up last night with a fever. We had to run some medicine by my mom's house and check on him. He'll be fine, but I had to spend a few minutes comforting him." Mike added, "We still would have made it on time except that there was a fender bender on the way that slowed traffic. But we enjoyed a nice sprint from the parking area."

Obadiah welcomed them. "No worries. Time is relative anyway. What seems like twenty minutes in here could be hours, and what seems like hours could be just a few minutes. There is always plenty of time." We all glanced at each other with puzzled expressions. "As soon as Catherine and Mike catch their breath and get some coffee, let's get started."

A few moments later we were all seated in our familiar spots and Obadiah began speaking, "Do you remember the assignment from last week?"

A few of us spoke up, "What is the primary tool of the prophet?"

"What did you come up with?" *listening talking timing*

Again, a number of us had some responses, "Revelation." "The Holy Spirit." "The voice of God." "Faith."

"Okay. Those are all good answers, but not quite what I am looking for. Think of it this way. Let's consider a carpenter who is building a house. He or she will have the plans to show what the house looks like. He will have wood and nails for the building material. He will have his experience to guide him in the proper timing and technique. But the tools that a carpenter uses to assemble the house are hammers and saws, and a few others. So think again about a prophet and tell me what you think the tools are, and which one is the primary tool." *speaking + action*

I noticed wheels spinning in Jerry's head. "Well, then revelation would be like the wood and nails and the voice of God would be like the plans."

Hayley added, "...and the Holy Spirit would be like the technique and faith would be like his experience."

"You're getting there," Obadiah said.

Jerry continued in his line of thinking. "Then the tools would be the way the prophet delivers and builds the prophecy...which would be speaking it out."

"Very good!" Obadiah cheered. "Speaking is the primary way that prophecy is delivered. We also talked about another way last time. What was that?"

Mike joined in, "Prophetic acts. We spent a half hour looking for them last time. So which is primary—speaking or actions?"

"What would you say was primary?" Obadiah shot back.

"I would say speaking. We see example after example of people speaking prophetic words, but we see far fewer examples of prophetic acts."

Obadiah nodded, "Very good. While there are far more prophetic acts than most people recognize, speaking is more often associated with the intentional delivery of a prophetic message than acts alone. Many times, prophetic acts are accompanied by spoken words."

He continued, "Let me ask you a question. When a prophet speaks a prophecy and it happens as he prophesied, is it because he accurately saw the future or did it happen because he spoke it?"

Andre quickly answered, "I think it can be either or both."

"Good answer. Why can a word spoken or a prophetic act cause the thing to happen?"

Andre blushed, "I don't really know. That question just seemed like a trick question and that seemed like a good answer. I actually spoke without thinking about it."

The room erupted in laughter and a few people spoke up with "me too."

"I will make a note to be cleverer with my trick questions in the future." Obadiah grinned.

There was a pause while the room settled down, and then Maria blurted out, "Are you going to tell us or are you going to keep us in the dark?"

"I will get us started and we'll see if you begin to catch on," Obadiah responded, "I will start by making a statement that you all already agree with at some level, and then we'll keep digging deeper.

"Words have power. All words have power, regardless of who speaks them. You recall the old chant 'Sticks and stones may break my bones, but words will never hurt me.' That is wishful thinking and provides a catchy response, but the truth is that words have tremendous power to hurt and to heal. You don't have to be a prophet to speak words of power. The prophet's words simply have more power because of the authority from God that accompanies them. Do you recall how God created the universe?"

"He spoke it into existence. He said 'Let there be light' and there was light." Jerry answered.

"Correct. Yet we know that sound is the vibration of air against our eardrums converted into electrical signals that our brains translate into meaning. But there was no air in the beginning. How did God speak if there was no air to be moved by His vocal cords?"

We all looked at each other, having never really considered this technicality before now.

"Okay. You all look puzzled enough. The vibration of air that results in sound is a vibration of a specific frequency. Frequency is a fancy word for how fast the vibration moves back and forth. But the vibrations and frequencies are key to understanding creation and how words have power. When God spoke, He purposed within Himself to see something happen. He could see the result—what it looked like, how big it was, the color and shape, and where it would be. From this thought deep within Himself, He created a vibration of the energy from which all things are made that we spoke about last time. The creation of the energy vibrations at specific frequencies resulted in an ordering of quantum material to bring forth the universe and all that is in it. He spoke without air because the essence of speaking is not air; it is frequency of vibration. This is a key spiritual principle that a prophet must comprehend in his heart, if not in his head. As you speak in faith, born in a heart of communion with God, and do not doubt the outcome, your words will create the necessary vibrations to align quantum material.

"This is similar to what Jesus said in Matthew 21 when He told his followers that if we have faith and do not doubt, we can say to the mountain 'Be taken up and cast into the sea', and it will happen. The spiritual principle here is that there must first be belief in the heart—belief that has no doubt. We must be able to see the outcome and no other outcome."

Hayley asked, "What do you mean have faith and do not doubt? If you have faith, doesn't that mean you don't have doubt?"

"Not exactly, Hayley. You may have faith that God can do something. You may have faith that He can provide for you financially. You know all the scriptures and promises about Him being your provision. But somewhere in your heart there may still be doubt that He will do something. Just because I can open a door for you doesn't mean that I will open the door for you. We think of God in the same way. We don't understand His love for us, or for others, and we devise backup plans in case He determines we don't get the promise.

"We all act in faith every day, but we may also have divided faith. Most of the time we do not have faith for the outcome we really desire. We have faith that a loved one can be healed, but we also have faith that the sickness can continue. We have faith that God will provide for us, but we also have faith that friends or the government will help us out if God does not provide. The reason we rarely see miracles is because we have faith in multiple outcomes. Miracles happen when we see one, and only one, outcome.

"How many times have you begun praying for someone who was sick, and as you started you began rehearsing in your head the explanations around why God sometimes does not heal? That reveals where you heart really was. You know that God can heal, but you don't know that He will heal. So you make a back-up plan and leave the outcome to someone or something else."

I looked over and saw Catherine weeping silently. Obadiah also noticed. "Catherine? What is happening?"

With a faltering voice, Catherine whispered, "I am such a terrible mother. My little Josh was sick all night last night and this morning. All I did was give him some medicine and tell him he would get over it. It never occurred to me that he could be healed. As I listen to you, I realize that if I had faith and no doubt, Josh would be completely over his fever. Why didn't I do more?"

Obadiah looked at Catherine and Mike with compassion. "Josh is fine. His fever has already broken and his body is strong. This is not anything you should ever look back at. What you did or did not do in the past is gone. You operated from the level of revelation you had, and you did a good job as a good mom. As you continue to gain new understanding in these sessions you, and everyone in here, will have ample opportunity to look back at what you could have done. Don't fall for that trap. Look forward to the future and live in the present.

"There is always grace for the things we have missed in the past. That doesn't mean that we can undo what happened in the past, but it does mean that we don't need to undo the past. If we spend our time looking backward, we will not be able to change the present and the future. We are all so quick to internalize our failures to take action that we did not know was available at the time. From this we often accuse ourselves and speak words about ourselves that have power to hold us down. Matthew 18 teaches us that unforgiveness will keep the one who does not forgive in prison. When we do not accept forgiveness for ourselves, we lock ourselves into a dark prison that does not allow us to walk in peace and power.

"All of the past is forgiven. You must understand that all the wrong that you have done is forgiven, and all the good that you did not do is also forgiven. Holding on to sin and to missed opportunities of the past is a door through which doubt will enter. You may come to a place where you are completely convinced that God can do something on your behalf, but then you look at your past and convince yourself that because of what you have done, you doubt that he will do it. You determine that you don't deserve it, and so you begin looking for other options."

Mike reached over and gently held Catherine's hand. I noticed that Hayley's and Maria's eyes were glistening with sympathy for Catherine. I realized my jaw had dropped as I watched the interaction between Obadiah and Catherine, and I closed my mouth. I had felt a tingle when he said that Josh is fine. I knew it was more than consoling words. I pictured a little boy in red pajamas and a sweaty forehead looking at an older woman who had concern in her eyes, and I heard him ask if he could have some breakfast and watch TV. The tension around the woman's eyes relaxed and she felt the boy's forehead. She visibly sighed and hugged the little boy.

"Catherine," I ventured, "What was Josh wearing this morning?"

"He had on his red 'Flash' pajamas. That is his favorite superhero right now."

I gulped. "What does he usually do on Saturday mornings with his Grandma?"

"Usually, he'll wake up and she will make him his favorite breakfast. Then he'll turn on the TV and watch videos while playing with his Granddad."

My voice broke as I told her what I had just seen in my imagination. Catherine and Mike both began to cry and hugged each other as I described the boy and the woman in great detail. Maria made her way over and began to encourage Catherine and pray for her. Hayley stepped over and stood behind Catherine and prayed silently as Maria continued to minister to her. Jerry, Andre, and I just looked at each other and watched what was going on. None of us was sure what had just happened, but we felt that we had just learned important lessons.

FREQUENCY

After a while—I'm not certain how long—the room felt different. Mike and Catherine had transitioned from crying to laughing, and everyone else followed them. We first felt the relief physically, like we had just walked a couple of miles at a fast pace. Then as the laughter subsided, the room got quiet and we just sat there and waited. We didn't know what we were waiting for, and when it eventually came we didn't really know what it was.

A tremendous peace came over us as one. I still can't describe it exactly. The sense of peace was like the feeling you get right after a time of intimate worship, but it was also like the resolve a team of special ops warriors feel just before they begin their mission. There was a sensation of complete calm in my body, and yet I felt something stirring in my spirit that seemed to provoke me to action. It was the most incredible experience I had ever had up to that point in my life.

As I look back at what happened, the best way I can describe it was a pulse. It was like a single booming note had been played at a quantum level and the vibration of the sound reverberated within us for a long time. I didn't realize I had closed my eyes, but when I opened them I saw Obadiah still sitting in his chair. I almost thought I could hear echoes of the note coming from him. He looked around at us and as he looked at me I felt my body relax. It was time to move on. Obadiah got things started again.

"There truly is power in words. When the frequency of the sound of those words are aligned with the One who created all things from frequency of energy, transformative power is released. We witnessed a touch of that power today. Do you have any questions about what just happened?"

Andre spoke up. "I have been present many times to witness people being healed. I've experienced the presence of God a number of times. This one was different. I'm not certain I can explain how it was different, but it was. Can you tell us what happened and why it was different?" Many of us were nodding our heads in agreement with Andre's question.

Obadiah nodded. "Sure. Most believers in the West don't experience quite what you experienced this morning. We have times of intimate worship that expose us to a presence of God, as you described. We pray for those who need healing and see them healed. But we don't typically experience what happened here. What just occurred was not something we did, but something we experienced. So often, we pray for healing out of obedience or some sense of religious obligation, and God honors it. We may worship and open our spirits to a touch from God, and He touches us. But what we just experienced was more than a touch. It was an encounter with the power of God. You are all in a place of training where you will experience encounters in an accelerated manner in order to heighten your senses."

Jerry asked, "Are you saying we shouldn't expect to experience things like this outside the cave?"

"That is not what I am saying. You should certainly expect these experiences. What I am saying is that much of the body of Christ today does not expect it because they don't have a paradigm for it to be possible.

"You aren't ready yet for a complete explanation of why you experienced this today, but I can explain some basics. What I am about to tell you is not exactly what happened, but it is like what happened. Have you seen what happens when a stone is thrown into water? I don't just mean the ripple effect, but I'm talking about what causes the ripples. The stone breaks the surface of the water and creates a depression in the place where it impacts. This depression means the water that was there is pushed somewhere else, so it is pushed above the level of the water around that point and continues outward. As the stone continues to sink, new water rushes up to replace the empty place left by the stone. The momentum of the upward motion eventually causes the rushing water to rise above the level surface and then to fall back down again due to gravity, displacing some of the water that had rushed in which start the cycle all over again, but with less intensity. The result is a series of circular waves rolling from the center point of impact. It happens very fast when you throw the stone, but it is very beautiful to watch in slow motion.

"There was a release of power from the heart and mouth of God like a stone being thrown into water. What you physically and emotionally felt was the result of riding along on the ripple wave of that power in the spirit just now. I spoke the words. The words inspired hope in your hearts and you saw the possibility of him being healed. Almost all of you instantly saw Josh healed and believed it was happening, never believing that there would be any other outcome. Many of you took action based on what you saw and power was released to bring about what you all agreed on. Josh was healed. There was alignment in the frequency of God's heart and the hope and belief in your hearts that changed the state of Josh's body."

"It is amazing that healing something as small as a little child's fever could cause a ripple that big," commented Maria.

"Every healing creates a big ripple. When God moves in power, His love is not muted for anyone. He is the stone that was cut without hands, and the ripple of His power fills the whole earth. Sadly, the hearts of most people are not open to feel Him."

Michael had the next question: "Will you teach us to release God's power in that way?"

Obadiah turned to Michael and looked directly into his eyes. "You already have within you everything you need to direct the power of God's love in ways that impact people and continue to ripple in their lives for decades." He slowly turned his head to look at each of us directly, almost daring us to challenge his statement and almost daring us to test it. Then again, maybe he was just checking to see if there were any more questions.

We sat for a few more moments waiting for more explanation. If we had the capability to release God's power as Obadiah had just done, we wanted the instruction manual for doing it. Surprisingly, Obadiah just stood up and said, "We've been here long enough this week. You all spent quite some time in the presence of God. We'll talk more about releasing power a little later. While you have what you need, you are not quite ready to be trusted with it all yet."

I was beginning to realize that Obadiah enjoyed cliffhangers. "But I will tell you this. You should expect your lives to be different this week. Just as we talked about the power of spoken words this week, you will find that your words will have more power. Be careful stewards of your speech. I will see you all next week."

CHAPTER THREE: BEHOLDING GOD

think it
speak it
it happens

Zach
H:10

SPEAKING

Obadiah was right. Everything he had been teaching both weeks seemed to add to each other. Not only did I experience what he taught us last week, but the insight I had begun to experience the previous week continued and became more natural to me. I still seemed to know things before they happened, but this week I began to recognize it sooner.

On Tuesday I was riding in the car with a coworker after lunch. We were in a hurry and decided to take a short cut through a residential area. We were just chatting and making small talk and I thought I saw a child run out into the street. I called out, "Slow down! Watch out!" My coworker hit the brakes hard and then looked at me. "What in the world are you shouting about?" I paused for a moment, thinking of what to say. Just then a child came running into the street about a half block ahead. Had we not stopped, we would have been right there. I pointed at the child and said, "I thought I saw something in the road, but it is a good thing we stopped anyway. That kid never even looked before running out." My friend turned back toward the road again, mumbling something unintelligible under his breath. I'm not sure if he said something about me being "amazing" or something about me being "crazy."

But I also took note of the words I was speaking. There were a few times when things happened that could be written off as random events. But at the same time, when you see a high number of random events happening at the time you have an intent for them to happen, you realize it takes a lot of faith to believe in that many coincidences. I am all for science, and I enjoy the study of numbers. But clinging to antiquated beliefs, simply because they are attributable to science, is a religion I want no part of.

The first speaking incident I noticed was nothing extraordinary. It didn't result in saving the life of a small child or anything really important. My wife and I had been invited to a play with some friends at a theater across town. When we left the house we realized we were running late. Having traveled the route before, I estimated that it would take about forty minutes to get there, allowing for traffic and intersections. We were supposed to meet our friend in thirty minutes. I had never made it across town in less than thirty-five minutes. Because of the venue of the event and the popularity of the show, arriving late would mean that we may lose our seats and would not be able to see the show. I looked at my wife and said, "We'll make it." She replied that I would have to break a number of traffic laws to make it in time. I don't know why I said this, but the words I spoke were, "If we hit every traffic light green on the way, we can make it just in time without breaking any traffic laws. So that's what we will do." We passed through fourteen traffic lights without having to stop once, with a few of them turning green just as we approached. Traffic was also working in our favor. Slow moving cars would change lanes as we approached them in order to get out of our way. Could this have been random? Scientists will tell us that the random status of lights means that at some time all fourteen lights will be green at an interval to allow someone to travel unhindered. But to have them all green at intervals of traffic that were also randomly unusual on a specific day when we just happened to need all of the conditions to be met seems a little too coincidental.

Later in the week, I was traveling to New York City for a business meeting. I was there for two days and had packed light because it was summer. On the second morning, I woke up to find it raining in the city and I remembered I had no umbrella. I realized that I was first on the presentation agenda in the morning and that I was going to get soaked walking to the meeting venue three blocks away. I began thinking about how to catch a cab or where to purchase an umbrella and then the thought just popped into my head to stop the rain. I looked out the window at the clouds and said, "I think we've had enough for a while. You can stop until I get to my meeting." I finished getting dressed and walked down to the lobby. When I stepped out of the hotel I saw many people folding their umbrellas. The rain had stopped just when I needed it to stop, and just as I had spoken. I walked to my meeting and a few moments into my presentation I glanced out the window and saw a hard rain had begun again. I could only smile.

As I pulled into the parking area this week, Mike and Catherine had just parked, too. It looked like Catherine had brought some baked goods. "What's in the container?" I called out to Catherine.

"Homemade cranberry oat bran muffins," she responded. The morning was already starting out well.

We walked through the opening and found that Maria, Hayley, Jerry, and Andre were already there. With our arrival we had a full crew, coffee brewing, and muffins. Yes. It was going to be a good day and everyone else seemed to sense that something was up too. After a few minutes of greetings and the distribution of muffins, Obadiah went to his seat and sat down. We were ready to start.

PRACTICE

Obadiah began, "Any questions about what happened this week?"

Maria didn't hesitate. "I don't have a question, but this week was wild. The level of revelation I was getting was remarkable. Even people around me who are not believers began to notice that something was going on with me. I either knew things in advance, or it looked like I was able to make things happen. Did everyone experience stuff like that?"

Most everyone nodded their heads in agreement with big smiles. Jerry added, "I know what you mean, Maria. I was shopping in the grocery store this week and the thought hit me that the man a few yards ahead of me was in a bad state of depression. Then I got the sense he was thinking of taking his life. I wheeled my cart next to his to grab a can of soup, and I noticed his buggy was empty. I glanced at him and caught his eye. Knowing I had an opening of just a few seconds I quickly blurted out, 'I love this type of soup. Days like today help me to appreciate how great life is these days and to appreciate even little things like...cream of mushroom soup. It sort of makes life worth living.' Now, I don't like cream of mushroom soup. I hadn't noticed what I had picked up when I began speaking to him. But I had to make it look convincing, so I put the can into my buggy, along with a can of cream of broccoli, which is what I had intended to pick up. The man shrugged and said, 'Yeah. Sure. Whatever.' I knew he didn't mean it. I left him in the soup aisle and went about my shopping.

"When I made it to the cashier's line, the same man pulled up behind me. He looked different. He was smiling. He recognized me and spoke. 'Can I thank you for what you said back there? I was not having a good day—or week—or month. In fact—I feel like I can be perfectly honest with you—I wasn't even sure I wanted to go on. Then you held up that can of soup and said life is worth living. Suddenly, I began to remember when I was a child and my mom would make cream of broccoli soup for my brother and me on cold days. We didn't have much going for us, but my mom made a good life for us anyway with things as simple as a can of soup. I don't know what came over me, but something inside of me changed. I wanted to see my mom again, and to have some soup with her.' He then pointed to a dozen cans of soup in his buggy. 'She isn't doing well, but she has been asking me to visit her. It would break her heart if I took my own life, and I decided that if she could bring happiness into the world I grew up in, then I can find some ray of hope for my life. I've decided it is time to visit mom, reminisce with her, and let her encourage me through my current place in life. She is really good at that and she always somehow makes things better. Thank you for reminding me that the simple things in life often bring the greatest joy and meaning.'

"All I could say was 'You're welcome. Tell your mom I send my blessings.' A hundred thoughts were running through my head. Mostly, I wondered if the words I had spoken had made a change in the life and spirit of the man, or if I had received revelation of what to do prophetically that would reach something that was already present in him. So, tell me, Obadiah...what happened?"

Obadiah smiled at Jerry. "You saved a man's life and a mother's heart."

Jerry tried again, being careful to ask the right question. "Okay. Then how did it happen?"

Obadiah began his explanation, "You accurately saw the condition of the man's spirit. It was depressed and without hope. He could find no reason within himself to live. The Lord put you and him in the right place at the right time and gave you the right tools to work with. When you spoke those words, they stirred up the memories of the man's childhood and found a tender place in his heart. Your words, with the power of the Holy Spirit behind them, hit that tender spot like a stone hits water and began to awaken a desire to live within him. At first it was to see his mother, but as the ripples widened he began to think of the hope his mom always exhibited. This setup a resonance in his spirit that was started in the days of his childhood and rang true. The words you spoke brought hope alive and changed the spirit of the man.

action walk

The revelation you saw stirred a desire in you to take action. The prophetic act you performed with the soup was the move of faith that brought authority of conviction and congruence to your words. What did you do with the cream of mushroom soup?"

"I actually have it with me. I was planning to stop by the store on the way home and exchange it."

"Would you be willing to let us put it on the shelf on the wall as a testimony of a life that was saved through the power of the spoken word?"

"Sure. I'll grab it during our break."

"Thank you. It is interesting that the Lord used something that neither you nor Robert liked in order to spark hope in him."

"Who is Robert?"

"Robert is the man at the grocery store that you just told us about."

"How do you know his name?"

"Practice." With that, Obadiah shifted in his seat and looked over at Andre.

"Did you have any interesting experiences this week, Andre?"

"I had a healing of my neighbor's cat. Nothing quite as dramatic as saving the life of someone who was going to kill himself."

"Andre, it is all significant. Don't ever undervalue the power of God based on what the power is exercised upon."

"I'm sorry. I didn't realize…"

Obadiah laughed out loud and interrupted Andre. "Don't fall into self-accusation. You did nothing wrong. You happened to be the one who mentioned what many others were thinking. I turned to you because you quickly recover and are the least likely to let the attention shake you. You have a thick skin. Most of the time that keeps you out of trouble."

There was a short pause and then Hayley raised her hand. Obadiah spied her and spoke with a wide grin. "Hayley, I appreciate the politeness of raising your hand, but that isn't necessary. However, I recognize that hand and give the floor to you to ask your question."

Hayley smiled, paused, and then asked her question. "When Jerry asked you how you knew Robert's name, you told him it was from practice. What is it that you practiced, how long did you have to practice, and how can we practice it?"

Obadiah settled back in his chair and thought for a few moments. "There isn't just one thing I practice. It takes many disciplines working together to step into high levels of the prophetic. We are going to cover them all over the next few weeks, but this is a great time to start with some very basic ideas.

"First and foremost, you must be able to hear the voice of God. We are told by Jesus that His sheep hear His voice. You must be able to hear His voice and be willing to step out in faith to follow it. There are many Christians who will teach that God doesn't speak to us anymore. Yet those same believers will affirm the scripture that says no one comes to Jesus unless the Father draws them. Every believer will attest to the still small voice inside that finally led them to the place of making a choice to follow Jesus. That is the Father speaking. Those who believe God no longer speaks to us became Christians because God does still speak to us—and to them.

"So having established that God still speaks, it is difficult to make a case that He only speaks to us for salvation, but not for other spiritual truths, direction, encouragement, and comfort. He is interested in our entire being, not just that we go to heaven. Why would He not continue to speak to us? Many will say it is because we have the Bible today and don't need Him to show us what to do. Yet, we still need Him to speak to us in addition to the Bible to help us understand, process, and accept Christ's love for us. In fact, the Bible tells us that God sends His Holy Spirit to teach us in all things. If the Bible were the only source of teaching, we wouldn't need the Holy Spirit, which is contrary to what the Bible says. How does the Holy Spirit teach us in all things? He does so by speaking to us at a spirit level through the revelatory methods identified in the Bible.

"Now that we know that God still speaks to us in our spirit, over and above the Bible but not contrary to it, then we have to decide if He will speak to us for others and not just for ourselves. The way we can find out about that is to consult the Bible. We are told to encourage one another, comfort one another, and build one another. We are also told that the purpose of prophecy is to encourage, comfort, and build up. If you look at all the evidence provided in scripture in the context of all the other evidence of scripture, there is no denying that God still speaks to us today for our own well-being and for the well-being of others. This is the voice of the Shepherd that all His sheep know."

"Then how does he speak to us?" asked Catherine.

"He speaks in many ways. But from a practical standpoint, we can use the framework of the five physical senses as a pattern for spiritual senses, except that there is one additional way He speaks. Just as we can hear, see, feel, smell, and taste in the natural realm, we can also hear, see, feel, smell, and taste in the spiritual realm. Let me explain a little more about these so that you can pay attention this week to hear from God in a different way than you have so far.

"Just as we can see light and color in the physical, we can also see things in the spiritual realm. Sometimes they will be superimposed on each other, or will appear so real as to think you have actually experienced something. These may be flashes of light, colors, or pictures; or they may be like a series of scenes in a movie; or anywhere in between. These can often come simply by waiting for them, or sometimes they just happen."

I spoke up. "This explains what I have been experiencing. A few weeks ago I thought I saw a glass falling off of a table and then it happened a few seconds later. This week I thought I saw a child running out into the road, and that also happened a few seconds later. Was this revelation? Was I seeing the future?"

"Yes," Obadiah answered. "That is exactly what it was. You saw both of those as if they were really happening, but you saw them prior to them happening. Sometimes you may see something similar, but it won't be about the future. It could be about someone's past, and knowing this will help you to encourage them in some way. There may also be times when you see something that looks like a future or past event, but it is really a symbolic picture. For example, you may see someone driving a school bus. This may not be literal, but it may represent that the person is leading a group of younger people through some sort of educational experience.

"There is also hearing in the spirit. This often starts with the still small voice of God that most of us recognized as having led us to Jesus. This same voice can continue to speak to us. But the voice can grow more sure and louder as we learn to listen. There are times when you may think you hear someone talking to you or whispering in your ear. This is often the voice of God or perhaps a messenger angel. Sometimes you may hear a song in your head. Not one of those songs that get stuck in your head and annoys you, but one that you hear until you understand the message being conveyed. Finally, you may simply remember having heard something. These are all common types of hearing in the spirit.

"Two less common ways to hear in the spirit happen when the message is more urgent, more important, or more difficult. There can be the voice of God that you hear plainly in your spirit word-for-word, and there is the audible voice of God. The internal voice of God is usually very clearly Him. You have no doubt about it being God or you. The audible voice of God is even more so."

Andre chimed in. "I had an experience once when I believe I heard the voice of God. It was very clear and it sounded like it was real. Could that have been the audible voice of God?"

Obadiah responded without hesitation, "No."

"How do you know?" Andre asked.

"Because if you only think you've heard the audible voice of God, then you haven't heard it. The audible voice of God is so overwhelming that it will usually terrify you. Had it been the audible voice, you wouldn't be asking me about it."

"So, have you heard the audible voice of God?"

Obadiah chuckled. "Oh yes. Many times and in many settings."

"Were you terrified?"

Obadiah tilted his head slightly and looked toward Andre, smiling while he pondered his answer. "Every single time." Then he turned back to the rest of the group.

"The other senses also play a part in revelation. You can smell things that others may not smell. This could be the presence of angels, or it could be the presence of sickness, disease, or some other sort of dark thing. Just as your physical nose recognizes pleasant smells and foul smells, so does your spiritual sense of smell.

"The same thing goes for taste. You may have a taste in your mouth that speaks to you in some way. For example, a sweet taste could be speaking of good things to come and a bitter taste could be saying the person is dealing with bitterness. Just be certain that there is no physical reason for what you are sensing. If you have just finished a cup of very strong, but very bad coffee, it is a good chance that the bitterness you taste is from the coffee and not spiritual revelation.

"Finally, there is the sense of touch or feeling. You may feel sensations in your body. A pain in your body where none existed before could be revelation about a healing that the Lord is about to release to someone. Emotional feeling may also be revelation about emotional conditions of people. If you begin to speak to someone and suddenly feel joy for no reason, it could be that the joy of the Lord is on them or is about to be. In the same way, if you are speaking to someone and you begin to feel depressed with no reason to be depressed based on what they have said, then the Lord may be showing you where they are so that you can help them in the same way that Jerry helped Robert this week."

"I've been sitting here listening to all that you have described." said Michael. "I realize I have experienced insight, or revelation, in all five of these senses. However, sometimes I seem to just know things and can't really tie it to an experience in one of these senses."

"That's right," Obadiah replied. "Sometimes you just know something. It is like remembering something that you were never actually told. This may be a memory of having heard something, but you can't recall anyone ever saying it. That would be the hearing example I gave. It may also just be the memory of the experience or a fact pulled from your memory banks that wasn't there previously. This is also quite common and sometimes this is called an impression. It is like someone touched your memory with the knowledge and left an impression there. Sometimes you are very certain of the impression, and sometimes you are not.

"There are other types of revelation that we will cover later like dreams and visions, trances, visitations from angels, and visitations from the Lord. Dreams are especially prevalent, so we will most likely spend some time on them. The others are less common and we may just touch on them until you have become skilled with these basics. Having skill with the basics entails more than simply recognizing revelation and capturing it. Skill also means you will know how to interpret it and process the message and then how to deliver the message in a way that leaves people better than you found them."

Catherine had a question. "You said that practice is important. How can we practice this without risking hurting people?"

"That is a very practical question, Catherine. Thank you for asking it. There are lots of ways to practice. In general, you do not need to worry too much about hurting people as long as you remember to practice love, to see them as God sees them, and to leave them better than you found them. The Golden Rule would apply in this realm.

"But there are some things you can do just for fun that will help you to recognize how the Lord generally speaks to you and to build up your confidence in hearing. One thing that I have heard of is to ask the Lord for words of knowledge about people driving in cars next to you while driving. This helps to sharpen your spiritual sensitivity. If you would like to pray for them after you get the revelation, without them knowing about it, go ahead and do so. You could be changing lives for people in that way.

"Another fun exercise I have seen is to go to a mall or other public venue with a couple of friends who also want to develop prophetic gifts. Pick someone at the top of an escalator or at a specific corner in a walkway, and ask the Lord to show you something about their past or current struggle before they get to the bottom of the escalator. Then, share what you got with your friend and have them share what they got. As time goes on, you will all begin to quickly see an increase in the agreement between what you see, which is an indicator of your accuracy."

Andre asked, "I've heard of people, or heard jokes about people, who claim to hear voices in their head. Usually, these people are thought to be crazy, and often they act out violence that these voices instruct them to do. How do we know that we are not opening ourselves up to hearing these voices instead?"

"That is one of the biggest fears about the prophetic, Andre, and it is why many people and even many denominations or movements do not embrace the prophetic. People are so afraid that they will be hearing from the devil that they choose to hear from no one. But there is a sure way to know that what you hear is God and not the devil. That is through abiding in Him—abiding in Jesus."

"And how do we do that?"

"Again, that takes practice. Since I know how astute this group is, I can bet that someone is going to ask how to practice abiding in Him. So I will tell you before you ask, but not before we take a short break. Let's take about ten minutes to rest and then we'll talk about abiding in Jesus."

Everyone got up and stretched, and Jerry slipped out to his car to get the can of soup.

PRESENCE

While everyone was getting more coffee and taking a bathroom break, Obadiah was drawing something on the whiteboard. When he finished, near the end of our break, he had drawn several horizontal lines on the board with an arrow pointing outward on the right end, and most had a vertical line in the center.

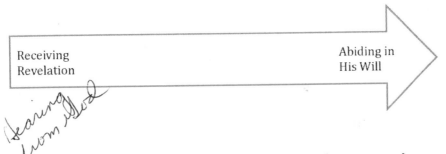

We all puzzled over the drawings as we began to take our seats again. Obadiah waited for everyone to get settled and then began.

"Most aspects of life move along a spectrum of progression. That is how we all grow in anything. We start at a beginning place, and then progress along a spectrum to more depth and proficiency. A child learns a few basic words for communication and then grows in his or her ability to speak more fluently and with a larger vocabulary."

Obadiah pointed to the first drawing. "It is the same way in spiritual things. We begin with basics and progress toward more depth. The things I was teaching earlier this morning were the basics of revelation. As you continue to practice the basics, you will move toward the other end of the spectrum which is abiding in His will. Abiding in His will is the place where you are so much a friend of Jesus that you begin to feel what He feels and see what He sees.

"You know what it is like with a husband and wife who have been together for years. They come to a place where they almost know what the other is thinking and what the other would say before it is said. They are content to just sit together without conversation. Abiding in His will is like that. You know Him so well that you can anticipate what He would do or what He would want you to do or say.

"There is also a quantum aspect to it." Obadiah now moved to the second drawing. "The spectrum awareness of the presence of God applies at the quantum physics level. You recall that we talked about creation earlier. We discussed how God created everything out of the material He had on hand, which was spirit. We also talked about Him putting creation in the only place available, which was within Himself. This condition of all creation being within Him and being made of part of Himself creates the state of omnipresence of God in all quantum material that is generally barely noticeable to us. Yet His presence is always there all the time. We simply don't recognize it. But as with everything else, our recognition of His presence grows along a spectrum. It begins at a point of a barely noticeable omnipresence that everyone experiences and ends with the overwhelming consuming fire of His full glory at the center of His being.

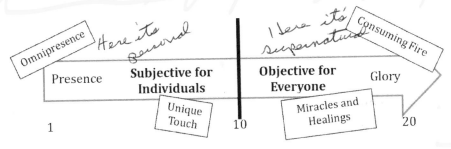

"If there was a dividing line midway between those points, everything to the left of it would be the subjective recognition of God. This is often experienced through a unique touch from God that an individual experiences. No one else can testify to that unique touch, but the individual knows that they experienced God in some way. The intensity of those touches can vary depending on where they occur along the spectrum.

"On the right side of the spectrum are the objective experiences of the presence of God—encounters that more than one person experiences. These often begin as healings or miracles that grow in scope and intensity. They are verifiable by eyewitnesses or doctors. These are the types of experiences that no one can argue about their validity. As the progression continues along the spectrum, the experiences grow more profound or impact entire populations of people and often show some sort of visible manifestation of the presence of God such as smoke, a cloud, fire, or very bright light. The furthest end of the spectrum is the light energy from which quantum material is created and where it is again broken down into the sub-quantum material which is the spirit of God."

Hayley had been studying the drawings as Obadiah spoke and decided to ask a question. "I see that both of the drawings move along similar spectrums. The first is a spectrum of spiritual hearing and seeing or even communing with God, and the second is a spectrum of the experienced presence of God. Are you saying that as one of these increases, the other will increase, too?"

"Not exactly, Hayley, but you are getting close. There is actually one other spectrum that must be considered before you can really say they move together. This is what I meant earlier when I said that there are many disciplines that must be practiced to obtain a high level of prophetic operation. So far, we have only looked at two, and we have only looked at the practical beginnings of one of them. All that we discuss this week and the following weeks must all work together. They are not things you master one at a time and move to the next one. You will gain understanding of one which will bring understanding of another, then another, and so on until you are able to gain further understanding of the first one again."

"Okay. So the next drawing looks like getting married. Are you going to tell me I have to get married to be a prophet?" Hayley was smiling slyly at this comment.

Obadiah grinned back at her. "Let's not go there, but no. I am not saying that. Let me explain the next drawing and then start bringing everything together.

"Abiding in His will and experiencing His presence requires growing in your relationship with Jesus. This next drawing shows the steps along the spectrum for a natural relationship between a man and a woman. It begins with an introduction to each other. After the introduction they begin to speak and find some things in common, and there is often talk about the positive things they see in each other. At some point they both realize they want to spend focused time getting to know each other and consider making a commitment to each other. The next step is an affirmation of that commitment before God and man, which is known as marriage.

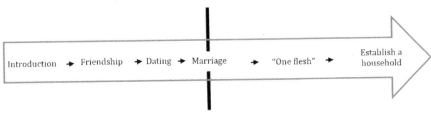

"But marriage isn't the end. It is just the beginning of the real relationship. Once there is a commitment, the couple will spend time learning how to act for each other's mutual benefit rather than only for their own benefit. They don't keep secrets from each other and they spend time being intimate. The Bible calls this becoming 'one flesh.' Once they have truly become one flesh, meaning they are of a single mind and vision, they will begin to establish a household that is uniquely the two of them. The household will usually include offspring, and will blend characteristics of both of them. In fact, their house may adopt a unique smell and unique feel and atmosphere, unique decorations and themes, and a unique diet that is shared. There will be no other household that is quite like theirs.

"Our life with Jesus should be the same way. We are the 'bride of Christ' and the purpose of becoming His bride is to establish a household after becoming one flesh with Him. Unfortunately, many Christians in the West today are still dating. They believe they are interested in Jesus and want to keep getting to know Him. However, they are not really ready to make a commitment and are happy with just 'going steady' with Jesus. But the real fun doesn't start until the commitment is made forever."

"Why do you think that is?" I asked. I recognized what Obadiah was describing in my dealings with most people who called themselves Christian, and I figured that since it was so widespread there must be some sort of cause behind it.

"There are many layers of factors that have brought this about. Among them are the cares of the world and pleasures of the flesh. There is also an increasing focus on self. Most people in the West act as if they were the only real person who exists. You can't have a relationship if you are focused on yourself. A relationship requires focus on someone other than yourself. In order to have a true relationship with Jesus, you must spend time focusing on Him.

"So one of the key reasons that this lack of commitment has been able to happen is because most of the church has set aside the discipline of biblical meditation, often called beholding. We simply don't teach people to do it, and those churches who talk about it rarely teach their members how to practice biblical meditation. You will not be able to advance to the place of a prophet without practicing biblical meditation. You will never experience a deep relationship with Jesus, or have the profound experiences of His presence, or abide in His will if you do not practice biblical meditation."

Maria piped in, "I sure hope that last drawing is going to tell us how to practice biblical meditation." The whole room erupted with laughter—partially because she had said what we were all thinking and partially because we all knew, including Maria, that she was exactly right about the last drawing.

BEHOLDING

Obadiah brought the room back to order. "This next drawing does show the different levels along the spectrum of biblical meditation. We'll talk about it a little, and then we'll actually put it to practice.

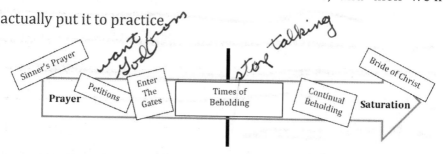

"The spectrum begins with talking to God, or prayer. The first prayer that results in an abiding type of experience for everyone is the sinner's prayer. This is when the Holy Spirit inhabits the person. The opposite end of the spectrum is saturation, which is when the Holy Spirit is so much a part of all you do that you are completely in communion with God at all times. This is the full meaning of 'walking in the Spirit' that Paul talks about. But we can take deliberate steps along the path in order to accelerate our journey through the spectrum. This path is what I have drawn out here.

"As you can see, everyone starts with the sinner's prayer and most people move quickly to prayers of petitions. It is a natural act of faith in God to believe that if you ask Him for something, He will hear you and act on it. But as we mature as believers, we learn that we enter His gates with thanksgiving, and we begin to add that to our conversations with God. But it is still mostly us talking at this point. There are various levels of these two types of prayers that most believers pray, and sadly, most believers do not move much beyond these.

"The next step is the hardest because it is the transition to biblical meditation. We are told many times in scripture to meditate on the word and on Him. But we typically just pray petitions and thanks. Moving into meditation, especially the type of meditation that is often called 'beholding' requires us to stop talking. In fact, it frequently doesn't even involve us listening either. When we begin beholding Him, we typically make a deliberate effort to do so, and then we stop beholding and go about our business. This is what I call 'times of beholding' and it is where we begin to learn how to commune with Him. With enough practice, which is the term that started this entire conversation, we can eventually maintain a state of continual beholding which is having the awareness of Christ in you and you in Him constantly before you. It is superimposed over all of your daily activities and you find that having the awareness of Him in you makes your day a day of power in the spirit.

"The final place is becoming the Bride of Christ, which means that you become one flesh with Him. You begin to have those characteristics that we described earlier about married couples. They start to think like each other, finish each other's sentences, and anticipate what the other would do in a situation. Sometimes, they even begin to look like each other. When you begin to look like Christ, you are letting your awareness of Christ in you become visible to those around you simply by watching you and listening to what you say and how you say it."

"I'm still not certain I understand what 'beholding' is," Catherine added. "What does it look like and how do I do it?"

Obadiah responded, "Beholding is simply sitting quietly in the presence of Jesus and seeing Him there. You don't talk to Him, ask Him for anything, or attempt to engage Him in any way. You simply see Him there and connect with the power of His presence. He may engage you. If He does, then you respond and interact as needed. But the point of beholding is not to get anything more than simply being in His presence. At the same time, it allows the quantum material in your body to become energized by the quantum material of His presence and it renews your spirit.

"We are going to spend some time beholding Him. Some people are able to go there right away. Others need help getting there. So the steps can be different, but I am going to describe two paths. If you can't get there on the first one, then take the second path. There are other ways to get there too. If these don't work for you, let me know and we'll try others.

when reading
the bible – ask God
want it means

CHAPTER THREE: BEHOLDING GOD   87

"A word of caution: don't try too hard, and don't set any expectations. Many people are expecting some major encounter in the spirit that lays them out on the ground for hours, or they expect God to speak some great secret of the universe to them. But most of the time, especially at first, nothing is said and there may not even be any interaction. You probably won't feel anything, and may even wonder if you really had an encounter at all. The thought that will come to your mind is that it was just your imagination. We'll talk more about the imagination later, but for now you just need to know that even if it was your imagination, that does not mean it didn't happen. God gave humans an imagination that is different from all other creatures, specifically so we can access the spirit with it.

"If you are ready, we'll begin." Obadiah looked around the room to see if there were any looks of concern. Some people in the room appeared calm, and may have actually experienced this before. Others were shifting in their seats as if they wanted to be in the right position to meet with Jesus. I was more in line with those shifting, though I couldn't really think of what the right or wrong posture would be.

"Okay. Go ahead and get comfortable. There is no right or wrong posture." Did he just read my mind? "But you don't want to get into a position that is likely to put you to sleep. We aren't going to have any soft music going in the background. That can sometimes help, but usually it ends up stopping us at the gates of thanksgiving and the courts of praise. This is a time just for you and Jesus. Let's start by closing our eyes.

"Now you want to clear your mind of everything. As soon as you start to clear your mind, your mind will try to fill itself again. If a thought comes into your mind that is important, like something you have to remember to do, then just write it down and close your eyes again. Eventually, you will have all the reminders captured and you can deal with the unimportant things by simply focusing on where you want to go. Pick a place where you want to meet Jesus. In your imagination, decide where He will be. Maybe He is at the top of a set of stairs. Perhaps He is sitting on the shore of a body of water or high up on a mountain. It can be anywhere you want to meet Him.

"Focus on the setting. If other thoughts try to come in, ignore them and re-envision again the place of meeting. As you see the place, look off and see Him there. Don't worry what He looks like. Some people see Him as a person similar to the historical paintings of Him. Other people see Him as someone else. Many people see Him as a human figure enveloped in white robes and white light, without a discernable face. It could even change each time you visit with Him. Whatever He looks like, see Him walking toward you. Now, in your imagination, sit down as He arrives where you are. Now just watch Him. He may stand there. He may sit with you. He may touch you or even speak to you. Whatever He does, just enjoy His presence. Now we will sit here for a few minutes and enjoy Him."

It was quiet for a while. I struggled a little bit. I had never been taught this, nor had I even been told this was possible. I kept getting stray thoughts in my head. I remembered that my wife had asked me to stop by the hardware store on the way home and pick up some fertilizer for the lawn. Then I remembered an important phone call I needed to make at work the following Monday. I dismissed both thoughts and continued to sit there. As other things to do came to mind, I dismissed them just as instructed. Then some really wild thoughts began to bubble up. I remembered my first grade teacher, then a tree I used to climb when I was a child. I remembered the second car I owned—a 1979 Chevy Camaro. It was if my mind was fighting against me having an encounter with Jesus.

I tried to focus on a place to meet with Jesus, but I couldn't decide where to meet Him. Then I realized that may be the problem. Maybe I couldn't get rid of the stray thought because I hadn't decided on a place to meet. If only I could decide on a place to meet, then it would work. Suddenly, I realized my mind was now occupied with trying to figure out why I was having stray thoughts. This seemed hopeless. No matter what I did I couldn't get my mind to settle down.

Obadiah's voice shook me out of my confusion. "Everyone just stay in that place with Jesus. Some of you are having trouble focusing. You can't manage the thoughts in your mind. Let's try approaching this a different way. The rest of you can continue as you are.

"Those who are having trouble should follow my instructions. Let's start by relaxing your body. I want you to start concentrating on each part of your body. For each part, focus on feeling the part of the body and then release all tension from it. Start with the top of your head, then your forehead." He paused. "Next feel your cheeks, then your neck." Another pause. "Now your shoulders, then your left arm and your right arm." He continued down the entire body and by the time he was finished I was completely relaxed. I hadn't realized I had become tense in my frustration about not being able to clear my thoughts.

"Now let's clear your thoughts. As every thought comes into your head, see it inflate like a balloon and float into the sky. Just stay in your relaxed physical state and let the thoughts float away. You have been trying too hard to make something happen. By placing yourself into the relaxed state, and letting your thoughts go, you will cease fighting with yourself and your own will.

"Now that you are in a place where you are no longer struggling, let's take one more step. Think of a place you enjoy going. This can be your favorite place to relax or to get away and be alone. Imagine yourself there. Breathe in and out slowly and enjoy the surroundings. This is your secret place. While you are sitting there, imagine the place beginning to sink. You and your surroundings are beginning to drop slowly like an elevator. You are going deeper into the spirit, which is the place that Jesus inhabits. This place in the spirit is within you. As a Christian, your spirit has been redeemed and renewed and is now the place where Jesus lives.

"Remain relaxed and let your imagination continue to let you sink into the spirit until you find a place where your descent settles. This is where your heart is most open to Jesus. Now continue to stay relaxed, and look off into the distance. Do you see Jesus walking toward you now?"

It was amazing. Before I realized it, I was sitting by the beach with Jesus walking toward me, and I was completely relaxed. I watched as He approached me, and then I saw myself standing to greet Him. He stopped about two yards in front of me. He reached out His hands toward me and I extended my hands to clasp His. I didn't feel power moving through me. I felt love. It wasn't just love. It was Love, flowing through every fiber of my being.

I looked into His eyes, the eyes of Love Himself, and I knew that I would never be the same. I recall how it felt when I first became a Christian and accepted Christ into my heart. This was similar to that experience. This was the "first love" experience spoken about to the church in Ephesus. The same excitement that flowed through me when I first "met" Jesus as my Savior was now flowing through me in this first meeting in the Spirit. I didn't realize that, like Ephesus, I had lost my first love. But there was a new spark ignited in me at this moment.

No words were spoken. I just stood there and gazed into His face and into His eyes. I saw Him seeing me and loving me. I saw with the eyes of my imagination, and I saw with the eyes of my emotions, and I saw with the eyes of my spirit. Yet it was not the type of experience where I was laid out on the floor or where I began shaking or shouting. I was simply sitting in the room, experiencing Jesus, in the place where my heart and spirit live together.

CHAPTER FOUR: HOPE

FAITH

I was looking forward to the meeting today more than ever. I had spent the week visiting with Jesus. The first four or five times I used the long method with the relaxation, but I eventually got comfortable enough that I found I could simply close my eyes and go to my secret place with Him without the full relaxation and focusing.

My visits with Jesus were the highlights of the week. I was surprised at the variety in the meetings. I guess that I expected that something many people called "beholding" would always be me beholding, or looking at, Jesus. But most of the meetings were quite different. There were still times of gazing into His eyes, and that never got old. There was always something new in His eyes. But what I found is that they really were visits.

There was one visit when Jesus stood in front of me and held my hands, and I felt energy being transferred. I don't know what type of energy or for what purpose, but I felt something flowing into me that seemed to energize and refresh me. Another time He sat down with me and we chatted about some people at work that I had been having some tension with. He helped me to understand them better and to be able to work with them. There was even a time when He suggested that we take a walk down the beach in my secret place together. We didn't speak during the walk, but there was a sense of peace and safety that stayed with me for days.

The most surprising thing was that there was one day when He didn't come. I tried the short method and the long method, and He never showed up. There was just the ocean and some sort of bird perched on top of a tree nearby that kept watching me. After a few minutes I stopped and went about my business. I was disappointed. But in spite of His absence that morning, revelation seemed to be coming faster and easier than ever before.

Apart from the one day when He didn't show up, though, the week was exciting. I looked forward to my quiet time when I could meet with Him. Today, I was excited to talk with the others about their times of visitation, too, and find out who had similar experiences.

When I pulled into the parking area, I realized I was the first to arrive. There was a spring in my step as I walked past the dogwood trees to the magnolias, and into the entrance to the cave. This week had, indeed, been a good week. As I stepped into the room, I saw Obadiah standing near the whiteboard checking his markers.

"Good morning, Obadiah." I called out.

"It always is, Jason," Obadiah replied. He never seemed to just give a simple response to anything, but that was part of what I liked about him.

"Do you have some good things planned for today? Last week was very life-changing for me."

"I think you'll find this week interesting. We have a lot to cover." Obadiah sat down in his chair and sat quietly, his head seeming to move slowly from one chair to the next as if we were sitting there. It was a few moments before I realized he was praying for each of us. Suddenly, I realized that he prayed for all of us. It must have been a regular thing for him. I had never considered this before, nor the impact his prayers had on my life. I found myself beginning to tear up a bit. I couldn't recall anyone except my mom and dad praying specifically for me.

After a few more moments the others began arriving. Mike and Catherine were first, then Maria and Hayley walked in, Maria chattering and making wild gestures as she spoke. About a minute after them, Jerry came in, and then Andre walked in about two minutes after Jerry. There was the usual buzz of greetings and joking while everyone got coffee or water. When everyone was finally seated, Obadiah began.

"How was your week?"

Everyone responded at once with "great," or "wonderful," or "best week ever," and similar expressions.

"Was there anything in particular that stood out to anyone?"

Everyone looked around at the others, and then Jerry spoke up, "I noticed that the revelation I got seemed to be more precise than previous weeks. This week it wasn't about the quantity or speed of the revelation, but it was more about how accurate it was."

Catherine chimed in, "I didn't notice the revelation so much, but my creativity level seemed to be much higher this week. I've been working on some new ideas for a couple of paintings for weeks, and suddenly everything seemed to open up. I've had weeks in the past where I've pushed past a blockage of creativity and found things explode open, but this was different. Instead of a sudden burst of creativity, this week seemed to just expand a little more each day. One day I would get a little bit of insight for an approach, the next day I would understand the previous insight better and gain some new insight, and the next day it would build again. Previous blockages have been more like a balloon of creativity bursting, and this week was more like a balloon of creativity being inflated to its fullest point." She paused a few seconds. "I don't think I am explaining it well."

"I understand what you mean," Maria responded. "Working with my clients this week felt clearer than before. It was like I could see them with better vision than in the past—almost as if someone had wiped away a film of residue from a windshield."

Obadiah asked, "Did everyone feel like you were living better in tune this week?"

Mike answered first. "I really hadn't thought of it that way and didn't make the connection. But I did notice that I seemed to have a lot of good breaks in work this week. I was able to close three very large deals that I had been working on for months. It wouldn't be unusual to close one of them after this amount of time, but three in one week is unheard of. Then, I was able to get some leads for additional business that looks to be on a fast track for closing. Is that what you mean by being better in tune?"

Obadiah nodded his head and answered. "That would count." He looked around. "Anyone else?" He seemed to stop and stare at me. I felt that I had to mention the day that Jesus didn't show up.

"I was going to ask you something in private, but I'll go ahead and bring it up now. The week was very good, except for one day. There was one day I went to meet with Jesus and He didn't show up. There was just some bird sitting in a tree near where we meet. But when I went about my business, it seemed like the heavens were opened up to me with revelation. There wasn't anything I couldn't see or know if I just asked for it. Can you tell me why Jesus didn't show up, and why that was the day when the power seemed greater?"

Obadiah pondered my questions for a few moments. "Was the bird an eagle of some sort?"

"Now that I think about it, it could have been an eagle. It had the beak of an eagle, and the color of the feathers looked right."

"Ok. What does an eagle mean to you symbolically?"

"I guess I usually think of the phrase 'eagle eye', so sharp vision would be the first thing that comes to mind." Then it hit me that the eagle was a prophetic symbol of the clearer revelation I had that day.

Obadiah started laughing. "The Lord has such a keen sense of humor. One of the ways that God speaks to us is through symbolic language. That's why much of what we get prophetically is in pictures or other visual means such as dreams, visions, and our imagination. You went to visit with Jesus and He met you as an eagle, which was a message to you that you would be able to see very clearly that day. As it turns out, you were able to see everything with such unprecedented clarity that nothing was hidden from you except Jesus Himself. The only thing you didn't see in the spirit was Jesus appearing to you. But don't feel bad. People have missed seeing God since the beginning of time when He appears to them in a way they don't expect."

Then, with a smile still on his face, he turned to the others and started talking to the group. "Don't dismiss anything during your time in your secret place. Jesus may come to you in many ways if there is a message He wants you to have and to walk in during the day. He will also change things up now and then to keep you sharp and so that you don't settle into a routine with Him. When things don't seem normal, look around and pay close attention. It could be that He has a matter for you to explore during the day."

He turned back to me. "You should feel honored that the Lord is allowing you to learn in this way. Thank you for sharing that with us."

Sensing that the topic was finished, Obadiah pivoted the conversation. "I want to ask you all a question. You have all been experiencing new things in the spirit. Some of you have even experienced miracles, or signs and wonders as some may call them. But you are all still at the beginning stages of this. It is like a door has been opened, but there is something still standing in your way. So my question is this. What do you think are typical barriers to operating in frequent signs and wonders?"

The room was quiet for a few moments. Finally, Andre called out "Faithlessness." Then a couple of other people suggested bad teaching, lack of training, and unbelief. I thought about it for a few moments and considered some of the teachings I had heard in the past and volunteered, "Not enough love?"

Obadiah finally saved us from our nervous attempts at insight. "You guys are very close. Some of what you have suggested is exactly what I would say, and some of it is related. I would start with two things that you have all mentioned. Lack of love is certainly a barrier to signs and wonders." I barely resisted whispering "yes!" when he started with the one I contributed. Obadiah's eyes darted my way briefly and I turned a little red. "In order to move in genuine signs and wonders you must have a desire to help others. Without love, you have little or no motivation to seek signs and wonders, except for your own benefit. But it is love that releases authority for us to move in signs and wonders consistently.

"The second one I would mention is a lack of faith. Faith is the actual working out of what we claim to believe. When James says that faith without works is dead, he is saying if you don't take a step toward a work in the area of faith you profess, then it isn't really faith at all. It is a statement. It is talk. But for it to be faith, you must be willing to take an action that demonstrates you really believe what you are saying. Anyone can say they believe God heals the sick. But only those with faith will lay hands on the sick to proclaim and release healing for the sick person. The works that you do—which may be as simple as actions; they don't have to be charitable or evangelistic actions—demonstrate what your real faith is. You are all here this morning because you have the faith to believe you can become a prophet. You are not the only people I spoke to about these meetings. Many of the others told me they believed they were called to be prophets and would be here. But when it came to showing up, you are the ones who took action on the very little information I provided. You acted in faith that the dreams and the meeting with me were for a purpose, and your works brought you here.

"Let me ask you this. Do you know what is required before you can have faith?"

Most of us sat motionless. Jerry shifted in his seat a little and answered. "Hebrews 11 says that faith is the assurance or substance of things hoped for and the proof or evidence of things that are not seen. Romans 8 says that hope that is seen is not hope because no one hopes for something that they have seen. It seems to me that faith is a physical manifestation of something that is not yet seen. So are you thinking that hope is required in order to have faith?"

Obadiah's face broke into a huge smile and his eyes twinkled a bit as he responded. "Jerry, you are exactly right. You have done some studying on this topic, haven't you?"

Jerry nodded sheepishly and replied, "A little, but I still have a lot to learn. I can't seem to get it working in my life in spite of knowing how to explain it."

"Then let's see if we can diagnose it for you and for others in the room." Obadiah answered. "Where does hope come from?"

"From the Lord," Andre said.

"Okay." Obadiah responded. "But let's get more specific. Let's take some time and really look into this. You all have some sort of Bible with you. Let's actually see where scripture tells us hope comes from. I'll give you all about fifteen minutes to look up some references. Break up into groups of two or three and work together."

Mike, Catherine, and Jerry quickly formed a group because of their proximity to each other. Hayley and Maria turned toward each other and I found myself pairing up again with Andre.

Each group had at least one electronic Bible, so we were able to do word searches. I was a little concerned that we would all have the same scriptures, so I decided to start from the end of the list instead of the beginning. After about fifteen minutes Obadiah cleared his throat and called everyone back into the larger conversation.

"So what did you find?"

Concerned that everyone else would have the same list, I decided to speak up first before the others quoted all the references Andre and I had found. "1 Peter 1:3 says that the resurrection of Jesus causes us to be born again into hope, so His resurrection would be a source of hope. Titus 1:2 says it comes from the promise of God. Colossian 1:27 says we get the hope of Glory from Christ in us. Romans 15:4 says we have hope through perseverance and encouragement of the scriptures..."

"Hold up a minute, Jason. Breathe for a few moments while someone else chimes in. You don't want to read off the whole list, do you?" Again, I turned a little red. This seemed like a day where I couldn't do the right thing, even when I had the right answers. I decided that it may be best if I refrained from any more talk for the remainder of the day.

Obadiah went over to the white board and began making a list: resurrection of Jesus, promises of God, Christ in us, encouragement of scriptures, and perseverance. "Did anyone else find some sources of hope?"

Catherine replied, "We found a few."

"Go ahead and share a handful of what you found."

"We found some references in the Old Testament, but I want to mention one more from the New Testament that I think is very important. Romans 15:13 says that the God of hope fills us with joy and peace, which causes us to abound with, hope. That seems to say that connecting with the joy and peace of God gives us hope, partly because God is hope and, when He gives us joy and peace, He gives us part of what He has to impart. That one seems to be connected to almost all of the ones that Jason mentioned."

"Very good, Catherine. We will discover how important those are as we continue to meet. What else did you find?" Obadiah asked.

"Well, it looks like Job 4:6 says that our fear of God, our confidence, and our integrity can be our hope. There are multiple places in the Psalms that say our hope is in God, and I sort of read that as meaning that He is a container, of sorts, of our hope. In a few other places it says our hope is from Him."

"Did you find any clues as to how we get that hope out of Him, if He is the container for it?"

Catherine smiled big. "As a matter of fact, we did. Psalm 119:49 says to remember the word of God to His servant in which He made the psalmist hope. So hearing a word from God is a sure source of hope."

"Very good," Obadiah concluded. "Does anyone have anything different from what has been said?"

Maria started to speak as she glanced at Hayley for confirmation. "We found some other scriptures, but I don't think they are looking at anything different. It all seems to be pointing back to God as the source of hope, and talking about how He delivers that hope to us." Hayley nodded her agreement.

"You guys are sharp today. You are exactly on target," Obadiah said.

"Well, it helps us to hit the target when we use the Bible as the weapon," Jerry mused. Everyone laughed. Even Obadiah laughed and we could see his appreciation of the joke in his eyes.

"So," Obadiah continued, "it looks like there is, indeed, a theme regarding hope. Catherine phrased it very well. True hope always comes from God, and He delivers that to us through His words to us—His promises. When we hope in other things, we set ourselves up for disappointment. But hope in what God has told us always comes through when we persevere in holding onto that hope."

"Now let's think about what can be a hindrance to hope. We said that lack of faith can be a hindrance to supernatural power, and hope is a necessary ingredient for faith. So what can cause a lack of hope?"

The room was quiet and there were a variety of expressions on faces as we all puzzled over the answer.

Maria finally ventured to break the silence. "I think I remember it saying somewhere that hope deferred makes a heart sick. I'm not sure what that means, but it keeps coming to mind. It seems to be saying that even true hope can bring disappointment if it doesn't come soon enough."

Obadiah nodded. "Great point." He paused. "Anyone else?"

After a few more moments with no one saying anything, Obadiah began speaking. "You are heading in the right direction, Maria. You are referring to Proverbs 13:12. That verse not only says that hope deferred makes the heart sick, but it also says that desire fulfilled is a tree of life. There are two sides of looking at hope in this verse. The first half of the verse is talking about having a hope for something—it may be a true hope or a false hope. But waiting for hope that is prolonged and extended until the will, emotions, and even thought patterns get worn and can no longer envision the hope. The second half of the verse says that when the thing that is longed for arrives, it brings a freshness to our existence. In other words, we are happy when we get what we want and we are unhappy when we don't get what we want.

"But the problem isn't about getting, and it isn't always about what we want. In the case of a hope based on a promise of God, as we were just discussing, hope deferred happens when we expect the fulfillment of that promise in a timeframe or a manner that is not what God promised. The root of the problem is that we tend to want to rush the promises of God, or we want them on our own terms."

"But how do we know what the right timing is or what the right terms are?" Andre challenged.

"Sometimes you have to settle for realizing that the timing and terms you were operating under are wrong. If you have a hope based on the promise of God, and you find the hope fading, which is the sick heart referred to, then you have missed the timing or the terms. That means it is time to reexamine the promise. That is the first step.

"The next step is to reestablish that the promise was from God. We do this by finding scriptural support for the promise. We have to apply practical wisdom at this stage, and it is usually good to consult other sound believers about what you believe you have heard. For example, you may be looking for a job and believe you heard from God that you are going to get a new job. Scriptural support for this may be the promises that He is your provider and that He does not make the righteous beg for bread. But that may be the support if you currently have no job. If you have a job that is providing adequate support, then that promise may not apply. You would have to dig deeper and find promises that He has called you to a purpose and a destiny that He will not forsake. If your current job does not carry you into that purpose, or cannot carry you there, then the promise can be supported in scripture. However, if your current job is able to release you into your destiny but it isn't yet, then you may need to re-evaluate the timing and the terms to see if perhaps your current job will grow into the hope you have for the future."

"That sounds like a lot of work," Andre said.

Obadiah smiled, understanding Andre's intent. "No one said the Christian life would be easy. At least, no one in the Bible said it would be easy. In fact, there are a lot of references that will teach just the opposite. However, much of the process I described can come out of your quiet time, beholding and listening to the Lord. He will bring understanding as you seek Him.

"Let's take a break for a few minutes and when we come back, I want to talk about the number one barrier to moving in power and the number one reason we don't have hope."

B E L I E F

Our break went a little longer than it had in the past. All of us except Obadiah found ourselves gathered near the coffeemaker, chatting about the idea of true hope requiring a promise from God. Eventually Mike broke it down in a way that was easier for me to understand. He said, "Hope without a promise from God is a verb. It is something we do, and maybe it will happen, but there is no guarantee. Hope based on a promise from God is a noun. It is something we possess inside, and so it doesn't waver with circumstances." Looking at it this way, I understood how hope is the foundation for faith that can lead to signs and wonders.

A few moments after this, we noticed that Obadiah was sitting in his chair. We made our way back to our seats as well.

When everyone was seated, Obadiah spoke. "I hope everyone got all settled with coffee. Mike, your summary regarding hope was very good. I am glad to see you are all helping each other to process what is being presented."

"We're going to switch into a little higher level now. We've been talking about moving in signs and wonders so far today. We talked about the requirement of love, the need for faith, which has a need for hope, which comes from the promises of God. So essentially, signs and wonders require love and the promises of God. Since God is love, and as believers we have the Holy Spirit in us, we all have the capacity to love. We also have the same promises of God in scripture, and some that have come to us prophetically. Yet we still find it difficult to move consistently in signs and wonders.

"The missing piece that brings about consistent signs and wonders, and other miracles in our lives, is congruence. We do not have congruence in our hearts."

Andre asked. "What do you mean by congruence?"

Obadiah smiled with a slight glint in his eye. "I'm glad you asked that, Andre. Let me explain.

"The basic definition of congruence speaks of the quality of agreeing or having harmony. Within each of us, there are different aspects that come together. We often hear about mind, body, and soul; or heart, mind, and spirit. The triad I am speaking of today is mind, emotions, and will. I don't want to get caught up in details about the terms that are often used by the church or other spiritual disciplines. What I want to speak about today applies only in the context of congruence."

Obadiah stepped to the whiteboard and began drawing an image of a girl looking to my left. Then he added a "thought balloon" behind and slightly above her head. It was the type of image you might see in a cartoon drawing to show what the character is thinking.

"Let's suppose we have someone contemplating a decision or some sort of issue in her life. The two main factors that will come into play will be her mind and her emotions." He wrote both of these words inside the balloon. "The solution her mind and her emotions agree upon becomes her will." He wrote the word "will" below mind and emotions and added arrows to show the relationship. "The will speaks of taking action. We say 'I will do this' or 'I will do that.' Thus the will drives our behavior." He wrote "behavior" below the thought balloon and an arrow to show that will leads to behavior.

"This interaction between the mind, emotions, and will is what we will call the heart. We have all heard people talking about making decisions based on what our heart is telling us. Often they will point to the chest to indicate something separate from the mind, but in this sense the heart is not the contracting muscle in our chest. It is the place where our mind and emotions agree on a matter and direct our will to manifest a behavior." Obadiah drew the outline of a valentine heart around the three words in the balloon and continued.

"Our hearts mature over time as our mind and emotions learn from two sources. They will receive input from things we are taught and from things we experience." He added the words "teaching" and "experience" to the right of the balloon. "Thus, our hearts are constantly trying to get what we have been taught to agree with what we have experienced. When the two don't agree, the emotions will usually win, and the mind will devise some explanation to reconcile with the emotions. This sets up a belief system that causes our will to drive behavior consistent with that belief system. I can spend a few minutes with anyone, asking a few questions about their current life, their successes and failures, and tell them what they really believe. When I do this, most people are surprised and will even argue with me at first. The place we are in life is a result of the collection of our behaviors."

I heard a few people shift in their seats and felt there might be disagreement. Obadiah handled the discomfort graciously.

"I understand there are many circumstances that just happen to us. Many children are abused by parents or other adults through no fault of their own. It often takes years for them to bring proper agreement between their mind and emotions based on that experience. However, their state today is a result of how they reconciled what has happened to them. Many live in a state of victimhood for their entire lives. Others overcome what happened and live as healed survivors. There is a spectrum of states in between.

"What I want us to be aware of today is that your state today, as adults, is a result of what you believe about yourself, about others, and about God. But there is good news." Obadiah turned back to the whiteboard and drew a large bolt of lightning above the girl and in her line of vision. It stretched far enough to nearly touch the heart inside the balloon. Inside the bolt of lightning he wrote the words "Revelation from God." *ask for revelation*

"When we seek the Lord, He can reveal things that can add true understanding to the mind and true interpretation of the emotions. He can redefine the belief system when we seek Him. This new belief system directs our will to behave differently, which brings about different results. You see, when our minds are forced to make sense of an emotional experience that doesn't agree with what we are taught, our heart knows it. Our mind is giving in to our heart as a compromise, but there is still doubt lingering. This compromise between the mind and emotions will cause us to be half-hearted in our behavior. When they fully agree, then we can act whole-heartedly. Revelation from God can accelerate the process to having a whole heart." *emotions + mind together is congruence*

Obadiah continued. "There is only one thing that can interfere with revelation from God. Many times we become so invested in our belief system that our hearts become hardened. We find that we've built our lives around the wrong thing, but making a change means admitting that much of our lives have been spent chasing shadows. *I was wrong* We realize that all we held dear— our thoughts, our past times, our hobbies, perhaps our careers, and maybe even our spiritual confessions—were the result of a deceived belief system. We had bad teaching. We had highly charged emotional events that didn't make sense. We *trama* compromised concerning something we knew deep down, but now our pride won't let us release the wrong beliefs. So we develop a stronghold." He drew a dotted line forming a five-sided shape around the heart shape, completing the entire diagram.

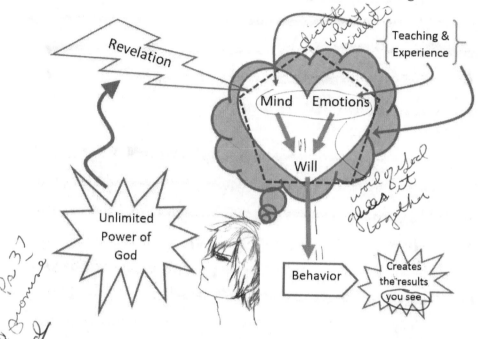

"We hold on tight to what we've been doing and hope to get different results. But this type of hope is the verb that Mike was speaking of. It is what we do when we hold onto those false promises that are the result of a compromised heart. Revelation from God provides 'a hope.' It provides a noun that we hold onto in our hearts to bind our mind and emotions. Holding this hope that is built on the promises of God releases power and authority into our lives."

"These strongholds seem like they can be very ingrained and subtle." Maria asked, "How can we know if we have them?"

Obadiah answered, "You play detective and look for clues. Take notice of your behavior, especially when you are beginning to do something that you acknowledge requires faith. These behaviors are the clues to your internal belief system. Look for inconsistencies between what you say and what you do. Look for evidence of hedging against disappointment."

"What do you mean by hedging against disappointment?" Hayley asked.

"I'll give you an example. I once had a student who had confessed for years that he believed God healed people today, and that God wants to heal everyone. But he rarely saw anyone healed. We talked for a bit and most of his questions to me were around why people sometimes don't get healed. I asked him why he was so concerned about why people don't get healed. He told me that he wants to have the right answer ready in case the person he prays for does not get healed. As soon as he gave me that answer it hit him. He said that he believed God wants to heal everyone, but he would get ready to explain to the person why they didn't get healed before he prayed for them. He had spent his life confessing a belief in healing, but building a faith for not seeing healing. His mind was fully engaged in creating the explanation that compromised what he thought he believed. There was still doubt in his mind about healing, and his emotions didn't want to deal with seeing people disappointed, so they built a belief system to let them both off the hook. His prayers for healing were half-hearted at best, but his explanation for why healing didn't happen were whole-hearted."

Now it was Catherine's turn. "How do we get rid of them?"

"We are going to take some steps in that direction right now. It is not likely we'll be able to deal with everything today. Much of this takes time to recognize, and then walk out the new belief in a way that lasts. But we'll look at some ways to start making changes.

"I would like everyone to close your eyes for a few moments and ask the Lord to show you some areas in your life where your behavior tells people what you believe. We'll start with some simple ones first. For example, Catherine, the way that you hold Josh when he is sleepy or tired tells anyone who watches you that you love him dearly. There is nothing about that to fix, but we want to start with things like that in order to learn how to be behavior detectives."

The room got quiet as everyone began doing what Obadiah asked us to do. I noticed that most of the group closed their eyes, but we all just sat in silence and considered our behaviors. After about a minute, Mike cleared his voice.

"This is pretty basic, but I might have an example." He paused, and then Obadiah nodded for him to go ahead. "Every morning before I go to work I take time to read the business and economic news. Could this be a behavior that says I believe that what happens in my business is related to what happens in the larger economy and marketplace?"

Obadiah smiled. "That's it exactly, Mike. Good example." Obadiah noticed Hayley eyeing her notes. "Do you have an example, Hayley?"

"I do. I was thinking about something I do frequently and it occurred to me that I take copious notes. In this class, at work, and in almost every situation I am usually the one person who is writing down something about what is being said. I thought about this and I think it might mean that I value words. When people say significant things, I recognize value in their words and I write them down so that they might be preserved."

Obadiah looked her in the eyes. "You should write that down." Laughter broke out in the room. Obadiah continued. "I am only partly joking about that. Part of the reason you are here with this group is your high regard for words, both spoken and written words. We have already discussed that the primary tool of the prophet is sound, usually in the form of spoken words. But there is also a very important place among the company of prophets for those who will record those words and steward them so that they may be remembered, recalled, and released when needed. This scribe function brings permanence to the message of the prophets."

We all stared at Hayley under the weight of Obadiah's words until we noticed she was blushing a little. Obadiah changed the subject.

"You all seem to understand how to play detective with your behavior. That last exercise was identifying behaviors that are consistent with what you confess. Now we want to take the next step. For this, you will probably need to ask the Holy Spirit to help you. He is very good at this, and is gentler with you than you would probably be with yourself.

"Take a few moments and try to identify a behavior in your life that is inconsistent with what you say you believe. These will be much harder to identify because we tend to want to deny the inconsistencies. There are some places you can begin to look that will help you discover your inconsistencies. First, look for areas of your life that are not going the way you want them to go. If you are getting results inconsistent with the desires that God has given to you, then it is probably because you believe something that is not congruent with that desire."

Andre spoke up, "Are you saying that we should expect to get everything we want? All of our desires should be fulfilled? I've never heard anyone teach that before. In fact, I've heard a lot about Christians having to face trials and to suffer for His sake. What you are saying doesn't seem consistent with what I read in the Bible."

Obadiah seemed unfazed by Andre's objection. "It does seem inconsistent, doesn't it? But that is because we have had an improper understanding of trials, persecution, and suffering. In fact, this incorrect understanding is the reason that most believers are not living a full life in the kingdom of heaven. Our immaturity and selfish desires get in the way, and we have developed a teaching that supports the consequences of our actions and allows us to blame it on God. Notice that when I spoke of desires earlier, I talked about desires that God has given you.

"There is more than one source of desire. The most base level of desire is selfish desire, and that is the one that we are warned about in scripture. We cannot expect to see all of our selfish desires fulfilled, and we should hope that none of them are fulfilled. But the Psalms tell us that if we delight ourselves in the Lord, He will give us the desires of our heart. We have to stop reading only the last half of that verse and begin reading the whole verse. We must first delight ourselves in the Lord. That means we spend time with Him. We behold Him. We converse with Him. We enjoy His presence. As we begin that close walk with God, then the source of our desires changes. We no longer pursue selfish desires, but we begin realizing desires that are from God Himself. Those are the desires that will be fulfilled.

"Suffering happens because of our immaturity. Much of the suffering we undergo is because we make choices that are not in alignment with the path that God is leading us along. We actually use an incorrect term for this type of suffering. Rather than suffering, we are actually experiencing the consequences of our own choices and actions. Many of these consequences create emotional events in our lives that we call suffering. Suffering can be physical or emotional or mental. He turned to Andre. "Does that help to clarify what you were understanding?"

"Yes, it does," Andre answered. "That actually makes a lot more sense. I always wondered how Jesus could promise abundant life knowing that most of His followers who heard Him make the promise would be persecuted or martyred. That just didn't seem very abundant to me. So the church made up this perspective of God that expects us to be downtrodden in order to be good believers. Is that right?"

Obadiah paused for a moment as if to carefully consider his response to Andre's assertion. Then he answered cryptically. "People often attribute God with very human characteristics." With that, he turned back to the original conversation.

S E E

"That was a great question Andre, but now we must get back to where we were. Let's take a few moments to identify at least one, and not more than two or three, areas in your life where your actions are inconsistent with what you think is your belief. Ask the Holy Spirit to help you."

Obadiah gave us quite a bit of time to write something down. It really was difficult. I found myself having a conversation, of sorts, with the Holy Spirit. While nothing was spoken out loud, the conversation sounded like this in my head.

"Okay, Holy Spirit, show me where I'm missing the boat."

"Nope. You have to do most of the digging yourself."

"Can you give me a hint?"

"Sure. Pick a major topic."

"Major topic? You mean like on Jeopardy? What sort of topic?"

"Something that applies to your life. Maybe finances or marriage or children or your career."

Instantly my thoughts went to finances.

"Okay. I have one. I'll take finances."

"What worries you about your finances, causes anxiety, or leaves you dissatisfied? By the way, I would have asked the same question for any topic you chose."

"I guess what bothers me the most is that I thought I would be earning more by now, that our home mortgage would be paid off, and that I would be on track to retire early."

Suddenly it hit me. I knew what was out of alignment. I have said, since before I got married, that God would always be my provision and the provision for my family. I could even quote multiple verses from the Old and New Testaments to support this promise of God to us. Yet I still go to work every day to a job that I don't really care for because I really believe that I am the one who provides for my family. With this revelation in hand, I began to write as Obadiah had told us.

As I finished writing and looked around, I saw some of the others were still writing, some seemed to have finished, and others still looked like they were thinking. I wondered if they had the same conversation with the Holy Spirit I had just had. Then Obadiah spoke softly.

"While you are still in your conversation with the Holy Spirit, ask Him what the root of this belief that you didn't know you had was?

Instantly, I was back in the place of conversation with the Holy Spirit. "Ok. Where did this come from?" I asked.

"You already know that." He answered.

"I'm pretty sure I don't. I didn't even know I believed this. I was just living my life providing for my family. I don't want to leave them helpless like Mikey's dad did."

Mikey's dad. I hadn't thought of Mikey for decades. We were neighbors when I was a child and that made us natural playmates. I remembered how we loved to play army in the neighborhood—sometimes we were in opposing armies, but most of the time we were saving our neighborhood from invading countries.

I remember the day when Mikey came over and it looked like he had been crying. He didn't really feel like playing. He just asked lots of questions about my parents, and talked about his dad being away for a long time. We were only ten years old and I didn't understand what had happened. A few days later my mom told me that I could invite Mikey to come over for dinner any time he wanted to come. She told me we needed to look out for him and his family because his dad had decided to move away from them and left them with no money and no way to take care of themselves. She explained to me that it is the job of the man of the house to provide for his family, and he doesn't get to decide not to provide for them just because it is inconvenient or because he gets interested in someone else like Mikey's dad did.

It was many years before I really understood what happened to Mikey's family, but the words of my mom took root deep inside of me. They had good fruit, but had also created a skewed view of family economics. Her words had implanted a responsibility and faithfulness to my family that kept us together through the good and the bad times. But it had also created a view of provision that said the husband was the provision for the family through the work of his hands. I hadn't realized until now that I had been leaving God out of it. Of course, I had a responsibility. But my responsibility was to be true to who God made me to be, and to be sensitive to Him and the opportunities He placed before me. By following Him, being authentic and developing skills that He gave to me, He would provide for my family through me.

The dissatisfaction I was feeling now is a result of trying to carry the full burden myself, and not allowing Him to work on my behalf. That's why I felt trapped. I was trying to sustain a place that had lost purpose for me. It was time to begin looking for a God-inspired transition, but I was living in a place of financial fear, rooted in the experience from my childhood.

Then I began to smile, and a few seconds later I noticed I was laughing quietly to myself. I never finished the conversation with the Holy Spirit. I was arguing with Him about not knowing the root, and in the middle of the argument I stumbled over my own answer. He was right, and I was laughing because I recognized He was right and He was laughing with me.

After a few more minutes, Obadiah brought us back to the discussion. He went around the room and asked who was willing to share what they had discovered. Because the group was curious about my laughing, I shared my experience with them. Everyone joined in the laughter and I was surprised when many of them told me they had similar conversations. The Holy Spirit had been very gentle with each of us. What was revealed didn't feel condemning like I expected conviction to feel. In fact, there was no negative emotion at all. Each one of us felt relief and freedom. It seemed to just be an understanding of a situation in our lives. While all of our inconsistent beliefs were actually a type of sin, realizing the inconsistency didn't lead any of us to feel shame. Each one of us who shared our stories embraced the understanding and had a feeling of empowerment to make a change in our lives.

Obadiah thought for a few moments and then began speaking again. "Your stories are all very good. I am glad you are able to see some of the inconsistencies in your lives. That is the first step, though a very important step. Now I would like to go one level deeper."

"Deeper?!" Andre almost shouted out before he realized what he was doing. His eyes were wide with incredulity. While we were startled by the outburst, we all felt exactly as he did. Even though the last exercise was surprisingly painless and freeing, none of us was looking forward to digging up more areas of our lives.

Obadiah smiled slyly. "I promise it won't be too painful. This next step will help you to see areas in your life where you are blocking hope and faith. Let's take that last step into closely held beliefs that drive our will and behavior to act without hope and faith in our lives.

"Without thinking about your behavior and any implications an event has had, I want you to write down one, two, or three things that happened to you in the past that impacted you emotionally. The way you know that it impacted you is that you will still feel the same emotion that you felt then. You may need to go way back into your childhood to find some of these. In fact, some of the most significant events happen in childhood for two reasons. First, we don't have the mental processing to make proper sense of the event. The second reason, which is more important, is that the enemy will often try to abort our destiny in our childhood.

"Let's take a few minutes to recall a few events from your past that impacted your emotions in a very significant way. Write down the one that really seems to still hurt. You may feel fear, anger, shame, embarrassment, or extreme sadness. After you write it down, then think for a few minutes about what you think that event meant about you."

The room got very quiet as we all thought for a few minutes. I could almost feel the emotions in the room beginning to come to the surface. I began to feel the presence of the Holy Spirit. Some people in the room seemed to be struggling. Others had already begun writing. After about five minutes everyone seemed to be finished. Obadiah asked if anyone wanted to share anything.

Catherine cleared her throat. "I guess I can share mine."

Obadiah gave her permission. "Thank you, Catherine. What was it you discovered?"

Catherine began, "I remember when I was little girl I was fascinated with drawing and of making things with my hands. When people would ask me what I would be when I grew up, I would say I'd like to be an artist. When I started middle school, I signed up for art class. My dad found out what I had done, and he was furious. He told me I could not take art class. He did not want me to waste my time on something that wouldn't allow me to make a living. I decided that meant that art was just a hobby. I could not pursue it professionally. It became something I only did on the side, and over time I did less and less of it. That belief stayed with me all through middle school and even through high school. It wasn't until college that I realized I could pursue art as my main expression of who I was."

"What is your belief today?" Obadiah asked.

"As I spoke with the Holy Spirit just now, I began to understand that I still believe I can't make a living producing art. Even though I identify myself as an artist, my dad's words still drive my belief system. Somewhere deep down I still believe I can't make a living with art.

"Do you have a new belief?

"Yes, I do. I now understand that my dad feared for my future. But now I see that art is my expression of who God made me to be. Everything that God makes has value. Therefore, my art has value and there are people who will pay for that value. All I need to do is find those people."

Obadiah smiled. "That is a great example, Catherine. As you begin to market your art with this new belief system, you will find that it sells more easily and for more money." He paused and looked around. "Anyone else?"

Hayley cleared her throat. Everyone turned their attention her direction. "I might have something." Obadiah nodded slightly. "A few years ago my grandmother was very sick. She was actually diagnosed with terminal cancer. I had recently learned about healing prayer and I decided that I should pray for my grandmother. I prayed quite a bit, and even spent many days fasting in prayer. She didn't make it. The cancer took her."

"What meaning did you attach to that?" Obadiah inquired.

"At the time, I began to wonder if healing prayer was real, or if maybe I didn't have enough faith or authority to see people healed. I eventually decided that healing prayer was real because I saw other people pray for the sick and they were healed, even some with cancer. So I decided that I was just not called to pray for the sick, and I stopped doing it. I believed I was not one of the people with the gift of praying for the sick."

"And your new belief?" Obadiah prompted.

"I don't have a new belief. I know that the old one is wrong because that is the point of the exercise and this is the event that the Holy Spirit brought to me. So it must be a wrong belief. But I don't have a new one yet. I am now just confused why my grandmother died."

I noticed compassion on Obadiah's face. He seemed to want to give her an answer. "I am not going to give you an answer, Hayley. That will be between you and the Holy Spirit. But what I will tell you is that the death of your grandmother had nothing to do with you and your prayers. It had everything to do with other family, friends, doctors, nurses, and even her. The simple fact concerning your grandmother is that she contracted cancer, and the physical realm took its normal course. But you have been found faithful. You just told us that you eventually realized that healing prayer is real and is for today. Jesus told His disciples, 'Blessed are those who have not seen and yet believe.' You did not see your grandmother healed as a result of your prayers, and yet you still believe in healing prayer. There are many who have simply given up at that same point."

Hayley took a deep breath and let it out slowly. "Thank you. That helps."

Obadiah noticed the time. "It looks like we went over on our time today. We won't be able to hear any more experiences in this session. Watch for differences in your life this week as a result of what we discovered today. Now that your belief system is changing, you should begin to see your results in life changing to align with your beliefs. Maybe we can have a few more of you report back next week. I apologize for keeping you all so late."

With that, Obadiah stood up. He seemed to be ready to go somewhere. The group sat for a few moments and then we each began to get up too. Most of us were still mentally and emotionally processing what had just happened. I was looking forward to testing Obadiah's claim that life would be different this week. I was certainly ready for different results in my life.

CHAPTER FIVE: LOVE

H E A L E D

I admit that this week didn't show a release of any extra measure of the miraculous. I felt like I was still moving in the same level of prophetic insight as I had been for the past couple of weeks. But there was still a difference. The pressure that had seemed to be weighing me down most of my life was now gone. It wasn't something that would be recognized externally by anyone who might be observing me, but I no longer felt the need to be successful. I was willing to take life as it came. There was a new realization that the things I was dealing with were not about me.

Even in this new understanding of household economics that released me from the responsibility to provide for my family, I found that the provision was still there. The difference is that now my only responsibility was to be my authentic self in my job and my home. Sometime during the afternoon on Tuesday, I recalled Matthew 6:33: "But seek first His kingdom and His righteousness, and all these things will be added to you." I had heard this many times before, but suddenly I understood that part of seeking His kingdom and His righteousness meant seeking to be the person He created me to be in His kingdom. It is impossible to fully seek His kingdom and leave out who He intended me to be if I am in His kingdom. Because I am in Christ and He is in me, I must be a part of His kingdom. I had been looking at myself as always having to be something that I was not in order to provide for my family or to be a good employee or even to be a good person. This new revelation released me from the sense that I had to perform apart from who I am.

After contemplating this for a couple of days, I began to recognize how things just seemed to work out for me since Tuesday. One employee that had been performing poorly gave his notice on Wednesday morning, which meant I didn't have to go through our lengthy termination process. Another project that had been missing milestones all along was unexpectedly redesigned to be simpler in scope and all of the milestones were changed. This was something our team had been requesting for over two months but had made no progress with, and the change happened because of a new executive that stepped in with our client.

Perhaps the most remarkable was a weather phenomenon. The leaves had been falling for a few weeks and I had been unable to rake them and dispose of them because of the weekly meetings with Obadiah. My wife had been asking me to clean the yard, and it never worked out. On Thursday evening a storm blew through town with very strong winds. When the storm was over, I stepped outside and every fallen leaf was gone. I checked to see if they had blown into the neighboring yards, and those lawns were also bare. There are those who may say this was a coincidence or a fluke. It doesn't matter to me what it was, because it still worked out in my favor. I am perfectly happy with a life full of flukes and coincidences that work out for me. If the revelation and subsequent release I received means that the rest of my life results in flukes that work out in my favor, then who am I to say there is no relationship to the revelation?

As I pulled up to the parking area, I saw Hayley get out of her car with a large paper bag. Maybe I imagined it, but she appeared to be glowing a soft gold. When she turned toward me, she had a smile that was different. This smile seemed to be coming from within her rather than from her face. We walked together to the cave. At first we made small talk, but after a few moments she could contain herself no longer.

"This was an incredible week for me."

"In what way?" I asked.

"I had the chance to pray for a number of sick people. That alone would be remarkable by itself, because I rarely come across people who have anything more than a headache. But this week I interacted with four different people who were in the hospital or who were about to go into the hospital."

"Wow. That many people in just one week?"

"I know, right? That never happens to most people. But it doesn't end there. Do you recall my story from last week?"

"Yeah. Your grandmother died from cancer and you felt that you had let her down because your prayers for healing didn't save her. But Obadiah said you still remained faithful and that her death had nothing to do with you."

"Right. I can't tell you how much difference that made for me. I felt like a big weight had been lifted from me. It was like I had been walking around since then with a heavy backpack that I didn't know about. It kept me from praying for people who needed healing."

"So did you pray for some of the sick people this week?"

"I prayed for all of them." Hayley's eyes were beaming. The golden glow I saw around her earlier seemed to grow stronger. "Every one of them was healed."

I stopped for a moment and Hayley had to stop and turn for me to catch up. I was stunned. "Every one of them? All four of them? None of them remained sick?"

"Incredible, isn't it? I met the first person on Sunday afternoon. I was visiting my aunt, and her neighbor came by. She said she was entering the hospital to have gallstones removed. I don't even know what that involves, but I felt the Lord prompt me to ask her if I could pray for her, and she was willing. I began praying some general things, and suddenly I found myself declaring that she was receiving an ability to forgive people who had hurt her years ago and that all bitterness would be gone from her. As soon as I said that, she made a loud noise and said she felt something move inside of her.

"The next day, I decided on a whim to stop by and see how she did with the gallstones. When I got to her room, I found her packing her things. She was being dismissed because the final x-rays couldn't find anything wrong with her, and her bloodwork came back with no signs of anything to do with gallstones or her gall bladder."

I realized we were no longer walking. She continued.

"She was in a shared room and she told me that she had mentioned our prayer time to the woman in the next bed and that the woman wanted me to pray for her. The woman was in her seventies and had fallen at home. Her hip was broken in two places. So I prayed for her and I even spoke to the quantum particles to materialize and join the broken bones together properly. She told me that while I was praying, she felt some tingling in her hip. I was optimistic about what might have been happening."

I wanted to hear more. "That's two. What about the third?"

"I walked out with my aunt's neighbor and she wanted to stop by the gift shop to get something to remember her healing by. I walked in with her to keep her company. While she was there, she saw one of the pastors from her church and chatted with him briefly. In the conversation she introduced me as the one who had saved her a huge hospital bill. I was actually beginning to feel embarrassed, but the pastor asked me if I would be willing to accompany him to visit a family in the Cardiac Care Unit. There was a man in their church who had a heart attack over the weekend. They had found some blockages in the arteries in his heart and were going to have to do something to his heart on the next day, which was Tuesday. I'm not real sure what it was they planned to do. But something about sticking something in his leg to remove the blockage in his heart.

"I went with the pastor to the room where there were a number of family members sitting and trying to be optimistic. The pastor introduced me as a friend of a friend who was willing to pray for the procedure the next day. I don't know what he actually expected me to do, but I figured it was a chance to pray, so I didn't get into a doctrinal discussion. I began praying, and at some point I just began making declarations about love and releasing love into him and through him. I found myself saying that all of the hurts from the past that had hindered his ability to love were being removed from him completely and that the Lord was making a new way for him to find love for those who had hurt him. Then it was finished. The family thanked me and I left. As I walked out, I noticed his eyes were moist and his breathing seemed to be stronger."

"And?" I asked.

Hayley smiled. "I went back the next day during my lunch hour, to see how the procedure went. The doctors said that when they went in to clear the blockages, nothing was there. In fact, they performed some additional tests to get a good look at his heart, and everything was fine. The only thing they noted is that there was one place where there had been a blockage, but his heart had somehow built another pathway around the blockage and was now working perfectly."

"You're making this up," I joked.

"As much as I like to joke around, I would never make light of what happened this week. Do you want to hear about the fourth one?"

"Of course."

"I was astounded about the news of the healing of the heart. I excused myself from the room and made my way to the hospital cafeteria to get some lunch. I found a table off to the side where I could reflect. I never would have believed that I would ever be able to see someone healed this dramatically, let alone three people in three days. Yet, there it was. I wasn't sure if I wanted to shout for joy or cry tears of joy. As I was beginning to get up, I overhead the people at the table next to me talking. One of them said the word 'grandma,' and the other one said the word 'cancer.' I didn't hear anything else they said. I felt strongly that this was a moment that had been setup by God. He had been showing me how much he loves to heal people for three days so that he could bring me back to the memory of my significant emotional event. Suddenly, I remembered seeing my own grandmother in bed as her life passed from her. But instead of feeling dread and fear, I felt a determination to face this cancer down. I heard myself softly whisper, 'Not again' as I resolved to help this family.

"I turned to the people at the next table and interrupted their conversation. 'Excuse me. I happened to hear you speak something about your grandmother and cancer. My grandmother suffered with cancer a few years back; I know what you are experiencing. I would like to encourage you, if you don't mind.' They smiled, a little startled, and welcomed me to join them. I briefly told them the type of cancer and they said their grandmother was dealing with the same thing. At this point I knew it was a setup, and I grew bolder. I recalled to them all the things the doctors had said while treating her, and they said the message they were getting was about the same. Then I asked them if I could pray for her. They hesitated a moment, trying to assess if I might be a Jesus freak or something. But after a moment the older one told me they would appreciate the prayer.

"Before I began to pray, I told them that the doctors are doing their best and they can only operate from a place of medical science and technology. While they should all be grateful that she is getting the best medical care and pain treatment available, their hope should not be in medical science and doctors. I looked them squarely in the eyes and said, 'This is not the time for your grandmother to pass. I know that she will live many more years. Your job is to believe what I am saying to you and to stand on her behalf between the words of the doctors and the promises of God.'

I paused just a moment to assess if my words were sinking into their spirits. I saw a sparkle of hope in the eyes of the younger one. I asked, 'Do you believe?' Almost inaudibly, the young one whispered, 'Yes'. I glanced over at her. She spoke again, 'I believe. I do. I believe she will live.' She began to smile. I glanced at the older one. He looked at the girl, and I saw him surrender his skepticism. 'Me too,' he said. 'I believe she will live'.

"Then I prayed a simple prayer. 'Jesus, we agree with your promise that this dear woman will not give in to the cancer and will live for many more years. I speak to the cancer, and I command the matter that makes up the cancer to dematerialize in the name of Jesus. I speak to organs and systems in her body that have been damaged, and I command matter to materialize where needed to repair and replace damaged tissue. I call for an end to pain and for a strong mind and body to be the outcome of this sickness. Amen.' We sat in silence for a moment, and then I started to get up. The young girl reached out and grabbed my hand. 'Thank you', she said. I looked at her and said you're welcome. I asked what room her grandmother was in so I could check back. Then I went back to work."

Hayley stopped talking. I waited a couple of moments before speaking. "Don't leave me hanging."

"I stopped back by yesterday. I was almost afraid to check in, but I knew it was something I had to do. I went to the room and found the young man I had encountered sitting in the room reading a magazine. He saw me at the door and stood up to greet me. He was smiling ear-to-ear, and I was surprised when he reached out to hug me. Then he told me that they had come down to the cafeteria that day while his grandmother was being taken in for some testing to update the extent of the cancer. It had been growing rapidly, and they only expected her to survive another month or so. While the technicians were running the x-rays, there was an equipment malfunction. They couldn't get a good image. They tried again and could not find any cancer. They sent her back to the room while they had the equipment checked and repaired. After a few hours, they took her back to a different machine, yet still could find no cancer. The doctor assured us this was not possible. They waited another day and tried again. Still no cancer. But this time the doctor commented that her organs looked in better shape than he would have expected for someone younger than her who had never had cancer. He said the doctor would have simply called it a bad initial diagnosis except they had a series of x-rays over several months showing a progression of advancing cancer, and she had exhibited all the symptoms. He and his sister had decided that one of them would be there around the clock until the doctors released their grandmother so that they could stand between their grandmother and the words of the doctors, nurses, and even family members."

I stood and stared at Hayley. She was having trouble finding words now, and I didn't want to push her.

"Then I looked over at his grandmother. For a moment it was uncanny how much she looked like my grandmother when she was healthy. I blinked a couple of times and then the woman looked like herself and I wondered why I had thought there was a resemblance. But I knew in my heart that my grandmother didn't die because of me. I don't know why she didn't survive, but it wasn't me. At that moment I was confident that I can speak words of healing and people will be healed. If they aren't, it isn't because of me. When people are healed, or when they aren't healed, it isn't about me. We live in a complicated existence, and some things can't be explained while we are in our physical states. At least not yet. But my part is to speak words of healing and freedom, and to inspire others to believe and to agree with the promises of God."

I swallowed hard. Maybe I was starting to get choked up, too. Suddenly, Andre came out of the cave and spoke to us.

"There you are. Obadiah told us you two were out here but that we couldn't disturb you until now." I felt myself shiver a little. "We're ready to start as soon as you come inside." With that, he turned and went back into the cave. Hayley and I followed him.

We walked into the room and took our seats. Obadiah welcomed us as we sat down. He asked if anyone had anything interesting happen this week. I looked over at Hayley and she looked back at me, and I burst out laughing. I explained, "If anyone has anything to share, you'd better do it before Hayley tells her story. She has had quite a week, and it will be very tough to top it."

Of course saying that was like throwing down the gauntlet, and no one wanted to take up the challenge. Before I'd said something, Maria had sat up in her seat like she had a story to tell, but when Hayley and I laughed, she'd sat back and turned to Hayley. Everyone was looking at Hayley, and she blushed slightly, which only augmented the golden glow around her face that seemed more obvious now that we were inside.

"Well," Andre said, "don't keep us in suspense!"

"Yes, tell us!" Catherine coaxed.

Hayley asked if everyone remembered her story about her grandmother from last week, and the whole group nodded. Obadiah smiled as if he already knew what Hayley was going to talk about.

She told her story, and even though it was my second time hearing it, I was just as amazed. It was so clear that God had set the whole thing up. People may have been able to write off the leaves disappearing from my yard as a coincidence, but four people being healed through one girl's prayers in one week? That was undeniably miraculous.

When Hayley finished her story, there was a buzz in the room. The entire group could sense something big was happening.

Catherine spoke. "Hayley, that's incredible in more ways than one. I love how God not only healed others through you; he also healed you!"

Hayley nodded, her eyes a little misty. "I see how God delivered me from my emotional damage and has freed me to speak words of healing to others." She was overcome with happy tears then, and Maria rubbed her shoulder.

Andre piped up, "That's a pretty long list for one week. Did you heal anyone else?"

"Honestly, I didn't try," Hayley responded. "I don't have any sense that I can just walk down the hallways of the hospital and heal everyone. I believe it was a divine appointment with me for these four, and I believe God will provide plenty of opportunities to heal people in the future. But as I was praying for healing, I remembered the words of Jesus from John 5:19, 'I only do what I see the Father doing.' These words encourage me that while I believe it's God's will to heal, I'm not expected to walk down a street and heal everyone in my path."

We sat for a moment in silence, and I thought back to the first week when we'd discussed specific prophetic acts. It was exciting to see how much we'd all been growing.

Obadiah smiled at Hayley and then said, "I see you brought something with you."

Hayley smiled as she pulled a little heart-shaped vase of flowers from the bag she had brought, "Yes. On the way out of the hospital I stopped by the gift shop and bought this small arrangement of silk flowers. I thought maybe it could go up on the shelf next to Jerry's can of soup?"

Obadiah grinned even bigger. "I think that's a wonderful idea." While Hayley stepped quietly across the room to the trophy shelf, Obadiah continued the conversation. "You're all starting to see more clearly outside the physical realm." Then he turned toward Maria and asked, "Does anyone else have anything to share?"

There was a rustling noise as Maria readjusted in her chair. She put her coffee cup on the floor and began, "Last week the Holy Spirit revealed to me that my behaviors reveal a mistrust in the area of relationship." She then gave a brief background of her dating relationships, culminating in a story about how she felt she'd recently lost "the one." "My behaviors through all of this reflect that I feel it's all on me to be attractive in a certain way, to find the right person, and to get myself married. When I really examined it, I saw I not only wasn't trusting in God's unconditional love, I also wasn't believing that He would provide the right community for me to move forward in my daily ministry. I guess I just feel like the pressure has been lifted, and this week I've enjoyed a more intimate relationship with Christ than ever before." Maria's joy seemed to fill the room. It was Hayley's turn to give Maria an encouraging hug.

"I can kind of relate to what Maria is talking about," I started. "I mean, not in the area of relationship. I'm happily married." Everyone laughed, including Maria. "I just mean that this week a wrong self-perception of mine was shattered." Although it felt harder for me to tell my story to the others than it had been to tell it to the Holy Spirit, I told my story of Mikey and his dad and how I'd felt freed from a false "provider" label. Mike nodded knowingly, and I was grateful I wasn't alone.

Obadiah looked around the room at each of us, almost through each of us, and said, "You've all been experiencing increasing moves of the Holy Spirit in your lives. You've been sitting before Jesus and visiting with him. You've been seeing the outcome of your declarations in the Spirit. And through all of this, you're beginning your journey into the spiritual, supernatural world of the Kingdom of Heaven."

I realized how different my perspective was from just a few weeks ago and how true Obadiah's statement was. I looked around to see everyone slowly nodding in agreement.

"Let's take a break for a couple of minutes, and when we come back we're going to start our discussion on how the Holy Spirit manifests in our lives."

FRUIT OF THE SPIRIT

As we settled back into the next session, the vibe in the room was lighthearted. Jerry playfully stole Catherine's seat, so she quickly sat down in Andre's. With the exceptions of Mike and Obadiah, the rest of us snatched up our study materials and hustled into new seats.

Obadiah laughed with us as we made more of a ruckus than kids playing musical chairs. I was glad to be in a group of people who knew when to be serious as well as how to have a little fun. Throwing myself into what had been Jerry's chair, I noted that the room looked different from this angle. It wasn't just that I was seeing from a new perspective, it was as if the ceiling was higher and the walls were a warmer color. I wondered if my mind was playing tricks on me, but Obadiah was opening up the next part of the session, and I didn't have time to further consider it.

"As I mentioned," Obadiah was saying, "you've all been growing in your spiritual perspectives. Now we need to talk a little more about the Holy Spirit and his gifts to us. One of the things I want to focus on the next few weeks is what we find in Galatians 5:22–23, the fruit of the Spirit. You know all the fruit of the Spirit: love, joy, peace, patience, kindness, goodness, faithfulness, gentleness, and self-control. I want us to begin giving serious thought to what each one truly is."

I'd been learning about the fruit of the Spirit since I was young, and I'd even taught on it in Sunday school. I was thinking I might have something valuable to share when Obadiah threw a curveball.

"Let me start with a challenging question: can anyone give an example of a fruit of the Spirit shown in the Old Testament?"

Jerry raised his eyebrows. "Did you say in the Old Testament?"

"Yes, that's right," Obadiah confirmed. The room was silent as we looked around to see if anyone had an answer; Hayley looked down at her notebook thoughtfully, but didn't write anything. Maria started to speak, but stopped short. Obadiah took the cue. "Okay, I know this might seem like a challenge at first, but I promise it's not. Why don't you all pair up and take twenty minutes or so to find examples in the Old Testament of each of the fruit of the Spirit as mentioned in Galatians 5."

Since I was now sitting closest to Mike, I turned toward him as he pulled out his tablet. "Howdy, Partner," I said and he smiled.

This time I noticed a difference in the way we were doing our research. No longer the quiet, hesitant group from the first week, we were talking openly about our ideas, eagerly highlighting passages and physically pointing out verses in our Bibles to our partners.

For an example of joy, Mike referenced how King David danced when the Ark of the Covenant entered his city, and I thought that was a good observation. Although the circumstances leading up to that moment had been hard for David, David knew that God had blessed and would continue to bless him and his people.

"I agree, Mike," I said, "even if it sounds like David's expression of joy looked a little silly."

"Can't say I haven't looked sillier," Mike said, and I had to admit that I probably had as well.

After some more thinking, I gave an example of faithfulness. I pointed out how Joseph had been sold into slavery and had served in captivity under Potiphar, yet because he continued working honestly, he went from prison all the way up to second in command.

Mike chimed in, "Yeah, I don't know if I'd be able to stay that faithful."

Obadiah overheard and gently corrected him. "You're going to have plenty of opportunities to grow and to show your faith, Mike." Mike raised his eyes, and I thought he looked like a little boy who had just been complimented by his dad. It was funny how guys like Mike and I could be so confident at work but not in our faith. Mike and I shared a look, and I knew he was thinking the same thing. We went back to work.

After we had a good list, Obadiah called the group back together. "All right, let's hear what each of you have. We'll go in the order they're listed in Galatians 5 for now. Who has an example of love?"

"I have an example," Maria giggled to herself. "I looove coffee." The rest of us laughed with her, getting used to her offbeat sense of humor.

"But Obadiah said to study the Old Testament, and 'He Brews' is in the New," Andre pointed out, and there was a collective groan at the old coffee making joke.

Obadiah chuckled. "Okay, let me rephrase. What is an example of love in someone's life in the Old Testament?"

"I have a real example," Maria chimed in. "How about how Ruth insisted on following Naomi back to her home country?"

"Good," Obadiah said. "Ruth was selfless in choosing to stay by Naomi's side no matter what."

Andre added, "That reminds me of the love of David and Jonathan."

"Yes, David and Jonathan showed love to each other," Obadiah agreed. "That love was so strong that years later, David showed favor to Jonathan's son, Mephibosheth. Those are both good examples of love. Who has an example of joy?"

I shared Mike's example of David's dancing. Then Catherine said, "I hadn't thought of this before, but when you mentioned dancing, I thought about how, in Exodus, Miriam danced for joy that first night when the Hebrews had crossed over the Red Sea."

"Those are both examples of times when joy followed some sort of difficulty," Obadiah pointed out. "You might notice that often the fruit of the Spirit are most evident in your lives when you're encountering hardship."

A thought struck me. "Are you saying that the fruit of the Spirit is for difficult times?"

Obadiah answered, "No, that's not quite what I am saying. The fruit of the Spirit may be consistently present in our lives in good times, and we'll notice them, but they are most evident when we're encountering hardship. It is like a candle on a table in a restaurant. You may notice the candle and think it is a nice touch. But when the restaurant dims the lights, you notice the candle even more. You recognize how it changes the feeling of the table with its flickering. It becomes more evident. The fruit of the Spirit is the same way with us. People may notice that you are different and may even appreciate the difference. But when times get dark, people will gather around you because of the fruit."

"Then it seems better to walk in the fruit of the Spirit during times of hardship. Is that right?" I asked.

"What I will tell you is that if you are not able to consistently practice living in the fruit of the Spirit during the good times, you will find it almost impossible to live in them in the dark times." Obadiah paused a moment to let that sink in. Then he continued, "Does anyone have an example for when someone in the Old Testament was at peace despite difficulty?"

"What about when Daniel was thrown into the lion's den?" asked Hayley. "It gives me goose bumps to even think about being surrounded by hungry animals, yet Daniel stayed calm and trusted in God to deliver him. That's the kind of peace I want!"

Several of us agreed. Then Jerry, who had been staring straight ahead, clearly mulling something over, shared, "I think Moses might also give us an example of peace."

"Go on," Obadiah encouraged.

Jerry held up his arm, acting out his story. "Imagine Moses standing in front of the Red Sea, holding the staff that has the sea parted, waiting for thousands and thousands of people to cross, and watching Pharaoh's army approaching from a distance. I think I'd get pretty nervous right about then and start to sweat, but Moses didn't. He just stood there, totally at peace, knowing that he was doing what he was supposed to be doing, and waited patiently for everyone to cross."

"That's an astute observation, Jerry," Obadiah said as Jerry brought his arm back down to his side. "And I like how you and Hayley both partnered peace with patience. Both Daniel and Moses were at peace while they were waiting for something to happen."

"Or maybe, in Daniel's case, while he was hoping that nothing happened," Hayley added.

Obadiah grinned at her. I appreciated how he always took the time to make each of us feel noticed and heard before moving on to the next thing. He was never rushed. He continued, "What are some other examples of patience?"

Andre mentioned how Jacob had worked for seven years to marry Rachel and how, when he had been given Leah instead, he had worked another seven years for Rachel. I pointed out the obvious patience of Job. Maria referenced Daniel 10:13 in which Daniel is praying and fasting and waiting for an answer yet finds out the angel who was sent to him was delayed.

Then Catherine said, "I think Sampson is another good example of patience. Even though his hair and his strength had been growing back for a while, he patiently waited until the moment when he could do the most damage to his captors to reveal his power."

Obadiah was clearly impressed with Catherine's example. "Very good, Catherine. You've all come up with some great examples. Who has something for kindness?"

Hayley brought up how Joseph showed kindness in giving provision and a warm welcome to the very brothers who had betrayed him. "Yes," Obadiah said.

Andre spoke up, "Jerry and I talked about two examples. One was how Rahab kept the spies, foreigners in Jericho, safe and gave them lodging. We also talked about how Boaz was kind to Ruth, providing for her as a master and as a husband."

"Boaz's relationship with Ruth is also a good example of gentleness, isn't it?" Catherine asked.

"This is all right on point," said Obadiah. "What other examples of gentleness are there in the Old Testament? Jerry, do you have one?"

Jerry was watching the wall again, so we knew he must have something good to share. "I was just thinking," he started, "about when the prophet Nathan went to David to confront him over what had happened with Bathsheba. He didn't just start condemning David for what he did. He didn't start yelling and accusing. Instead, he used a story and allowed David to recognize his own sin. Only then did Nathan point out what David had done and how it was wrong."

"That's an excellent point, Jerry," Obadiah said. "Often when we hear the word 'gentleness,' we think of something akin to taking care of a baby bird with a broken wing. But gentleness doesn't have to be quiet and soft. Sometimes being gentle means taking a considerate, yet tough, approach. We can learn a lot from the story of Nathan and David about choosing our words carefully and being wise with our delivery of truth. Often the best way to speak into someone's life isn't to speak at all, but to ask them questions and guide them to the truth based on their answers."

All of a sudden, a work memory flooded my mind. It was of a coworker who had asked me about church once. Instead of figuring out why he was suddenly interested in God, I had simply given him directions to my church and told him the service times. He never showed up. At the time, I remembered feeling guilty that I hadn't spent more time talking to him about God. Now I realized I should have asked more questions.

"Remember," Obadiah said, as if reading my mind, "when we're going over these examples, we shouldn't be thinking of moments in the past where we feel we have failed or not done enough. Rather, we should look for ways to implement the fruit of the Spirit in our lives moving forward." I caught his eye and nodded my head. He might have winked at me, or it might have been the light playing tricks.

After that, our group gained momentum and went through the rest of the list rather quickly. For goodness, examples were given of Noah finding grace in the eyes of the Lord and of Deborah, who was known as a holy prophetess and a righteous judge. For faithfulness, I shared my example of Joseph, and Andre mentioned that when Nehemiah began rebuilding the wall, even though he was under opposition from Sanballat, Tobiah, Geshem the Arab, and that whole crowd, he remained faithful to the vision he was given and the mission he was undertaking. Finally, Obadiah opened up the discussion on self-control.

Maria spoke up. "I need more of that when it comes to chocolate!" We all laughed.

Mike said, "I need more self-control when it comes to anger. The first example of self-control in the Old Testament that pops into my mind is when David was hiding in that cave, and Saul came in to relieve himself. Saul was hunting David down to kill him, but even when Saul was vulnerable and David could have killed him, David instead just cut off a corner of his robe. I aspire to be that calm and controlled!"

"It's interesting to see how you're all already tying examples of the fruit of the Spirit to your own lives. The Spirit is certainly at work as you continue seeking Him and His purposes. Another good example of self-control is when Samuel went to Jessie's house because the Lord had told him that was where he would find the next king. Jessie brought his sons, but Samuel passed them all over. I think it would have been tempting to just pick one of them and move on with the process, but instead he exercised self-control and asked, 'Isn't there someone else?' That's when they brought David in, and that's when Samuel knew that David was the right man and anointed him."

The girls all agreed with Obadiah in unison. It was obvious they had also talked about this example.

I was kind of disappointed to come to the end of the discussion. Searching for examples in the Bible was like a game, and it was a game that was transforming the way I understood my world. I had a feeling it was making me a man more like how God would want me to be.

Obadiah interrupted my thoughts, asking, "What was interesting about this exercise? I asked you to look for examples of the nine fruit of the Spirit in the Old Testament, and you were able to find them fairly easily. What does that tell us?"

We pondered his question. Obadiah let us think for a minute. Then Andre said, "I give up. What is it supposed to tell us?"

Obadiah continued, "This tells us two things. First, you can look at behaviors and pinpoint the fruit. You saw that Ruth behaved with love. You saw that Joseph behaved with kindness. You saw that Nathan behaved with gentleness. These were outward behaviors that we observed. Just like a fruit is an outward manifestation of what's going on in the tree, these things are outward manifestations of what's going on within us. And these behaviors existed all the way back in the Old Testament."

Hayley raised her hand and then quickly brought it down. "Sorry," she said, "habit." Obadiah motioned for her to ask her question. "I was just wondering if we can call it the fruit of the Spirit in the Old Testament. How does that work if this all occurred before Christ sent His Spirit to us?"

"Wonderful question," Obadiah said. "You're right that there wasn't an indwelling of the Spirit in the Old Testament, because we don't see that occur until the New. But there was a ministry of the Spirit acting in and on the lives of the individuals we mentioned. Consider how many people in the Old Testament did not have an understanding of who the Messiah would be, and yet had faith to believe in a yet-to-come Messiah. That alone presents the possibility of a ministry of the Holy Spirit in the Old

Testament. The Spirit has been at work bringing about good fruit for centuries."

Obadiah paused, but we were all too lost in thought to ask questions. He continued, broadening his subject, "Often in the Church, when we talk about the fruit of the Spirit, we say we can't produce the fruit on our own, and that's only something God can do. That's partially true, because God is our source of life, but if He did everything and we did nothing, there would be no reason to instruct us to cultivate the fruit of the Spirit. It would just present itself in our lives, already ripe."

Andre commented, "Yeah, but just the other day I was kind to a guy who really gets under my skin. That was all thanks to God. If it would have been up to me, I would have punched him in the gut."

We laughed as Andre pantomimed a fight from his seat.

When the frivolity died down, Obadiah continued. "There's truth to that, Andre. The Spirit does enable us to be more than ourselves. But the truth is that you have been cultivating your relationship with the Spirit, which kept you from acting on your own impulses. We are active participants in producing the fruit of the Spirit. That's why Paul told us to exhibit the fruit. While the Holy Spirit does the developing, we have to participate, taking responsibility for our own maturity, because God won't mature us against our will. Our participation centers on developing a relationship with the Holy Spirit that allows Him to influence us and help us build good, long-lasting, unshakeable character. You see, non-believers can build good character, but without the Spirit, their character can be manipulated by circumstances and can change in a heartbeat. The fruit of the Spirit, however, does not change because of circumstances. It also doesn't spontaneously spring up overnight; it's something that has to be grown and cultivated."

Everyone let the gravity of that challenge to cultivate the fruit of the Spirit sink in. After a few moments, Obadiah continued.

"Over the next few weeks, we're going to be studying each of the fruit of the Spirit in more detail. The order in which we're going to study them has incredible significance for the prophet. Today, we're going to look at love because it's the foundation. Without love, none of the other fruit could be produced. Then we're going to talk about goodness and joy, two related fruit. They're the natural next step as they flow out of love. Goodness and joy help cultivate kindness and gentleness in our lives. Then will come patience. Then faithfulness. Then peace. And finally self-control. Next week I'll talk more about that order and why it's important, but for now, just trust me that it's important for the development of prophetic insight. I know we're tackling a lot today, so why don't you take one more quick break before we dive into what a biblical understanding of love looks like?"

Hayley made a heart with her hands at Maria, and they both smiled. Everyone stood up and stretched, but no one said much, as all of us were already thinking about our definitions of love.

L O V E

After a quick break, we returned to our seats and Obadiah jumped right in. "I already told you that love is foundational to all of our other subjects. To begin, we need to ask ourselves, 'What is love, and how do we express it?'"

"Love is unconditional, like how I feel about my son and how God cares about us," Catherine said.

Andre joined in, "Love is giving of yourself for others."

"To me," said Hayley, "love means different things in different forms. It can be an action verb expressing how you show you value something or someone, an adjective to describe something or someone that gives affection, or a noun that describes who God is."

Mike, who had been typing on his tablet, said, "Well, Merriam-Webster says that love is 'strong affection for another arising out of kinship or personal ties, attraction based on sexual desire, affection based on admiration, benevolence, or common interests, or an assurance of affection.'"

"It's agape," Jerry said. "It's unselfish, loyal concern for our fellow man."

"That's all good," said Obadiah. "And all true. But let me give you my definition of love for this class." Hayley grabbed her pen and notebook and leaned forward in her chair. Obadiah paused until she was ready and then continued. "'Love is the desire for others to do well regardless of their response for you.' That's basically how God loves us. His desire is for the best for all of us—regardless of how we treat Him. He wants all of us to be with Him and to have abundant and eternal life. God loves everyone. That said, He doesn't necessarily like everyone."

Jerry raised his eyebrows, and Maria looked confused. Obadiah caught their expressions.

"Don't worry, I'm not talking bad about God. You too are able to love people without liking them. You can hope that people succeed in life and do well, all the while wishing that they do well in life somewhere far, far away from you." I said 'yes' a little too strongly and immediately felt my cheeks redden. Obadiah pretended he didn't notice. "Let me give you an extreme example. Tell me, did God love Hitler?" We nodded. "Yes, He loves everyone. But did God like Hitler? Absolutely not. He hated what Hitler did. He hated that Hitler was a bigot who killed Jewish people and anyone who didn't fit a certain mold. God loved Hitler and had the desire for him to turn from his awful ways, but He didn't like him. In other words, Hitler had no favor from God. We can take action to increase God's liking of us, and that's called 'favor.' We gain favor by spending time with Him and growing more like Him."

"Like what we're learning about biblical meditation?" Hayley asked.

"Exactly," Obadiah responded. "God loves those who love to draw near to Him. He loves to be close to us. In scripture, when God says to the goats that have been separated from the sheep, 'Depart from me; I never knew you,' he's implying a lack of intimacy. God knows who every person is and knows everything each person has done, but some people don't enjoy an intimate relationship with God. When we grow in intimacy with God, we learn to love like He loves. So let's look at scripture to see if we can define God's idea of love. Why don't you take a few minutes to find some references to or ideas about love in the New Testament? When you find one, write it on the white board so we can look at them together."

We eagerly pulled out our Bibles and our tablets and began the search. After fifteen minutes or so, our list of verses and notes included:

Luke 6:27: "Love your enemies, do good to those who hate you"

Romans 12:10: "Be devoted to one another in brotherly love; give preference to one another in honor."

1 John 3:17: If God's love abides in you, when you see a brother in need, you will help him out.

1 John 5:3: "For this is the love of God, that we keep His commandments" These commandments are not burdensome; they don't weigh us down.

John 15:13: "Greater love has no one than this, that one lay down his life for his friends." Jesus died for those he loved.

As Hayley capped the marker and started back to her seat, Obadiah said, "Good work. Let's take a look at each of these. Start with Luke 6:27. What does it mean to do good to those who hate you? What does this look like in our lives?"

Catherine pointedly looked at Michael, and he took the cue, "You know how last week I told you guys about those three big deals I closed? And about how everything was starting to click into place at work? Well some of the guys who I work with aren't big fans of the favor I've been receiving. I feel like they're trying to undermine me at every step, always looking for issues in my work or a complaint they can take to my boss. I know I can't allow this to impact how I love them. I know I need to cooperate with the Spirit to grow, and I need to desire for them to do well."

"Thanks for sharing, Mike," Obadiah said. "It's not easy, but it sounds like you know the right thing to do. Let's move on to Romans 12:10 now. Who has an idea of what it means to 'give preference' to one another?"

Catherine barely let Obadiah finish his question before chiming in. "Listen, I'm a mother of a small child. I know all about giving preference to another person."

"Can you give us some examples, Catherine?" Obadiah asked.

"Sure, let's see. I never get to eat when my food is hot anymore because I have to help Josh. I had to permanently cancel my weekly girls' luncheon because I'm always driving my son to a lesson here or a practice there. And I've learned that I need to be in bed way earlier than I'd prefer to be because otherwise I'm exhausted when I wake up at the crack of dawn to the sound of crying." She shook her head. "All that said, I'm honestly glad to do these things because I consider it an honor to be a mother and to care for such an amazing, little human being." She smiled, and it was evident how much she cared for her son.

"That's definitely love. Does anyone have an example for 1 John 3:17? What does it mean to see your brother in need?" Obadiah asked.

Immediately, Maria replied, "You know, I was just thinking something about that one. When I hear the phrase 'a brother in need,' I think of homeless people. I'm not sure why I've made the two synonymous. But this week I learned a new definition. I was in line at lunch a couple days ago, and the woman in front of me ordered food for herself and her two children. When they told her the amount, she started rummaging around in her purse. She took everything out, placing her lipstick, her car keys, coupons, and various other items on the counter. She practically turned the purse inside out. Normally this kind of wait would annoy me and

I'd get impatient. But instead I felt sorry for this woman. When it finally dawned on me that she had forgotten her wallet and was probably deeply embarrassed that her kids and everyone else was waiting on her, I offered to pay for her order. It only cost about $15. At the time, I didn't see this as helping someone 'in need,' but I guess that's what it was."

"I like that story, Maria," Obadiah said. "One of the reasons why I like it is because it shows that you are in transition. You're learning how to perceive need. The more all of you hone this instinct, the quicker you'll respond, and the more people you'll serve." Although clearly pleased with the praise, Maria looked shyly away. Obadiah said, "There are two more verses on the board. What does 1 John 5:3 mean when it talks about keeping commandments without being weighed down by the law?"

As I looked down at the floor, I noticed others tilt their heads to look at the ceiling or stare at their notebooks; everyone was avoiding eye contact.

Obadiah graciously moved ahead. "Lots of times when we talk about keeping God's commandments, we get into a law-versus-grace discussion, but that's not really what 1 John 5:3 is talking about. Jesus came to fulfill the law, yet he gave us a number of commandments. Paul and other writers of the New Testament also gave instructions. In Galatians, Paul spends a lot of time talking about how we're saved by grace, which is true, but then at the end of the book he gives a list of things to do and a list of things not to do. There's obviously a behavioral aspect at play here. You see, your behavior is how you know whether or not you're operating in grace. If you're fully in grace, you will walk in the fruit of the Spirit. Being under the law means keeping God's commandments to cause Him to love us, but keeping God's commandments is a natural way both of showing we love Him and of understanding how He loves us. Is that a little clearer?"

We murmured our agreement. Obadiah continued, "Okay, last one, John 15:13. What does it mean to lay down your life for others? I mean without actually ceasing to live."

Maria snickered and covered her mouth, but it was too late. "I hope that's what you mean!" The rest of us couldn't help but laugh a little with her.

Ever patient, Obadiah picked up where he'd left off, "You only get to physically lay down your life once, but that's not all this verse is saying. What it's saying is similar to the 'giving preference' that we talked about earlier, but it's more extreme. Giving preference can be inconvenient, but laying down your life costs you something, and it costs you something serious. It could cost you a lot of money, a prized possession, a relationship—something that will alter your way of living for some time."

"For me, I think it would mean something like quitting my job because I needed to spend more time with my family," Mike suggested.

"Another good example," Obadiah said. "Now that we have a better idea of what love is, let's consider the definition of the actions of love. Would someone read 1 Corinthians 13:4–7?"

"I have it memorized," Jerry said. "Love is patient and kind; love does not envy or boast; it is not arrogant or rude. It does not insist on its own way; it is not irritable or resentful; it does not rejoice at wrongdoing, but rejoices with the truth. Love bears all things, believes all things—"

At that word, Obadiah raised his hand and Jerry paused, "Let me say one thing about that. To 'believe all things' means that love believes in good things that reflect God's love for us; love believes that there are better things than may appear in a seemingly negative situation. For example, love won't believe a scandalous rumor; instead it will search out what is true about an individual." He motioned for Jerry to continue.

"Love bears all things, believes all things, hopes all things, endures all things. Love never fails" he finished.

"Right," Obadiah said. "When it says that love isn't arrogant or rude—some translations say 'doesn't act unbecomingly'—it means that love never acts immaturely. It always acts in a way that is appropriate for the situation. Does anyone else have a definition to add?"

Andre pointed out that "keeps no record of wrongs" means that love truly forgives and forgets as if the offence never happened.

Looking up and pushing her hair back from her face, Hayley added, "Love doesn't rejoice in unrighteousness. I think that means that, for example, when a kid is getting bullied or someone is struggling with alcoholism, love doesn't laugh along or turn away from the issue. Love grieves when we're disrespectful to the kingdom of God and His creation."

Standing up, Obadiah replied, "Well said, Hayley. With that, I'm afraid we're out of time. Let me just reiterate that love is the foundational key to success as a prophet. If you don't get love right, you won't get anything else right. Love should be manifest in everything you do and say. That's not to say you're going to love perfectly all the time, but it does mean that the more you grow in love, the more of a true prophet you become."

I committed that line to memory. The more you grow in love, the more of a true prophet you become.

"Your assignment this week then is to be very conscious and aware of opportunities to love those inside your family, to love the people you meet on the street, to love those who hate you, and to love people you don't like. We'll report back next week."

We shared knowing glances as we stood to go. It was going to be a challenging but rewarding week. I couldn't wait to see what love was going to do in my life and in the lives of my friends over the course of the next seven days.

CHAPTER SIX: GOODNESS & JOY

LOVE WEEK

I never knew love was so hard. Although I'd expected to have a heightened sense of love because of the assignment, I didn't think my new awareness would reveal a huge absence of love in my life. I've always considered myself a pretty nice guy, and maybe outwardly I am, but this week I realized my thoughts about people are less than generous. Somewhere around midweek it dawned on me that I wasn't loving people at all; I was just being nice to them. Being polite isn't love; it's just acceptable societal behavior. I win points with people by being cordial, but that's not love. This week I realized that although I was smiling and making small talk about people's lives, I wasn't actually desiring the best for them.

As I pulled in the clearing, I was so preoccupied with my mental review of my week that I only subconsciously noticed Andre making his way down the incline and Maria pulling into a space. Taking the space next to Maria a little too quickly, I came within an inch of hitting her door when she opened it to get out. She looked at me with wide eyes as I finishing pulling in, and I shook my head at myself for being so careless.

I turned off my car, and jumped out. We were both still in shock, but, as usual, Maria was the first to talk, "You scared me there! Jason, are you all right? You look frazzled. Is something wrong?"

"I think I'm okay," I started. "Maria, I am sorry— I was just lost in thought about my week and wasn't paying attention."

"It's okay," she said. "I've had quite the week as well."

"Oh?" I raised my eyebrows, willing myself to calm down so I could commiserate with Maria about our rough weeks.

She smiled. "Yes, this was the best week ever!"

"Righ—," I stopped and turned towards her. "Wait...best week ever?"

"Absolutely. It did start out a little rough, but once I realized what was going on, I jumped into the whole experience head first," she said, still beaming.

"Catch me up here. What do you mean?"

"I mean I struggled with the concept at first, but once I chose to love and gave it my all, things really clicked into place."

Wow, I thought. Maria had simply chosen to love? Was it really that simple? Had I missed out on a week of blessings because I hadn't made that choice? "Can you give me an example?"

"I definitely have examples to share, but we're about to go inside, so you're just going to have to wait to hear about my week with everyone else," she said with a grin.

Turning to shake my head at her, I stepped into the cave and ran smack into Andre.

"Whoa there!" He turned, still unzipping his jacket.

"Sorry, Andre, I didn't expect you to be stopped right inside the door." I nodded my hellos to the rest of the group and sat down before I could do any more damage.

Maria, right behind me, seemed to float into the room. "Hello, everyone!" she sang.

"Someone's in a good mood," Andre murmured to me.

"Yeah, I think she has something good to share."

Everyone else took their seats, and Obadiah dove right into the session: "How was everyone's week?"

Sentiments around the room ranged from my awful week to Maria's glorious one and everywhere in-between. It seemed to be the majority consensus that none of us had really nailed the whole love thing; it seemed like more people felt they'd failed than had succeeded, but I was encouraged by several comments.

Catherine pointed out that once she'd recognized how she was beating herself up for not doing well enough, she was thankful that she'd had second and third chances to improve.

Nodding alongside Catherine, Michael noted, "Catherine and I talked about our assignment a couple days ago, and we were saying how we've noticed shifts in each others' attitudes. Even though it was a huge challenge at the beginning of the week to think about doing everything in love, it became more natural—

although never easy—as the days progressed. I know it was only one week, but I feel like Catherine and I are already closer because of it, and that's not even mentioning the good it has done in our relationship with our son and with people outside our home."

As others shared, I squirmed in my seat. I knew that if I didn't share about my difficult week, it would eat at me for the entire session. Finally I spoke up. "This week," I cleared my throat, "I discovered that what I thought was love was really just politeness and obligation in a thin disguise. Or worse, when I wasn't being cordial, I was being rude and harsh with people, with people I didn't even know that well!" I shook my head at myself and continued, "The Lord really spoke to me this week when I was driving home from work on Thursday though. I was driving through this underpass that's right before a traffic light. It's always pretty tight under there, even for just a couple cars, but on Thursday, this tractor-trailer cut me off. He pulled right in front of me, and I had to slam on my breaks to keep from hitting him. Recovering slightly, my eyes caught a sticker on the back of his truck that asked, 'How's my driving?' Then there was a number to call to report any issues. I squinted to see it, but he pulled away too soon and I couldn't quite read it.

"I couldn't calm myself down. Fueled by anger and adrenaline, I followed him five miles out of my way just to get that phone number. Finally I got a clear view, wrote the number down, and pulled out my cell phone. But as soon as I typed the first two numbers in, I heard the Lord ask, 'What are you doing, Jason?' I thought it was pretty obvious, so I told the Lord, 'I'm reporting that jerk for his bad driving.' And then God asked the big question, 'Why do you think that man is in a hurry to get home?' As I considered it, I realized that driver probably also has a family. He probably also has obligations at home and was just in a rush to return his truck and get back to his wife and kids. It hit me that I hadn't been choosing love. God asked me, 'What would love look like in this situation?' Well, love would pray that he would make it safely home. That he wouldn't be in any accidents. That he and his family would be blessed. So I began praying all of that out loud. I guess in that way, this moment was a success, even if it started off as a terrible failure. I had moments like that all week long. After the fact, the Lord would reveal what I'd missed. It was an awful week, but at least now I'm painfully aware of how much love is lacking in my life and how far I have to go."

"It's not easy, is it?" Jerry asked rhetorically.

Obadiah strangely didn't comment. He just nodded and turned to Andre. "Andre, how was your week?"

Andre hesitated for a few moments and then said, "It was an interesting week for me. I ran into someone I hadn't seen in years." Andre looked around the room. "Most of you guys don't know this, but I have a past I'm not too proud of. I've done a lot of things I wish I hadn't done. Let's just say that I fell into the wrong crowd back in the day, and they got me involved in some pretty bad things. To state it generously, they didn't have such a good influence on me. Anyway, when I met the Lord, he really helped me straighten up my life." Andre looked like he might get emotional, but he recovered and continued, "Well, I ran into one of those old friends this week. Totally unexpected. I just saw him on the street, and he waved me over to talk. My first thought was, 'Oh no, not again.' But then I realized I'd been set free from that life. The Lord reminded me that I didn't have to like him, but I did have to hope for the best for him. Looking at him, I thought to myself that not much had changed. He still dressed the same, acted the same, and talked the same. He was the same person, just fifteen years older. While I don't want to invite him back into my life, that conversation reminded me that he is still one of my old friends. I still want to see him do well. The thing that has changed is that my definition of 'doing well' is way different now than it was all those years ago.

"When our conversation died down and it was obvious we were about to part ways, I heard myself ask him if I could pray for him. Now, in our background, prayer isn't too unusual. There's a religious history there, even if there isn't a godly one. He looked straight at me, and I thought I saw a little spark in his eye. He said, 'Sure, man.' So I asked the Lord to be with him and protect him and keep him safe and to just show His face to him. That was about it. We shook hands, and he walked away. For fifteen years I've hoped I'd never see him again, and now I catch myself hoping I do run into him again."

We all sat quietly for a moment. It was the first time Andre had opened up like that, and I think all of us were searching for the right words to encourage him.

Surprisingly, Hayley was the one to break the silence. "Thanks for sharing, Andre. While I can't identify with your entire story, I do know how hard it can be to love people who have led us astray in the past. I think you took a huge step in the Spirit this week."

I looked at Maria. "I think Maria has something to share with all of us as well."

"Yes, I do," Maria began. "I started out this week like a lot of you. I felt like I was failing the assignment. You may be surprised to hear this because you all met me in a specific environment under specific circumstances, but I'm not like Jason. I'm not typically too polite or cordial to people I don't care to be around. If I like you, I like you, but if I don't, then don't expect me to go out of my way to be nice. On Monday, I was convicted about this attitude, and I decided I was going to do this love thing right. I discovered that I could learn to love, starting with a compliment here and small piece of encouragement there. What Obadiah mentioned last week about loving people even if we don't like them really resonated with me. I found that setting out with the intent to help others and with the desire for them to do well helped me become a nicer person. After all, if I believe every person needs to know Jesus and needs to be cared for, why wouldn't I make my walk reflect my talk?"

If I wasn't convinced to take the step of faith to love better last week, I certainly was now. I looked around the room and saw everyone intently listening to Maria.

Maria continued, "When I started out, I was thinking about that verse in Proverbs about how if you're kind to your enemy, you 'heap burning coals of fire' on his head. I kind of thought of love as a nice form of revenge. As I changed my attitude, however, I found it wasn't like that at all. When I started being nicer to people, they started being nice back. Through this practice, I uncovered a couple things I had in common with people who I wasn't too fond of before, and I actually made a few new friends! It's funny, I probably would have liked them all along if I'd given them a chance."

"Isn't it freeing to know that we don't have to like everyone in order to love them?" Catherine asked.

"You know," Michael said, "it occurred to me that the definition of love that Obadiah gave us last week—'wanting someone to do well regardless of their response to you'—doesn't have any emotion attached to it. People often tie love to an emotion, but in this definition, it's more of a choice."

"And it's a hard choice that we have to keep making every day," I added.

"Yeah, that's true too," Mike agreed.

"Did you have a question, Hayley?" Obadiah asked.

I turned to look at Hayley, whose brow was furrowed with a pensive look. She began, "I've just been thinking about something. Last week you made a point about God loving everyone but liking some people. I began to wonder how to know if God likes me or not."

"That's a great question Hayley," Obadiah said. "How do you know if God likes you or not? Can you know? Can you do anything to cause him to like you more? Well, let's look at what the Bible tells us. When you think of people from the Bible, who do you think God liked more than others?"

Jerry said, "David immediately comes to mind for me. Scripture refers to him as the 'apple of God's eye.' He's also identified as a 'man after God's own heart.' That's pretty high praise."

"Exactly right. God liked David," Obadiah confirmed. "Any other ideas?"

"When the angel appeared to Mary, he called her a 'highly favored one,'" Maria pointed out.

"Yes, good," Obadiah said. "That shows that not only can God like people, he can like people a lot. We can get a lot out of these two examples of David from the Old Testament and Mary from the New. What caused God to like them? Note that David was called the 'apple of God's eye' before he was anointed to be king.

He spent a lot of time out in the fields just worshiping and praying and communing with God. Those intimate moments with his Lord are what caused God to like him and to favor him. I think it's a fairly safe guess to say that it was something similar with Mary. She was probably very devoted to spending time with the Lord and faithful to whatever he asked her to do. Mary honored the Lord and gained favor in that way.

"So the short answer, Hayley, is yes. You can cause God to like you. To oversimplify it, He likes people who like to hang out with Him. It's a similar principle to how we choose friends. We also like people who like spending time with us. Even if you don't like someone at first, you may find that the longer you know her and the more experiences you have with her, the more you like her.

"Think about when you guys first entered this cave. You assessed one another and made some quick decisions, even if subconsciously at first, about who you liked, who you thought you'd get along with, and who wasn't really your cup of tea. Now, after meeting with each other every week and sharing who you are with one another, I'd venture to say you like everyone else in the room."

"Well, maybe not everyone" I teased, and everyone laughed. "I'm just kidding. It's true that I've come to love and like you guys."

"We love and like you back, Jason," Andre said.

After a few moments, Obadiah continued, "You've been sharing some significant emotional events, and those draw people together. Relationships are built over time. In the same way, your relationship with God is built over time. If you want God to like you, you have to work on your relationship with Him. He says that if you draw near to Him, He'll draw near to you. Drawing near to Him involves spending time and sharing some experiences and some adventures with Him. You'll start seeing how God shows up when you take a step of faith. You get to know Him even better as He reveals more and more of Himself to you. Favor on your life will continue to grow and grow. Does that help, Hayley?"

Looking up from her notebook, Hayley gave a small nod. "Yes, thank you."

"I have a question as well," Jerry said, and Obadiah motioned for him to continue. "I was thinking about love this week and was looking over scriptures about things like loving your brother and taking care of your brother. The question that came to mind was, who is my brother? Am I only commanded to love other believers, or am I commanded to love everyone in this way?"

Obadiah said, "That's another good question. What were your thoughts on it, Jerry?"

"I gave it a lot of thought," Jerry said, and none of us was surprised. "There are times when we're instructed to love our enemies, but more often than not, when the Bible talks about loving others, it's in the context of loving other believers. For example, in Romans, Paul is writing to believers when he says 'love one another.' He's not really telling them to love people outside the Christian circle. Then there's Jesus who says that the world will know that we are His followers based on our love for one another. Again, that seems to be talking about inter-Christianity love, not outward love. Does the Bible command us to love people who aren't believers? It seems to say that we can but that it's not our central command."

"I'm not going to give you an outright answer," Obadiah said, "but let me give you something to think about. Remember when we talked about quantum physics and time and the creation of the world? You guys know that God is eternal and outside human time. While we see and think linearly, when God looks at a person, He doesn't see that person only in a specific place or time. He sees all that he or she will become. So say He looked at Andre twenty years ago. Would He see Andre before he came to know the Lord or after he'd built a relationship with Jesus? He sees Andre the believer. In other words, God sees how each of us is going to end up."

Obadiah paused for a moment to let us think over his words. "We don't have that advantage. We may think that because someone isn't a believer, we aren't required to love that person. But if that person becomes a believer later in life, then when the Lord is watching you interacting with that person, he's seeing you treat a fellow believer poorly. My answer, then, is that it's up to you whether you think linearly or nonlinearly. But for me, because I don't know who might become a believer later in life, I'd rather err on the side of love. I'd rather love those who might be far from God and who are difficult to love so I don't make the mistake of not caring for one of God's beloved. I want God to see the fruit of the Spirit of love flowing through me to every person."

"Thanks for your perspective," Jerry said.

"Absolutely," Obadiah said. "Before we move from love to the next fruit of the Spirit we're going to discuss, goodness and joy, I want to make sure we're all on the same page about prophecy. We know 1 Corinthians 14:31 says all believers can prophesy in the Spirit. Every believer has access to the realm of the Spirit and can see, discern, and speak prophetic truth. Every believer has, to some extent, the ability to speak for the Lord and to encourage and build up others. Every believer has access to the entry-level, developmental stage of prophecy, yet Paul says some are prophets. We know, therefore, that there is some sort of spectrum to prophecy. All are called to prophesy, but not everyone is called to be a prophet. Some are called to be teachers, and some are called to be evangelists and et cetera. That's how Christ's Church functions.

"Now, I believe that each individual who is called to be a prophet follows a specific path, and I've broken down its development into five stages."

With this, Obadiah stood up, walked over to the whiteboard, and drew something that looked like this:

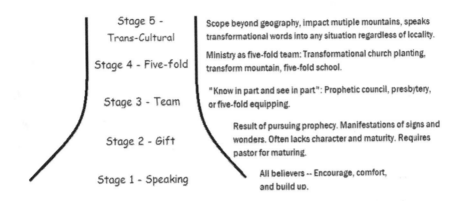

Stage 5 - Trans-Cultural — Scope beyond geography, impact mutiple mountains, speaks transformational words into any situation regardless of locality.

Stage 4 - Five-fold — Ministry as five-fold team: Transformational church planting, transform mountain, five-fold school.

Stage 3 - Team — "Know in part and see in part": Prophetic council, presbytery, or five-fold equipping.

Stage 2 - Gift — Result of pursuing prophecy. Manifestations of signs and wonders. Often lacks character and maturity. Requires pastor for maturing.

Stage 1 - Speaking — All believers -- Encourage, comfort, and build up.

Pointing to the first stage, Obadiah said, "I call this stage 'Speaking.' This is the stage that is available to all believers. This is where we speak words to encourage and build up others. We look at them and love them, wanting them to do better. We ask the Lord to help us see them through His eyes and to give us a word for that person. Then we prophesy, encouraging them with what is to come and what good plans the Lord has for them. Then we speak what is evident in the Spirit, and He delivers. All right, so every believer has access to this level. Are you all tracking?"

Taking time to look up from the diagram I was copying, I nodded. I wasn't quite sure what all of this was going to mean for my life or how I was supposed to move up the path, but Obadiah was a good teacher, and I was excited to learn what all this was going to mean for both my life and the lives of others God would bring into my life.

Seeing that we were all following, Obadiah continued, "The next stage up is what I call 'Gift.' This is a result of pursuing prophecy. At this stage, people often see manifestations of signs and wonders. People may be able to prophesy with amazing accuracy in this stage. They're able to give words of knowledge and tell people about themselves, and often they're able to identify things in others' lives that they would have no way of knowing. They find that they're able to operate at a higher level, and they aim to grow in it, pursue it, and practice it. At this stage, however, if a rising prophet doesn't have a certain level of maturity, he or she can go wrong. For one, she might deliver correction in untimely or inappropriate ways. Or lack of intimacy with the Lord, combined with personal opinions and biases, can get in the way. A person who is prophetically gifted needs to be closely connected with someone who has the gift of—or ideally who holds the office of—being a pastor who can help them grow in maturity and character to hone their gift.

"The next stage is what I call 'Team Ministry.' At this stage, the prophetic person realizes that no matter how gifted he is, he still only knows in part and sees in part. He realizes that he isn't the end all and be all of prophetic ministry and that he needs insight from others to grow, so he looks for others who are mature and who have similar giftings, and he begins ministering with them. When people with a combination of prophetic gifts and insights team up, it's sometimes referred to as a 'prophetic counsel.' This is contrasted with a 'presbytery,' in which elders of the church or people who are very experienced in ministry, such as pastors or even spiritually wise businessmen, serve as a board to offer godly perspective and to be a sort of chorus with the prophet. The third option for this stage is a 'five-fold equipping ministry.' In a five-fold equipping ministry, believers with other callings—such as to be a pastor or an apostle or an evangelist— work together, share with one another, and aid each other as they mentor others in their area of gifts. For example, a prophetic person might see in the Spirit and speak words that transform the natural, while the apostolic person shifts the culture of the group, and the pastor helps others to grow in maturity. This could be a ministry to a small group or a local church. The key point here is that the group works together both to minister and to train up and equip others in their giftings.

"Stage four, or 'Five-Fold,' is a significant jump. This is where the prophet and the rest of his five-fold group, who have probably already been ministering informally, begin to really cast vision for a city or a geographic area. Perhaps they hear the Lord's call to plant a church. Or maybe the group feels led to address or transform a particular cultural area or belief. Or perhaps instead of just equipping a few individuals, the team decides to start a full-fledged training school. No matter what the direction, in this stage the whole team decides to move forward to take a certain territory and begins working together toward that vision.

"The final stage, stage five, is what I call 'Transcultural' At this point, the prophet operates with a scope that's beyond geography and that impacts multiple cultural spheres of influence. A stage five prophet speaks transformational words into any situation, regardless of locality. To clarify, a stage four prophet may have authority in his church but not in another, or he may have prophetic clarity concerning a certain city but not another. Contrastingly, a stage five prophet pretty much has authority anywhere he or she goes."

Uncapping his pen again, Obadiah drew a dotted line between stages three and four. Below the dotted line, he wrote "Function," and above it he wrote "Office."

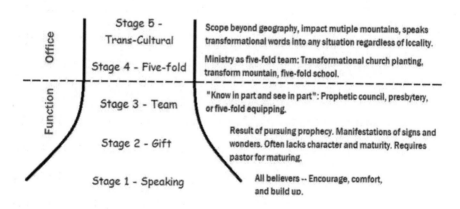

Obadiah explained, "What you can see here is that anything in stages one through three is what I consider normal church life. I usually use the term 'prophetic' to explain giftings at this level as this is where you see the function of the prophetic voice in the church. Above the line is where a prophetic person steps into the governmental office of a prophet. Again, a stage four prophet is part of a five-fold team with a specific mission to transform a church or a city, and a stage five prophet can prophesy concerning nation-wide and even global events. While it's not necessary to be at stage five to be a prophet, those in stages one through three need further development. Sometimes the Lord will immediately elevate someone to stage four or five, but that's not usually the way things are done. In the same way you don't make someone the pastor of a church the minute you recognize his pastoral gift but rather grow and disciple him, you also need to disciple and grow a prophet.

Taking a deep breath, Obadiah said, "All right. I know that was a lot of information to take in. I don't like to stop in the middle of the explanation because I think it's helpful to consider the full path to being a prophet, but does anyone have any questions now?"

No one spoke up. Several of us were still writing, and others were looking thoughtfully at their notes. I eyed the board nervously. That first time I'd met Obadiah, he'd said something about me being one of an army of prophets. Looking at his diagram, however, I couldn't see how I could get past level two, let alone reach level four or five.

"Okay. I have a question for you then," Obadiah said. "Where do you think you currently fall regarding these levels of prophetic maturity? Let me say, if you're sitting here today thinking you're at stage five, you're not."

Jerry let out a nervous sigh, and Maria chuckled. "Yikes," Maria said. "I thought I was doing okay with the whole learning-to-love-better thing, but I don't know if I'll ever master that level, let alone the others!"

Obadiah was quick to respond, "We're not here to master anything, Maria. Remember, we're working toward greater giftings and greater expressions of the Spirit. When you rely on Him, He will slowly reveal the next steps to you and will go before you and with you as you proceed. And you'll have a team beside you to support you as well. Don't get discouraged."

Maria smiled back at him, and I felt encouraged too.

"I have a question," Hayley said. "The descriptions of stage three and stage four seem very similar to me. What's the distinction there?"

"Yes, they can look similar," began Obadiah. "In stage three, you may work with people in developing a five-fold ministry, but it's usually small in scope. Stage four is when there's a shared vision or a shared mission in mind. For example, anyone in any stage can plant a church. You could do this at stage three without your five-fold ministry team and have a happy, healthy church body. But in stage four, because you have a five-fold ministry that is anointed and that has accountability, you may plant a church and see an impact on the surrounding city. The economy may improve, the divorce rate may drop, crime may decrease, land values may go up; there are dozens of ways the city might be transformed. Your impact as a stage four prophet and as part of a team is far greater. I see the difference between stages three and four mainly in the scope of the impact.

"I think it's worth noting that a lot of times a stage three prophetic person is ready to become a prophet and just hasn't found the rest of the five-fold team to balance them out and augment and empower them to be the most they can be. It's possible to develop the confidence of being in the office of a prophet while not yet being anointed to bring transcultural transformation as a prophet. Does that answer your question, Hayley?"

"Yes," she said, drawing in her notebook.

Mike cleared his throat. "You said that a person with a prophetic gifting in stage two often lacks character and maturity. Is that always the case?"

"The Gift stage is really the tipping point. Everyone starts at stage one, a lot of people get to stage two, and it's those who have the opportunity to develop character and opportunity who are able to progress to stage three and beyond. Most people have a hard time maintaining the discipline it takes to build character and maturity in stage two and plateau there or even get discouraged and fall away. Some people, because they start seeing what should be, begin trying to correct others in an unloving way; those types of actions reveal a lack of character maturity that will hold a prophetic person back. That's why pairing up with a pastor and being dedicated to both growing personally as well as in the prophetic gifting is so important."

"That makes sense," said Mike. "And I actually have another question if that's all right." Obadiah nodded for him to go ahead. "When you were talking about stage five, you mentioned having an impact on 'multiple cultural spheres of influence.' What did you mean?"

"A number of people have studied the way people in different societies interact, and they've come up with what they call 'spheres of influence.' Essentially these are categories describing a certain set of beliefs and behaviors. Religion could be one of these as it influences the way we think and act. Our family and family structure is another. Our education is also a societal categorization. Media and entertainment has become an increasingly influential sphere; everything we consume influences us in certain ways. And of course the laws and policies of our government also have an impact on how we think and act and maybe on what we are and are not allowed to do. Another sphere is commerce and trade or our idea of success in business. The final one I'm going to mention is the arts and sciences. This sphere is more internal than the others as it's where we get in touch with what's inside of us and bring it out through creative art or invention and innovation; a lot of these creations become new information and data that shift our perception of the other spheres. So these are what I'm talking about when I talk about a prophet shifting a sphere of influence."

"I hate to break up our good flow, but speaking of internal influences, my coffee is having one on me," Maria ventured.

Obadiah chuckled. "That's quite all right. It's time for a break anyway. When we come back, we'll dive into the next fruit of Spirit: goodness and joy."

I stood up and stretched, smiling at Hayley who was still bent over her notebook, writing as fast as she could. Then, feeling like I needed a little caffeine boost for this session, I headed over to join Andre in grabbing a cup of coffee.

GOODNESS AND JOY

Our break was shorter than normal. Even though we'd already received a lot of information, we were eager to push forward. After only a couple of minutes, everyone was back in their seats and looking at Obadiah.

"Are we all ready?" He asked. "Okay, let's start with the question: what is goodness?"

Catherine asked, "Isn't it like being kind to people?"

"Well remember," Obadiah said, "kindness is a different fruit of the Spirit. We can't define one fruit by calling it another. While it's true that the fruit overlap in a lot of areas, we're going to be looking at the things that distinguish them from one another."

"God is goodness," ventured Andre.

"That's true," responded Obadiah. "But God is also love, so our definition has to be smaller."

"Dictionary.com gives a couple of different definitions for 'goodness,'" Mike said, looking up from his tablet. "It lists 'moral excellence or virtue,' 'kindly feelings and generosity,' 'excellence of quality,' and 'the best part of anything or its essence.'"

"Those are all interesting," said Obadiah. "'Moral excellence' particularly resonates for me as a definition of goodness because building your character and behavior so that they are wholly pleasing to God does result in goodness. Genesis 1:31 says that 'God saw all that He had made, and behold, it was very good.' So part of our goodness is given to us by God by virtue of being part of His entire creation. Would someone read Ephesians 5:7–10?"

We raced to find the verse, and Jerry got there first. It was impressive to see how he turned almost directly to the page in his worn Bible, putting those of us using tablets to shame. "Ephesians 5:7–10 says," Jerry began, "'Therefore do not be partakers with them; for you were formerly darkness, but now you are Light in the Lord; walk as children of Light (for the fruit of the Light consists in all goodness and righteousness and truth, trying to learn what is pleasing to the Lord).'"

"Remember when we talked about how everything in creation is made from quantum material? You go from the body to the systems, from the systems to the organs, from the organs to the cells, from the cells to the molecules, from the molecules to the atoms, from the atoms to the subatomic particles, and from those to quantum particles. All of this boils down to the extradimensional fields of light energy. We're all made of light. We were 'formally darkness, but now [we] are Light in the Lord.' And the 'fruit of the Light consists in all goodness and righteousness and truth.' This light is the very fiber of our being. We are actually made to be good; the very substance of our being results in goodness. When we are not exhibiting goodness, we are behaving in rebellion against the very fiber of our beings. How often have you heard someone describe unrighteous behavior as 'self-destructive'?

"Our calling, then, is to walk as children of the Light. We have to learn, through the Spirit, what is pleasing to the Lord so we can live it out. God enables us to do that good work. Hebrews 13:20–21 tells us, 'May the God of peace...equip you with everything good for doing His will, and may He work in us what is pleasing to Him, through Jesus Christ.' You see, goodness is being closer to the Lord and becoming more like His image every day. Why do you think I've paired goodness and joy then? How is joy related to goodness?"

"If goodness is moral excellence," Jerry replied, "and if sinning robs you of joy, then joy and goodness must both be the result of an upright life."

"Joy and peace are foundational to a Christian character, right?" Andre said. "Then I guess goodness could be an outflow to others as a result of joy and peace."

Maria asked, "Could joy be the outward expression of the inward reality of goodness? Or, the other way around too, I guess, because if your heart is joyful, then being morally excellent, or good, would follow. It seems like the two go hand-in-hand."

"Very good," Obadiah said. "Joy flows from goodness. There's clear evidence that walking with a clean heart brings joy into your life and into the lives of others. In John 15:10–11, Jesus tells us to keep His commandments, which is goodness, 'so your joy may be complete.' In Romans 15:31–32, Paul asks that his service would be favorably received, or perceived as good, so that he might come in joy. In 3 John 1:4, John says, "I have no greater joy than this, to hear of my children walking in the truth." Again, walking in the truth, finding what is pleasing to the Lord, is goodness, and that brings about joy. Jason, you have probably seen this in the lives of your Sunday school students."

I was unprepared to be called on, but I knew that what Obadiah was saying was true. "Yes, actually. I've had several students who have made the choice to live by God's commands, and that brings both them and me joy."

"I feel that way about some of my interns," Mike chimed in.

"Yes," Obadiah replied. "It gives us joy when we see our protégés learning and growing. In the same way, it pleases God when we learn and grow. 2 Thessalonians 1:11–12 says, 'To this end also we pray for you always, that our God will count you worthy of your calling, and fulfill every desire for goodness and the work of faith with power, so that the name of our Lord Jesus will be glorified in you, and you in Him, according to the grace of our God and the Lord Jesus Christ.' In other words, doing the right thing pleases God, and that brings joy. Or for another example, in the doxology at the end of Jude 1, in verse 24, it says, "To him who is able to keep you from stumbling and to present you before his glorious presence without fault and with great joy." You see, in every instance we've examined, joy is a result of walking in truth, being blameless before God, and keeping his commandments.

"Here's a thought, then: lack of real joy in the church is a lack of real goodness in the church. If we were truly good, motivated by love and not the law, then joy would increase. Conversely, the absence of goodness leads to darkness and robs us of joy. There is not joy in hell because there is no goodness in hell. You can be happy without goodness, but you can't have joy."

"That makes me think of Jonah," Jerry said.

"Can you explain, Jerry?" Obadiah asked.

After taking a moment to collect his thoughts, Jerry continued. "While Jonah eventually obeyed God, he didn't have excellent moral character. He didn't enjoy the salvation of Nineveh because he was bent on judgment. Jonah could have entered into the goodness of God and celebrated His goodness with Him, but he didn't, so he missed out on the joy."

"Maybe Jonah was a stage two prophet," Andre said. "Maybe he didn't have the character to reach stage five."

"Or maybe he was being called to be a stage five prophet but allowed himself to be held back by his own emotional wounds," Maria offered.

"Sometimes God elevates you to a certain level for a specific purpose," Obadiah added. "It could be that Jonah just happened to be the person who had to go to Nineveh. Traditionally we refer to

Jonah as a high level prophet, but by our definitions, Andre is right. Jonah might not have had the character and sustained support to be at stage five. That said, he was the one who was available, and God gave him a specific assignment, so he operated at a stage five level for a period of time. This might happen to you as you develop as well. You might be on stage one or two and go on a mission trip where people are believing for big things like healing and serious words from the Lord. Because the Lord uses whoever is available and anoints that person with whatever gifting is needed at the time, you might walk into that specific calling and perform miracles or give extremely insightful words and think you've reached the next level...only to discover that when you return home, you're back where you started. That's because God will give you the gifts you need to perform His miracles. But He also wants you to develop your character so you can be trusted with that level of authority long-term.

"To recap the main point of this week: how do we cultivate goodness? First, we learn what it means to be pleasing to the Lord. Second, we become worthy of the calling. Part of being worthy means understanding your calling and authentically behaving in a manner that is consistent with that calling. Many people are miserable in ministry because God didn't call them into ministry. Just because you don't have a 'church-y' calling on your life doesn't mean it's not from God. Remember, God created you, and when He made creation, He said that it was good. That means it can be good for you to have a calling that is outside ministry. You need to walk in the truth of who God created you to be. Third, in order to cultivate goodness, we have to keep God's commandments. Jesus gives us at least fifty commands in the New Testament. Research them. Write them down. Memorize them. Keep them.

"Goodness opens the door for joy in our lives. When we cultivate goodness, we cultivate joy. We can choose to exercise joy regardless of our circumstances," Obadiah said.

"You're saying we can choose to live in joy no matter what is happening to us and around us?" Catherine asked.

"Absolutely," Obadiah responded. "And you don't have to push the circumstances out of your mind to experience joy. You can focus on and work through difficult circumstances while maintaining your joy. Let's do an exercise. Did you know that just by appearing joyful physically, you can increase your feelings of joy? Relax your eyes to what photographers call 'soft eyes'; release any strain, and let your face go into a neutral position. Sit up straight and relax your shoulders. Now, and don't overthink this, we're going to laugh."

"We're just going to laugh?" Andre said, squinting dubiously at Obadiah.

"Exactly," Obadiah said, beginning a soft chuckle.

The rest of us exchanged glances and tentatively joined in with a forced laugh here and there. About ten seconds in, Maria lost it. It was hard to tell if she had just gotten into the exercise or if all of us sitting in a room trying to laugh struck her funny, but she really cracked up. That loosened the rest of us up, and we all started genuinely laughing. It felt good to laugh, and I could feel tension I hadn't even realized I was carrying start to ease out of my shoulders.

After about thirty seconds, however, I started feeling ridiculous and wondered how much longer Obadiah was going to make us keep this up. Around the fifty-second mark, our laughter died down until it came to a complete stop.

Obadiah smiled. "I know this made some of you feel uncomfortable, but I promise it's a valuable exercise. Now I want everyone to pull out a pen and a piece of paper and write down the main thing stealing your joy right now. Once you have it written down, get into a group of two or three and discuss what you wrote as well as the dominant emotion, such as fear or anger or depression, you have to overcome in order to defeat it."

Immediately I wrote the words "false identity" on my paper. When Maria had finished writing, I turned toward her and explained how I'd been struggling with feeling like I wasn't a good enough provider for my family. "Without realizing it, I put a lot of weight in my career, which is funny because I don't even like my job that much. I've pretended to love being a businessman and everything that comes with it all these years, but the truth is that I feel like a fraud. For a while I had to work late every night because of a big project, and my guilt over never being at home made me feel awful. When I finished that project, I found I was reluctant to return home on time. The thing that's supposed to make me feel like I'm taking care of my family—having a job—actually makes me feel like I'm drifting further away. All these years my idea of success has been me being a good provider. Turns out I'm not so great at it, and my feelings of lack of self-worth have really been stealing my joy." This was the first time I'd admitted any of these feelings, and I was almost surprised to hear them come out of my mouth. It was a relief when Maria started sharing and I could take my mind off myself.

"I have a big event tomorrow," she began. "I will be attending a family reunion barbeque with relatives that I haven't seen in years. Most of my extended family are not believers and they know I take my faith quite seriously. I am not looking forward to the grilling—no pun intended—that I will probably get from the rest of the family. My cousins, especially the boys for some reason, always teased me relentlessly about being a follower of Jesus." She paused a moment as she considered her next statement. "With all that I've been learning and growing in these past few weeks, it will only get worse. I can already hear them saying 'Here comes the family prophet. Everyone get quiet so we can hear what God is going to say.'"

I imagined myself in the same situation and I also began to get butterflies in my gut. It occurred to me that when this training is over, life may get a little more uncomfortable for all of us.

After a few minutes, Obadiah said, "We're not done here yet. Now I want you to begin laughing again, and while you're laughing, I want you to tell the same story. If it's too hard for you to look at your partner while you're talking, that's okay; you can just speak it to yourself, as if you're telling a joke. You already know that you can tell the story and that you can make yourself laugh, and I promise you that you'll be able to do both at the same time. As you do this, you're going to train yourself to experience joy in your circumstance, and you'll find that you're the one in control of your situation. Ready?"

Most of us nodded, and Obadiah called, "Go!"

I looked at the wall across from me and tried to think of something funny to make me laugh. When that failed, I forced a loud "HA." It didn't help. Finally I just smiled and started telling my story. As I continued, I realized it was kind of like telling a joke. My situation didn't have any real power over me, so why should I let it weigh me down? Gaining momentum from the rest of the room, I began laughing. When I finished my story, I was in tears, and I think they were the good kind. Looking around, I saw others crying as well. Andre was the only one who wasn't smiling.

Obadiah was moving on. "I'd love to discuss what you all experienced more, but we're tight on time, so I'm just going to give you your assignment and then those who need to leave can and those who would like to stay a little longer can talk about what they felt. Your assignment this week is to experience goodness and joy. This week, pay attention to situations in which you find it difficult to enter into joy. When the Holy Spirit reveals a situation to you, take stock of your physiology. Take a joy stance; relax your eyes, roll your shoulders back, and hold your head high. If it's okay to laugh, then laugh and claim that your circumstances will not define your reactions. Decide to experience joy regardless of your circumstances. In addition, whenever you run into someone this week, enter into a physiology of joy, and see if you don't start seeing more favor from others.

"Next week we're going to talk about kindness and gentleness. If you want to think ahead a little, consider how you would define each of these from a spiritual behavior perspective." With this, Obadiah stood up and walked toward the restrooms.

Michael and Catherine waved their goodbyes and headed for the door. Jerry and Andre followed. Hayley pulled Maria over, and the two of them began praying together in hushed voices. Being the odd man out and feeling as if I'd learned enough in one session to last me a lifetime, I decided to head out as well. I grabbed my coat and headed for the door as concepts of goodness and joy, having joy through difficult circumstances, and moving up the path to prophetic maturity floated around my head. "Holy Spirit, help me grow," I prayed as I exited the cave and walked up the gravel path to my car.

CHAPTER SEVEN:
KINDNESS & GENTLENESS

MATURITY

It took me awhile to figure out how to smile with soft eyes. For the first few days, I was overly conscious of my efforts. One day I was practicing my look in the mirror in the men's room at work and almost got caught when another guy came in. Finally I realized that if I just made the choice to be happy, it was much easier than trying to figure out how to manipulate my facial muscles. In trying to get a handle on goodness, I gave a lot of thought to what it means to be pleasing to God, but a lot of what I came up with ended up sounding like rules. Then I remembered that love is the foundation for all the fruit. I realized I could do things that would express God's love for others, and I could choose to act in ways that would honor Him. Changing my way of thinking from forcing myself to do the right thing to choosing to honor God made showing love much easier.

Later in the week, I started recognizing favor in my life. As I worked on developing goodness and joy, everything else just seemed to start working out for me. I didn't have to try to make good things happen, which made my days easier, and my joy began to spiral upwards. At one point, I even caught myself whistling as I walked down the hallway. It was amazing the difference one little attitude shift made.

Pulling into the clearing, I was surprised to see that all the other cars were already there. I glanced down toward the entrance of the cave and caught a glimpse of someone going in. I couldn't tell who it was, but I knew it wasn't Hayley, because her red hair glowed like fire in sunlight. I checked my car clock and saw I was still ten minutes early, but I had the feeling that I was late.

Breaking off from my ruminations about goodness, joy, and favor, I jumped out of my car and hustled down the path. When I entered, everyone was already seated and relatively quiet. "What's going on here?" I asked. "Did we change the meeting time, or is my clock just slow or something?"

Obadiah laughed. "Don't worry, Jason. You aren't late, and we wouldn't start without you anyway. Apparently everyone was just eager to talk about goodness and joy."

I let out a sigh of relief and everyone laughed. "Calm down, Jason," Maria urged. "I don't think I've ever seen someone take being on time so seriously."

Smiling, I pulled my jacket off and took my seat. "I just want to make sure I don't miss any of your stories about your weeks. They wouldn't be the same in the retelling," I said, secretly relieved that the group hadn't decided to vote me out or something.

"You're an important part of this group, Jason," Obadiah reassured me. "You all are. And now that we're all here, who has something to share from this week's assignment? Did any of you find an opportunity to take the 'joy test'?"

"Well," I started, "I must be a week behind here, because this week I learned Maria's lesson from last week. She said she decided to choose to love others and discovered that, through that choice, she became more loving. This week I decided I would make a choice to have joy and be happy, and it became a whole lot easier to experience joy. Going further, I made the choice to pursue goodness and the things that please God. I decided to do everything in my power to show God's love to others and to accept it for myself. It appears, then, that walking in the fruit of the Spirit, at least so far, is a matter of choice to follow where the Holy Spirit leads. And just like you said last week, I also noticed that after I started choosing joy and goodness, I began to experience favor. This week was amazing in that respect; things seemed to just work out for me."

"Yeah, I experienced favor this week, too," Andre said. "I'd been practicing the physiology of joy for a couple days when, for lunch on Wednesday, I went to that burrito place downtown where they assemble the burritos in front of you. You all know the one, right?" Several of us nodded, and Andre continued, "Anyway, while I was in line, I struck up a conversation with the people making the food. I ordered a burrito, and one person added the rice, one person added the beans, and when it got to the meat, I made some comment about how good the steak looked. The person put on the normal amount of steak, looked at me, smiled, and added another heaping scoop. I know that seems like a small thing, but if you've ever had a burrito from that place, you know they never do that. In fact, they're usually pretty skimpy with their serving sizes. It was like that guy saw something in me—like what Obadiah was talking about—and showed me favor as a result."

"Hey, never call extra steak a 'small thing,'" Jerry said, winking at Andre. "I know exactly what place you're talking about, and that was definitely a moment of favor."

Hayley spoke up, "I'm glad you shared, Andre, because I experienced something similar and was debating on whether or not to share. This Tuesday morning I really needed a coffee, so I stopped into a place near my apartment on my way to work. When I got to the counter, I realized I only had a couple of dollars in my wallet, and the place didn't accept credit cards. I'd already placed my order and didn't know what to do. Remembering our lesson, I smiled, stood up straight, and relaxed my eyes. A minute or so later, the barista called me over and said, 'I accidentally made you a large instead of the medium you ordered. I can remake you a medium, or you can have this one on the house.' I smiled even bigger, thanked him very sincerely, took the drink, and walked out knowing that God had shown me some serious favor!"

"Wow, free steak and free coffee?" Maria said. "If I wasn't convinced I needed more goodness and joy in my life before, I certainly am now!"

When our laughter died down, Mike asked, "Obadiah, last week it seemed like you intentionally tied favor to goodness and joy. Are those three joined somehow, and if so, are there other gifts tied to other fruit of the Spirit?"

"Let me explain that a little further," Obadiah said as he stood and walked over to the whiteboard. "Let's see here," he paused with the marker over the board. "There are specific gifts you can expect to see as you develop each of the fruit of the Spirit. And if we're going to be prophets who speak for God, we need to have good, developed fruit.

"We talked last week about how there are five stages of progression in the life of the prophet. We can use a similar format to tie those stages to the fruit of the Spirit." With that, Obadiah drew a long rectangle across bottom of the board. Inside the rectangle he wrote 'LOVE'.

"We already talked about how love is the foundation," Obadiah said. "Love corresponds to the first, basic stage of prophecy to which every believer has access. If you remember, that's the stage corresponding to 1 Corinthians 14:3, prophesying to encourage and build each other up."

Obadiah drew a smaller rectangle on top of the first one and wrote 'Goodnes and Joy' inside it, right above 'Love'. "The next level is Goodness and Joy, which correspond to the Gift stage. As I mentioned last week, many people don't move past phase two because they don't seek out and do what's pleasing to the Lord. In other words, they miss out on goodness, and as we learned, there's no joy without goodness. As Mike brought up, when your life is rich in goodness and joy, you begin to see favor. But to be clear, doing good things to get favor won't work. We do good things because it pleases God and allows us to honor Him, and that in turn brings about character, maturity, and joy. Favor is an added blessing, or the cherry on top of the goodness and joy sundae. So what is favor?"

"You know," Mike said, "I was just thinking about the other day when I called up one of my company's clients and he said, 'I don't normally do this, but something about you gives me a good feeling,' and he proceeded to move forward on a deal that had been stuck for months. Is that favor?"

"That's a great example, Mike," Obadiah said. "Favor causes other people to want to help make things work out for you. What they're actually doing is seeing and being motivated by something that God has placed in you because He likes you. And when He likes you, that favor exudes from you, and others see it in a spiritual sense—whether they believe in the spiritual sense or not. It's also partially visible physically. Think about it; you're not going to have favor if you're exuding negativity. Joy changes our body language, which makes people more inclined to like us.

Obadiah continued speaking as he added other smaller boxes for the next levels of the pyramid. "The next tier is kindness and gentleness. Goodness has to do with being pleasing to the Lord; kindness, however, involves how we behave toward others. At this level, we start seeing signs and wonders. Sometimes when you pray for someone, something will happen. Sometimes, for example, healings occur, but sometimes they don't. At any rate, you start catching glimpses of the miraculous, which build your faith and your vision. When you work on increasing kindness and gentleness in your life, you'll find yourself building relationships with others who will come alongside and work with you. As I said, goodness and joy are more about your relationship with the Lord. Kindness and gentleness impact your relationships with other people.

"When you're working with a group of people, you're going to have to develop patience, so that's the next tier. This is where we gain understanding, which is seeing things how God sees things. It's also where we grow in learning that not everything occurs within our concept of time. Here a prophetic person will start identifying what motivates people and what holds them back. As we learn more about others from God's perspective, we grow more in patience, which helps us grow in understanding. Somewhere between kindness and gentleness and patience is where stage three—the small team ministry—comes into play, because growing in these fruits allows a prophet to develop and sustain healthy relationships with other believers.

"The next tier up is faithfulness. Contrary to the popular belief that faith is a requirement for miracles, faith is actually more necessary when miracles don't happen. As you grow in patience and understanding, you develop the fortitude to push past setbacks and continue trusting in God's purposes. At this level, you are no longer discouraged by scoffers, mockers, and those who resist you.

"Peace, the next tier, comes from patience and faithfulness. When you're at peace, you begin to see miracles. There are different types of miracles; some are for you personally and some are for others. One type of miracle, signs and wonders, are for a specific purpose. When you begin to prophesy, you should expect to see signs and wonders. As you continue to develop, you'll see additional miracles that exceed the realm of signs and wonders. When we're at peace, we have an acceptance that things will occur in the Lord's timing, and this removes anxiety and worry. We also grow an enduring faithfulness that vanquishes our fears. This is where we start moving into stage four, which is the five-fold ministry.

Here, Obadiah finished his pyramid and pointed at the last box. "Finally at the top, we have self-control. A transcultural level-five prophet with self-control will speak words that make things happen, and he or she will do this on a consistent basis."

Andre moved a little, looking uncomfortable, and said, "Obadiah, I'm glad you brought that up, because I'm still not clear about the question you posed a few weeks ago. You asked us, when a prophet says something, is he seeing into the future and declaring what's going to happen or is he actually causing the future thing to happen."

"Good question, Andre," Obadiah said, nodding affirmingly, "There's no real way to distinguish which is happening at any given time, because it can be both. What is one hundred percent clear is that if you're gifted with such authority that your words have power, you need great self-control. Without self-control, your words—which have the power to change the course of a life—could be damaging and manipulative."

Obadiah stood back to examine the whole drawing, which, with all his notes, looked something like this:

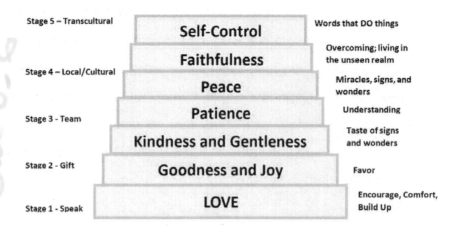

"Your pyramid is missing its top," Jerry pointed out.

"It looks more like a wedding cake than a pyramid to me," Catherine said.

Maria started laughing, and we looked questioningly at here. She explained, "It does kind of look like a cake! Because it relates to the fruit of the Spirit, it must be a fruitcake."

The room simultaneously laughed and groaned. Andre announced, "I think of fruitcakes as those inedible things I get at Christmas or the people who send them to me." Maria laughed and protested, "Hey now!" Andre quickly covered, "But I guess some of them are good. Like this one."

Obadiah just shook his head, smiled, and continued. "To be a prophet, you have to have a strong foundation of each of the fruit. Some people may find kindness or faithfulness easier to develop than patience, so it is possible to build them in a slightly different order, but no matter what, in order to be a prophet, you have to have all of them, and they do feed from the bottom to the top. Without love, the entire cake will fall. Does anyone have any questions about our 'fruitcake'?" Obadiah asked, nodding at Maria.

I said, "You mentioned signs and wonders around the kindness and gentleness stage, but then when you talked about peace, you said something about miracles following signs and wonders. I'm not following the distinction between miracles and signs and wonders."

"Thanks for asking that, Jason, because I think several of you are wondering that same thing," Obadiah said. "To confuse you more, signs and wonders are miracles. Think back to your grade school math class where you had to learn about sets. You drew circles, and in each circle was a collection of like things. Well, signs and wonders would be a circle inside the circle of miracles. In other words, all signs and wonders are miracles, but not all miracles are signs and wonders. I'm not going to delve into what all that means right now, because we're going to talk about it more in depth when we get to peace, but the short definition is that signs and wonders are miracles that occur for a very specific purpose."

"For now," Obadiah continued, "I want to stay focused on goodness and joy, and I have a question about your weeks. Did anyone notice, although many of you had success in growing this fruit, that there were times when you didn't seem to have access to it? Did any of you face a situation where you struggled to conjure up any goodness or where you felt like your joy was under attack?"

All of us except Hayley raised our hands, and she might have only kept her hand down because she was writing and didn't look up.

Obadiah asked, "Does anyone want to venture a guess as to why that was?"

Mike suggested, "A lot of it I think is due to all the hard things we face in our lives. When you see all the darkness in this world—like natural disasters and people struggling to make ends meet and the spread of disease—it can be hard to maintain joy. Our circumstances beat us down."

"You're on the right track there," Obadiah said. "Mike, you said that when you hear what's going on in the world, it's hard to maintain your joy. But where are you hearing about all the awful things that are occurring?"

Mike thought for a moment and answered, "Mostly on the evening news or the radio, I guess."

Obadiah nodded and said, "We are under the constant bombardment of negativity from the media. One of the reasons for the reemergence of prophets at this time is to combat a cultural deception that's been encouraged by media and entertainment outlets. Movies, TV shows, the news, and the Internet are full of upsetting information that's hard for us to swallow. What if I told you that was partially intentional? Think back to some specific things you heard this week, and see if media was the cause of your inability to practice joy. Media causes people to be discomforted, fearful, and alarmed.

"Twenty or thirty years ago, you wouldn't have heard all you're hearing today. Back then, people got news maybe three or four times a day, but now news is thrust in front of us 24/7. Because news outlets want your attention, they try to make their stories interesting, often at the cost of manipulating facts. Reporters and journalists try to pitch information in such a way that it builds an emotional response, which can cause you to lose your internal sense of joy. For example, over the past couple decades, we've been told time and time again that our economy is collapsing, which creates fear. Politicians tell us that their opponents lie to us, which creates mistrust. Media outlets have grown so powerful that they can manipulate the outcome of an election based on the way they choose to portray the candidates. Journalists can give us facts without telling the entire story, which colors our perception of truth. I'm not saying that our media outlets are actively involved in some sort of conspiracy, but they definitely are trying to bring about a certain mindset or response. On a spiritual level, Satan's objective is to kill, steal, and destroy, and if he can rob you of your happiness and destroy your confidence and peace, he can wear away at your strongholds of goodness and joy. The Enemy uses media to put you in a state of fear, turmoil, and depression. The more you listen to the media, the more you're influenced by its dark messages. The question we need to ask ourselves, then, is how do we deal with this media message of deception? Without using Christian platitudes, what do you think we can do to confront this situation?"

Maria said, "Before I can answer that, I need to know what a 'platitude' is."

Obadiah smiled and then explained, "A platitude is an overused expression, like a cliché, but it's used to try to say something profound. An example of a Christian platitude might be when someone says, 'God lets things get really bad before He steps in.' God loves us, so why would He want things to go poorly for us? Sometimes we give a response like that because it's an easy explanation for us, and we never challenge its validity. In the example I just gave, there are lots of reasons God might not immediately step into a situation. Maybe He's prompting someone else to grow in their faith and come alongside you. Maybe He's growing patience in you. He may even be giving you an opportunity to take action in His name and make a change yourself. Just because you don't actively see Him at work doesn't mean He has abandoned you—far from it!

"Another example of a platitude is when something doesn't happen that you've been praying for or something happens that you have been interceding against and the excuse is given that 'The Church just didn't pray and fast enough.' Maybe that's true, but it's not a reason to give up. Maybe you realize that praying and fasting wasn't the means to an end but was what God wanted His Church to do in order to grow for some other purpose. Perhaps God didn't even call for a fast at all, and it was just something we were doing because it is what we always do. In other words, a platitude oversimplifies a situation and haphazardly applies a semi-Christian perspective, which avoids engaging ourselves into the fullness of what God is doing. Given that definition, without using a platitude, what do you think the role of a prophet is in engaging the cultural deceptions of media?"

"What do you mean by 'cultural deception'?" Andre asked.

"Cultural deception occurs when mass amounts of people believe something without testing whether or not it's true, and this is accomplished by a coordinated repetition of the same line by multiple, high-level people who have a reputable platform. Eventually these people could collectively say anything, and it will be accepted as truth. It's the theory that if people hear a lie repeated enough times through enough sources, they'll begin to believe it. Often if you get enough people to believe something, it becomes a self-fulfilling prophecy."

Obadiah continued, "Joy is a powerful tool for believers, but the media is one of the biggest attacks on this great weapon. The good news is that we're living in a time of emerging prophets who will counteract the lies of the media. The hard news is that as you grow in your prophetic role, you're going to face opposition. Remember that Jesus himself was tempted by the devil. In order to quiet the lies of the enemy, you need to learn to distinguish your inner voice and the prompting of the Holy Spirit from the voice of the enemy. It's possible to get tripped up and start telling yourself lies. You need to bring messages of discouragement and accusation to the Lord so He can replace them with His messages of truth and encouragement. Remember, the truth isn't the same thing as the facts. The enemy will present facts to you in a certain way in order to discourage you, but God has a truth that's higher than facts that can give us joy even in circumstances that seem impossibly far removed from joy.

"Just as Jesus faced Satan who tried to hold Him back from His rightful purpose and position, you will face strong resistance to the things God has promised to you. The land you're about to possess as prophets is the ability to speak God's truth, or things that are true in the supernatural world. The enemy is testing you now to see if you can hold on to those truths in the face of repeated deception and whether you can continue to speak those truths when the world around you has bought into a different message of deception. That's quite a test."

Hayley cleared her throat and asked in a timid voice, "How do we know what that will look like? How do we tell what is God's voice and what's a voice of deception?"

"Don't worry, Hayley," Obadiah said, his eyes kind and gentle. "When you grow in love, you learn what kind of language is encouraging and comforting and what kind of language is discouraging and detrimental. Then when you grow in goodness, in discovering what is pleasing to God, you learn His ways and you become more in tune with His thoughts. The closer you draw to God, the easier it is to hear His voice and to know what is true. Often when we're deceived, it's because we aren't testing what we're hearing against what God has said. First Thessalonians 5:20–21 tells us, 'Do not treat prophecies with contempt but test them all; hold on to what is good.' As all of you become more aware of the workings of the supernatural and as you test the messages you're hearing against God's absolute truths, you will find it easier and easier to discern the deceptive voice of the enemy. Think of it this way. Experts who handle money don't learn to recognize counterfeit bills by studying counterfeit bills. They learn by studying the real thing very extensively. They know the real thing so well that they instantly know when they are holding something that is not real. In the same way, as you grow in recognizing God's voice through time spent with Him in biblical meditation, the easier it will become to identify the voice of the deceiver."

"To rewind a little," Mike said, "can you further explain what you meant when you said that if you get enough people to believe something, it becomes a self-fulfilling prophecy?"

Obadiah responded, "Yes, I mean that the more that people are told an idea, the more they begin to fixate on it, and the more they fixate on it, the more they believe it, and the more they believe it, the more they live it out as truth. For example, if you tell a child she is stupid, she will start to obsess over it. Every bad grade will become, instead of just one bad grade, a confirmation that she isn't intelligent. And the more she begins to believe that, the less she'll talk in class. The less she discusses ideas, the worse her grades will become. As she scales back the effort she put into learning, she will fall behind and will eventually be less knowledgeable than others her age, thus fulfilling the original lie spoken into her life. It's the same way on a massive scale. The longer, for example, you tell people that there is still a race issue in

America, the more people will begin to look for signs of it. When they see any conflict between people of different races, they will see it as confirmation and begin steering clear of the race they perceived as instigating the conflict. When they withdraw from interactions with the person of that race, a divide is built resulting in mutual mistrust, which, ironically, increases racial tensions. Prophets are called to counteract lies in their incubation stage, before they hatch into truths."

Obadiah sat back and stretched his arms behind him. "I think we need an encouraging break to refresh us a little before diving into kindness and gentleness. What do you all say to a ten minute pause?"

We all agreed a break would be good, and side conversations immediately sparked up around the room. Andre turned to me, "Man, this is serious stuff, isn't it?"

"Yes," I agreed. "Seriously good but seriously challenging." I paused a minute to think about what it would mean to speak truth when everyone around me believed something different and then decided I better take this whole prophet thing one challenge at a time. As I stood up to go to the restroom, I prayed under my breath, "Help me know your voice, Father. I need you like never before."

KINDNESS AND GENTLENESS

After we all settled back into place, Obadiah said, "Now let's look at the third tier of what Maria has named the 'fruitcake,' kindness and gentleness. How do we define kindness?"

We thought for a moment, and then Maria said, "Being nice? Being selfless when it's not natural to me?"

Mike followed with, "The dictionary on my tablet gives these words to define 'kindness': 'Mild, indulgent, considerate, affectionate.'"

"Romans 2:4 says that the kindness of God leads us to repentance," Jerry quoted.

"That's a good verse to pull out, Jerry," Obadiah said. "Why do you think God's kindness leads people to repentance instead of to license and lawlessness? Generally we might assume that if someone is 'kind,' we can get away with anything because that person will be too nice to stop us. If 'lawless' means you can do whatever you want and get away with it, and kindness also means 'indulgent,' then how can God be kind and yet convict people of their sins?"

We all thought for a moment, and Jerry responded, "I know God doesn't indulge sin, so being kind must be expressed differently through Him. I also know that kindness removes condemnation and judgment and opens the opportunity for us to choose to change."

"You're on the right track, Jerry," Obadiah said. "Our concept of kindness tends to be one of indulgence. God, however, doesn't give us license to do whatever we want. Instead, He is kind in allowing us time to seek truth. Titus 3:4–5 says, 'When the kindness and love of God our Savior appeared, he saved us, not because of righteous things we had done, but because of his mercy.' Kindness is a type of mercy. When we're in sin, God will never approve of what we're doing, but because of His kindness, He doesn't bring immediate judgment but instead gives us time and space to repent. The indulgence or kindness here isn't permission to sin; the indulgence is giving us time to choose to no longer sin. Kindness has to do with being fair and even generous to people you don't know. When you're in a situation where there's no reason to give preference and you do anyway, that's kindness. By modeling God's love to strangers, we show them kindness. What's freeing about God's kindness is that it doesn't mean we have to roll over and let people do whatever they want. Instead, it means we show them the same grace God shows them in encouraging them and giving them time to come to repentance. Now we need to relate this to gentleness. How would you define 'gentleness'?"

"I was waiting for that question," Andre said. "My dictionary says 'gentleness' is 'amiable; not severe, rough, or violent; noble.'"

"That's a pretty good definition," Obadiah said, "and now we need the spiritual application. Galatians 6:1 says, 'Brothers, if anyone is caught in any transgression, you who are spiritual should restore him in a spirit of gentleness.' So how does gentleness treat those who are in sin?"

Catherine said, "Gentleness protects the dignity of a person and leaves room for repentance."

"Good, Catherine," Obadiah said. "You're right to point out that gentleness leaves room for correction. That's the reason that gentleness, like kindness, doesn't lead to lawlessness. Gentleness doesn't keep us from correcting someone; instead it speaks to the way in which we correct them. Kindness is what you do for another person. Gentleness is how you perform that act of kindness. You have a responsibility to correct those who are in opposition to the Lord, but you have to do it in such a way that they feel as if they've gained, rather than lost, something."

Obadiah suggested we look at 2 Timothy 2:24–25, and Mike read the verses aloud: "'The Lord's servant must not be quarrelsome but must be kind to everyone, able to teach, not resentful. Opponents must be gently instructed, in the hope that God will grant them repentance leading them to a knowledge of the truth.'"

"Some translations say we 'must be kind to all, patient when wrong, with gentleness correcting those who are in opposition,'" Obadiah responded.

"That 'patient when wrong' part really stands out to me," Andre said, "because I know that the pride in me resists correction." I was encouraged by how much more Andre had been sharing since telling us a little more about his past.

"Yes, we often get in our own way when we're trying to be kind and gentle," Obadiah responded. "To help, here are some guidelines for when you have to correct someone in gentleness. First, only correct people with whom you have a relationship. You need to either have an established friend relationship with the person you're going to correct, or you two need to have mutually recognized pastoral relationship. If a person never asked you to hold him accountable or gave you permission to speak into his life, you cannot just decide you're his pastor. Make sure you're on the same page with a person before you try to correct his behavior.

"Second, get permission to share an observation, and then begin with a positive, or redemptive, observation. Where possible, connect the observation of the sin you're going to bring up to a misuse of a gift that God has given that person. This won't always be the case, but frequently sin is an overextension of a gift or calling on a person's life. Look for the redeeming part of what's driving the sin, and pinpoint the misuse of the gift. Of course, in some cases, the sin might be avoiding a gift God has given the person, so use your best discretion here.

"Third, deliver your correction. Then end with an affirmation. Remind the person that the Lord loves them and that you also love them and want to see them do well. Offer to help them walk through their situation and to provide any assistance you can to help them step away from their wrongdoing.

"When you're correcting someone, you want to be careful not to fall into an accusatory role. It's wrong to falsely accuse someone or to use gossip and slander to accuse indirectly, and people aren't going to listen to you if you come at them with an accusatory tone, even if you're speaking truth. The accuser of the brethren, Satan, will try to get you to go to everyone other than the person who has the problem. He'll try to get you to stir up gossip and trouble, but remember that you need to talk to one person and one person only—the person who needs correction."

"As a prophet, you're going to perceive many things spiritually before they manifest in the natural world. You can't correct a person on everything you see in the Spirit because the timing might not be right. An immature prophet will share everything they receive, but the more a prophet matures, the more he keeps secrets with God until the appropriate time to release the information. When you see something prophetically, you need to watch the person and look for the outward signs of the inward truth. When you see the outward signs, then you can address the situation. Being accusatory in this instance would be to make the criticism about the person, saying that he or she is evil or lost or messed up. Instead you want to approach the person in love and explain that he or she has a greater destiny but inappropriate behavior is getting in the way. Notice how in the second approach you are condemning the action, not the person. Remember to always confront the person with redemption in mind."

"Making an accusation will be uncomfortable because it's not the way most American relationships function. You have to remember that your purpose is to restore the person to a right relationship with Christ, not to make that person like you. And then when someone corrects something about your behavior, remember that they are making that hard choice in love." Obadiah paused and looked at Andre, who was fidgeting. "Andre, you look like you have a story to share."

Seeming surprised, Andre looked at Obadiah and said, "Not really a story. I just find both of those things hard—both giving and receiving correction. I didn't grow up in an environment where you could freely critique things, and I didn't grow up being very patient with reproof. I shared with you all that I'm not proud of who I was when I was younger, but I'm probably more ashamed of how I treated my family during that time than anything. They tried to correct me in love, but I wouldn't have any of it. We're still not back on track because of the damage I did back then." Andre sat forward and hunched over his knees, shaking his head.

"You know, Andre, you're not that person anymore. God has restored you, and He'll work with you to rebuild what was broken," Obadiah said, and Andre looked up at him with a glimmer of hope in his eyes. "And thanks for sharing, because your example also brings up an important point. When we correct people, we have to be prepared to have our relationship take a hit if the correction isn't well received. That doesn't mean we've done something wrong but rather that their heart isn't in the right place yet."

"How do I know if it's my heart or their heart that's not in the right place?" Hayley asked.

Obadiah responded, "Look back at the steps I outlined. If you are in a relationship with a person, if you share something redemptive that God is doing, and if you wait to confront the sin until it physically manifests in that person's life, then you will be showing kindness and gentleness and goodness and love and patience, which will keep your heart in the right place."

Hayley breathed a sigh of relief—I could see she put a lot of pressure on herself to be a good student.

"Continuing on," Obadiah said, "I have a question about Matthew 5:5, where it says, 'Blessed are the meek, for they will inherit the earth.' What does it mean to 'inherit the earth'?"

Mike said, "If I inherit a house, it means it is put in my name and I can choose to do with it what I want, so I guess it means to have authority over the earth."

"That's a good way to break it down, Mike," Obadiah said. "When we walk in a calm and steady gentleness, grounded in a state of truth, we have authority over the earth—including animals, places, and weather. A gentle spirit has authority over creation. Many of you have seen your own pets reflect the state that they observe in you. When you are calm, they are calm. When you are excited, they are excited.

"I don't know about with animals," Catherine said, "but I've noticed that my frame of mind has a deep impact on my son Josh. If I'm frazzled, he goes crazy. But if I'm calm, he also tends to be relaxed. So in that sense, I can see the immediate impact of my authority on a daily basis."

"That makes me think of a more extreme example," Jerry began, "from one time when I went hiking. I was with a buddy of mine, and we'd been out for a few hours when we rounded a ridge and found ourselves feet away from a mama bear. My first instinct was to run, but I knew that that would only escalate the situation. Oddly in that moment, I experienced an overwhelming peace. I took a step forward, and I spoke to the bear and politely told her to leave. My friend looked at me wide-eyed like I was crazy, but the bear just looked back and forth at both of us, turned, and walked into the woods."

"That's a great example of having authority over creatures of the earth," Obadiah affirmed.

"That's nothing short of miraculous!" Maria exclaimed. "So, Obadiah, I have a question. You mentioned that kindness and gentleness can lead to signs and wonders. Is this the kind of thing you meant—mama bears just walking away? How does this all work?"

"Kindness and gentleness disarm people's preconceptions and create a space of safety," Obadiah explained. "They adjust the frequency of the quantum field to align with the character and nature of God, and that opens up the potential for transformation. Again, we talked about how God's heartbeat has a specific vibration that is repeating and resounding at the quantum level. Part of practicing kindness and gentleness is syncing our quantum material with that frequency. When we are in tune with God, so to speak, we have the power to impact other material and other situations and bring about transformation. Getting connected on this deep level is what allows signs and wonders to happen.

"There's a second practical way in which kindness and gentleness shift our reality. Repentance is a change of heart. If a person really believes in their heart that there's a reason they're sick, we can, through kindness, change their heart, which is the act of repentance. In other words, kindness and gentleness, manifested through us, can lead them to repent, or change their heart about what they believe is making them sick, which can actually free them from the sickness."

"That's so interesting," Maria said. "I've seen people be healed and have been aware of big changes occurring within them, but I never really considered what was happening at a molecular level or what was being shared, so to speak, from the heart of the person speaking truth into that sick person's life. How incredible!"

Obadiah smiled, and he radiated such a warmth that we all smiled back. "We're about out of time," he said, "so let's end on that high note, shall we?"

As we began packing up our things, Obadiah said, "I know you're getting used to your weekly challenges, so this week it should be more natural for you to pay attention to moments when a kind and gentle spirit will go a long way. As you grow closer to God's heart and as you learn to care for others, you may even experience something of the miraculous. Be on the lookout for how God is at work."

Slipping my notebook into my briefcase, I considered how much more of the Spirit I was already noticing. It felt like He'd been giving me His perspective in a thousand little ways—from knowing when my wife needed a word of encouragement to having fresh insight into how to deal with my temperamental boss. Saying my goodbyes, I reflected on how much of my life up until this point had felt fruitless. As I walked out into the warm light, I thanked God for showing me, bit-by-bit, just how transformational the fruit of the Spirit is—and I smiled as I remembered our Fruitcake.

CHAPTER EIGHT: PATIENCE

GENTLENESS

Over the past week, I thought back over all the areas I'd grown and all the things I'd learned and discovered about myself, and I realized that God has been very kind to me. There has been and still is so much in my life that isn't where it should be. While there aren't any huge sins to speak of since I've tried to live a moral life, my life has still been tainted by sin, and I've been missing out on the abundant life Jesus promised me. All of this is because I've been focused on myself more than others. Even when I've done something selfless, I've done it because I want to appear selfless, which makes my own reputation my real focus.

Through all this, God has been kind enough not to give up on me, allowing me time to learn and make changes. He has also allowed me to recognize most of what has been missing. He chose me as "one of the many," to use the words of Obadiah, and invited me to these weekly sessions. Through this, He knew that I would discover my own shortcomings in a way that wasn't condemning. He allowed me to see myself and willingly make choices to change, while at the same time honoring me by choosing me to participate in what He's doing. This is gentleness at its best. Up until this week, I didn't even realize He was correcting me and leading me into repentance. But I see now that I've made changes in my life as a result of what He's doing, and I'm not the same person I was when I started this journey. All along, I never realized He'd been leading me down a path that would result in such a big change of heart. In church I've heard the conversation where one person says, "God is good," and the next person responds, "All the time." This week I began to fully understand the truth of that saying. Even when I didn't know I was falling short, God was treating me with a kindness and gentleness that honored what good He saw in me. And it's not the good He saw in me in the present; it's the good He saw in the entirety of my life, including the part I haven't even lived yet.

I was thanking God for all these things when I pulled into the parking area and saw Mike, Catherine, and Andre standing just outside the entrance to the cave. Catherine was lightly hugging Andre, and Mike had his hand on Andre's back. As I approached, they all stepped back a bit, and I heard one of them sigh. They turned toward me, and Mike and Catherine greeted me with a smile and said, "Good morning" in unison. When Andre looked at me, I saw his eyes were a little wet. He wiped his arm across his face and said, "Hey, Jason." I paused a split-second, decided I didn't need to ask just yet, and responded with "Good morning, everyone." We all walked down the path and into the cave together.

When we entered, we found that the rest of the group was already there. I made a mental note to come early next week and went directly to my seat. After a couple of moments of greeting one another, we settled into place. I noticed Mike and Catherine nod at Andre a couple times, and I saw that Andre's eyes were still moist. He wasn't saying much, but that was normal Andre.

"It's good to see you all here," Obadiah began, walking behind my chair and startling me. I looked back to see where he'd come from and decided I must have been too caught up in my thoughts to see him walk in. He sat down and said, "Let's get right into it. Who has a story from this week?"

It seemed that everyone had noticed Andre's demeanor because none of us jumped to talk. We all waited, looking around the room, pausing to look at Andre a little longer each time.

Finally Andre wiped his hands over his face and said, "I have a story." Catherine sighed and smiled, and Andre continued, "You all remember my friend I mentioned running into a couple weeks ago?" We all nodded. "Well I randomly—or you know, not so randomly," he said, pointing upward, "ran into him again on Wednesday."

"What was his name, Andre? I don't remember," Maria said.

"I don't think I told you," Andre responded. "His name is Jake." Maria nodded, and Andre went on, "So Jake and I talked for a couple minutes, and then he asked if I wanted to hear about this dream he'd had. It was odd for him to share something like that with me, but of course I said yes. In his dream, a man in his early thirties approached him on the street and told Jake his life was in danger. Jake then followed the man into an old warehouse building that transformed into a garden with beautiful trees and flowers. The man turned to him and said, 'You'll be safe here. This is the place you were created for.' Then the man left."

"The next night he had another dream and the man appeared again, this time in his living room. The man said, 'You and I need to spend time together and get to know each other. I have the answers you seek.' Then Jake woke up. The next evening, the third night in a row, the man visited him again in a dream. In this one, Jake was driving a car with the man in the passenger seat. The man said, 'Just ahead you are coming to a crossroads. There will be no turning back from that point. Choose right.' Jake looked in his rearview mirror and saw cars chasing him. The cars then turned into some sort of large animals with angry, red eyes. He woke up in a sweat."

Andre shook his head. "Guys, it was so clear to me what it all meant. It was like reading one of Jesus's parables and then reading the explanation, only the explanation was already in my head before he even finished talking about his dreams." Here Andre got a little choked up.

"Go on, man," Mike encouraged. "This is good stuff."

After a couple of seconds, Andre cleared his throat and continued, "So I told Jake that the man in the dream was Jesus. You see, when I prayed for Jake I had asked Jesus to visit him, and that was exactly what Jesus was doing in the dream. In the first dream, Jesus was telling Jake that he was created to live in communion with Him in a place of beauty and rest. It was like the Garden of Eden, a holy place of endless provision. The next night Jesus was asking for a relationship with Jake so he could learn Truth and begin to make sense of his life. The third dream was a warning that time is running out. I had to tell Jake that there are dark forces—demonic forces—that are pursuing him and that want to consume him. When I said that, he shuddered. But I also told him that he had the opportunity to make a choice. Jesus showed him a crossroads and told him to 'choose right.' The 'right' way is the way of the cross." Andre sat back and looked like he was done talking.

With big eyes, Hayley asked, "Then what happened, Andre? Did Jake accept Jesus?"

Tears began to slide down Andre's face as he responded, "Yes, yes he did. I asked him if he was ready to make the choice to begin a relationship with Jesus and put all the darkness and danger behind him for good. And he said yes. He said yes!"

We all clapped, and Andre was obviously moved. "God has been kind to Jake to preserve him all these years. Most of my buddies from fifteen years ago are either in jail or dead. But God saved me, and now Jake, too, has a chance for mercy and grace. The way Jesus spoke to him was so gentle. He didn't harshly correct him; He just asked to be friends, and that really resonated with Jake."

When Andre finished, we were all smiling. Andre then pulled out a small silver cross on a silver chain and held it up. "When I ran with the old crowd, we all wore these around our necks. At the time, it didn't mean anything to any of us. But this week, this became a symbol of God's love to Jake, as well as to me. I'd like to place this up on the shelf in memory of what God did this week."

Everyone echoed agreement with the idea as Andre walked over and hung the chain around the can of soup so that the cross dangled down off the shelf.

"That's just an incredible story, and we're all so glad you could be used in this way, Andre," Catherine said, and we all agreed. She continued, "I also love how you pointed out how Jesus modeled gentleness in the dreams. Because we were focusing on kindness and gentleness this week, I noticed so many areas where my natural tendency is to correct rather than to determine the most loving, most beneficial response. For example, this week at the grocery store I refused to let Josh put a premade sandwich in the cart, and he threw a temper tantrum, kicking and screaming in his cart seat. I was already having a rough day with him and that was my last straw. I grabbed his shoulders and harshly told him to settle down. Through his tears, he said, 'But momma, we have to get that man some food!' I let go and paid attention. 'What man?' I asked. 'The man outside the store!' Josh had seen something I hadn't. He'd noticed a man sitting outside the store who looked hungry, and he wanted to help. Because I responded in anger, I missed an opportunity to encourage my son. Because I didn't wait to get the full story, I didn't have the chance to practice gentleness."

Mike jumped in, "Catherine is being too hard on herself, though. Later in the week she came to me with a question. I was sitting in my easy chair after dinner and she said, 'Honey, it means a lot to me to see you off to work in the morning. Tomorrow would you come give me a kiss before you go?' There's a lot behind this story. Catherine usually makes me breakfast and then goes to get ready. I often scarf down my food, take my coffee to go, and head off to work. Her gentle question made me realize how underappreciated she had to be feeling and convicted me to show her I care for her in many more ways. I was impressed by how she carefully chose her timing and didn't condemn but rather let me recognize how I could be a better husband."

"Thanks for sharing that, Mike," I said. "I think sometimes I'm so eager to fix a situation that I don't take the time to consider whether the other person is even going to hear my point when it's surrounded by criticism. I appreciate how Catherine chose her timing for when you were at peace and could listen."

"That's a good thing to notice, Jason," Obadiah said. "And it leads us right into our discussion on patience. In Mike's example,

Catherine showed patience in waiting for the right moment to approach him. Our culture, however, is not typically very patient. Can you guys think of some examples of impatience in our culture today?"

"I sure can," Maria began. "When I'm in the line at the grocery store and someone picks up an item without a price sticker on it so the cashier has to call for a price check, I am the first person to start complaining, and I'm never alone in my annoyance." She shook her head. "Just so we're clear, I know my reaction isn't a good thing!" She laughed and we smiled back at her.

"I know what you're talking about, Maria," Mike said. "Nothing gets under my skin like when I'm driving and the road I'm on is narrowing down to a couple lanes and some guy goes zipping past me in the lane that's closing. I always have to count to ten to keep from laying on my horn."

"I personally don't have the patience to cook," Hayley said. "The other day I saw a recipe that took two hours to prepare and thought that sounded absolutely crazy. I cook everything in my microwave, and sometimes that even takes too long."

"I'm with you, Hayley," Mike said. "When my wife is away, I eat nothing but microwave dinners." He and Catherine shared a knowing glance. "In terms of impatience, I'm also thinking about how so many companies have forced themselves into short-term thinking because they have to report their earnings to their stockholders each quarter. They push to have better and better quarter-over-quarter reports, ignoring what's in the best interest for their mission and their customers in the long run."

"You all came up with those answers quickly," Obadiah said, "and I'm sure there are many more ways we and our culture are impatient. What about in the Church? Where do you see impatience there?"

"It's possible to become impatient with young believers' immaturity," Jerry said. "Seeing restoration in someone's life takes time, and we often aren't interested in making the investment."

"Yes," Maria agreed. "And on the flipside, new converts often want to know their calling and get involved in ministry immediately, but they first need to grow a loving relationship with Jesus."

"What about the length of our church services?" I asked. Obadiah asked me to explain, so I said, "We schedule a service to last an hour or an hour and a half and that's it. We basically plan when the Holy Spirit can spend time with us as a group of believers, and extending that time is often met with complaining."

"That's true, Jason," Jerry said. "In the early days of the American church, services lasted hours. Even today in the Amish Church, which is separate from our rushed culture, services can run half a day, and I've heard that in African churches, revival services last weeks. American churches are definitely the anomaly now with our hour-long, in-and-out services."

"Great points," Obadiah said. "How do you think our concept of the miraculous, or of God's supernatural power, is impacted by this impatient culture?"

"I've been thinking about healing since my experiences a few weeks back," said Hayley. "And I realized that now I almost expect people to be healed instantaneously. Like if I pray with others for a few minutes, I want to see immediate results. But sometimes God waits to act and allows us to grow our faith."

"That's right, Hayley," Obadiah said. "We also limit the miraculous with our impatience when we want fast conversions instead of discipling people. In the same way we want to pray and see immediate healing, we also want to talk to someone about Jesus for five minutes and have that person choose to trade their entire lifestyle for a very different one. That's a big thing to ask. We all want to see people come to Christ, but we often don't want to do the long-term discipling that leads to the miracle of their acceptance into God's kingdom. Let me be clear: there's nothing wrong with asking someone if they'd like to make a decision for Christ even if you've only talked to the person for ten minutes. But if you get discouraged when that person needs more time, that's impatience."

I'd never considered how our culture's lack of patience might be impacting my spiritual life, so I sat up and prepared to take serious notes.

Obadiah said, "Before we start blaming impatience on our culture though, let's take a look at Scripture. Take five minutes or so, pair up, and discuss some examples of impatience in the Bible."

We immediately went to work, and the room was abuzz with conversation. After a few minutes we quieted down, and Obadiah asked who had an example.

Andre said, "I immediately thought of Moses when he hit the rock to get water instead of speaking to it as God had commanded."

Maria said, "What about Abraham when he wanted a son and was waiting on the child who would be Isaac but then got impatient and had Ishmael?"

"In Luke there's the example of James and John who asked Jesus if they should call down fire from heaven to destroy the Samaritans who didn't welcome them," Jerry offered.

"Maria and I had a question," Hayley said. "What about examples like when Jesus cursed the fig tree or when He healed the boy after His disciples had tried and not been successful and then asked how long He had to put up with them? To me, it sounds like Jesus was impatient in these instances. So is it possible to be righteously impatient?"

"That's a great question," Obadiah said. "More than likely, it was a question of timing for Jesus. If it was time for His disciples to cast out spirits and they didn't do it, then being frustrated with them wasn't impatience but accountability. You see, impatience is when we want something sooner than it's supposed to happen. That's very different from when something was supposed to happen in God's perfect timing and instead it's being held back due to rebellion, disobedience, or what have you; responding with a rebuke when someone is delaying God's promise isn't impatience. This leads me to the question: what is the root of impatience?"

The room thought on this for a minute. "Thinking our schedules are more important?" I ventured.

"That's halfway there, yes," Obadiah said. "The root of impatience is selfishness. When we're impatient, we focus on what we desire at the moment and how we look to other people. Often miracles performed today, like healings, are done in front of groups of people, and when you're the one praying, often people are watching you and expecting you to make something happen. Sometimes we want something to happen not for the miracle's sake but so our faith and work gains recognition. We don't want to let down the crowd. As you begin performing miracles, you'll find that a crowd will grow and begin following you. You'll start feeling a lot of pressure to perform and see things happen. If things don't happen in your timing, you might even blame God for embarrassing you and letting you down. That's why it's so important to grow the fruit of patience now so you're prepared to stand firm when the crowds come and you have to remind them that God's timing is not our timing."

Obadiah let the gravity of this challenge settle and then asked, "So what can we do, practically speaking, to make a change in Christian culture concerning this impatience?"

"It certainly helps to know the Holy Spirit more," Catherine said, "and to ask Him to lead us rather than set our own agenda."

"That's true, Catherine," Obadiah responded. "And we need a proper understanding of eternity to learn patience." Obadiah walked to the whiteboard and drew a long line horizontally from one side to the other. Then he drew an arrow on the right side and explained, "This arrow represents eternity. The far left-hand side is when God spoke creation into existence and time began." Then Obadiah turned the marker to use just the tip and touched it to the board toward the left-hand side. "That's you," he said. I squinted but couldn't even see the dot. Obadiah continued, "If we map out the beginning of time until the end, your life is only a tiny, tiny sliver. The good news, however, is that we are part of eternity, if only a very small part. You need to understand that God is acting out a piece of eternity through your life. If you can keep that in context and understand that there's a much bigger story happening around you, it's much easier to maintain patience. Remember, just because you don't see immediate impact where you are doesn't mean there wasn't impact elsewhere."

"Hebrews 11," Jerry interrupted, "lists all the heroes of the faith down through the years and then says they did not see what they were hoping for, yet they continued to move in faith. They knew that what God was doing was bigger than them. They had an eternal concept that freed them to have faith in their time on earth."

"Great reference, Jerry," Obadiah said. "That makes me think of all the times in Scripture when there's a list of how this person begat that person and that person begat this person and so on. Then there's narrative and then another list of begats. This all culminates in the long list of genealogy preceding the announcement of Christ. If any one of those people in the list of begats hadn't existed, the bridge would have been broken. The stories of individuals like Noah and David and even Jesus were all dependent on every person in those lists. Each person had an important part to play in God's plan, but not every generation experienced a story of biblical proportion. There are long bridges that are only names, but those people were vital to building to the climactic moment of Christ's death and resurrection. These people were significant to eternity because they continued the line.

"Imagine if Billy Graham's great-grandparents wouldn't have given birth to his grandfather and so on? Hundreds of thousands if not millions of people came to know Jesus through Billy Graham and continued to walk with Christ as a result of his crusades. Let's take it a step further. After being born into a specific family, Billy Graham was saved in a small tent revival. Imagine if the person leading that revival hadn't been born? Billy Graham may not have come to Lord under the anointing he did.

"None of us would be alive without our forefathers' existence, and we have significance in eternity because of who will follow us in our bloodline. We do not have this vision of time now. Instead, we expect everything of significance to happen in our lifetime—and preferably when we're in our thirties through fifties so we can really enjoy it. It would help us to be far more patient if we realized that our significance comes from doing what we're called to do and that that could be a big thing for God or it could be having a son or daughter who will do something huge to advance God's master plan. We just need to be what we were created to be and do what we were created to do."

"That relieves so much pressure!" Maria interrupted. "I'm always worried about whether or not I'm doing enough for God's kingdom, but now I see I could be fulfilling God's purpose for me without being aware."

Obadiah responded, "Yes, God's expectations are the only things that matter. There are people who serve the Lord by having a child and raising him or her up to continue the line. You're beginning to see that to make a shift toward patience in the church, you have to develop your concept of eternity. Our part in the grand scheme of things may be small, but it's still significant. For centuries, the great cloud of witnesses has been watching the progression of our stories and God's overall story. Your life may not be a story of biblical proportions, but all our actions and lives add up to continue God's great story. We must live our lives without visions of grandeur and must be faithful to take the steps assigned to us. We don't want to be remembered for having done something notable on earth; instead we want to be known on earth because we've done something notable in heaven."

Andre began, "So you're saying that if an anonymous Christian performs miracles without getting credit for it, their significance is defined by heaven's perspective?"

"Yes, for example, the widow who gave two coins would have gone completely unnoticed if Jesus hadn't drawn attention to it. Because Jesus was making a point about what was happening concerning money in the temples, the widow was mentioned in Scripture. What she did was significant in and of itself, but it was only when she was recognized in heaven for what was in her heart that she became known on earth," Obadiah said.

Hayley's hand went up and she quickly brought it back down. "Oops. I keep forgetting," she said. "My question is: how do I know if I'm doing what I'm supposed to be doing? I feel like I'm following God and His purposes, but sometimes everything goes sideways and I wonder if I'm all wrong."

"That's a loaded question but an important one," Obadiah responded. "To help develop patience in our window of eternity, it helps to understand that every dream and calling has stages, and each stage can take time to unfold. If you're feeling frustrated with how things are developing, it could be because of the stage you're in. Let me take a moment to really break this down, because it's integral for moving forward."

D R E A M   S T A G E S

Picking up the eraser, Obadiah cleaned off the white board and then sketched a chart. When he finished, it looked something like this:

Death	Transition
Demonstration	Skills, understanding, and ability to deliver
Development	Recognize what is needed and pursues skills and understanding
Distress	Nothing seems to work; does not recognize what is lacking
Dream	Heal the sick; lead thousands to the Lord

Pointing to the bottom block on the board, Obadiah said, "The first stage—where everything starts—is the dream stage. This can be your dream to alleviate poverty or lead ten thousand people to the Lord or whatever you want. When you're growing in your relationship with Jesus and are following Him, something is born in your heart as a result of your communion with Him. This starts as a desire to do something and then becomes your dream.

"The very next stage is called the distress stage. Hayley, this could be what you were referencing with your question. Just as Jesus was immediately sent into the desert to be tested after being baptized, you will quickly hit a phase after your dream stage in which nothing works out. As you try to pursue your dream, everything will seem to go wrong, and you'll be at a loss as to how to move forward. Most people bail on their dream at this stage. Dreams require skills and patience, but when you start out, you're so full of hope that you don't consider needing time to build the correct abilities; you just want to make your dream a reality. The truth is that you have to give yourself time to develop to be able to bring about your dream."

"Those who press forward continue to the development stage. Here you realize that if you're going to accomplish your dream, you're going to need some help. You need to find out what you don't know and where you're weak so you can build up those areas. When you develop, you become aware of what's lacking in yourself and begin acquiring the necessary skills and relationships to make your dream a reality.

"After developing maturity concerning your dream, you move into the demonstration phase. At this level, you have skills and maturity plus your original passion for your dream. You know what you need to do, and you have the ability to do it. When you combine all these things—hope and wisdom and goodness and patience and faithfulness and closeness with the Spirit—and you're doing what you're called to do with all the skill it requires, you begin demonstrating the reality of your dream. Your dream comes to pass.

"The last stage you go into, the one everybody loves," Obadiah said smiling, "is death." We laughed a little and he continued. "This is not a physical death but a transition time where the Lord takes you to something new, to something higher. You'll be demonstrating the reality of your dream and then you'll realize that it's just the first step to a bigger dream. It's obvious when you've reached the death stage because you'll find there's no longer any passion to your old dream and that it's time for a new dream. In the death stage, you realize your dream was something you needed to develop and needed to be able to do in order to reach a higher calling. You die to your old dream and birth a new, more inclusive dream and start the process all over again. You cycle back to the dream phase. Although you may continue demonstrating the old dream, you get to add your new dream to it. As you begin asking the Lord, 'What's next?' you realize some new desires in your heart and a new vision and new dream to work toward. Hayley, did that help answer your question?"

Not looking up from her notebook, Hayley said, "I think it answered most of it, but I'm still wondering how to know if I'm in the distress stage or if I'm just out of God's will."

After acknowledging her question with a short "mm," Obadiah sat silent for a moment. Then he said, "Hayley, can I ask you a question to help answer your question?" She nodded and he asked, "How did you know that you'd done something wrong as a child? How did you know you shouldn't take your dad's wallet or color all over the walls?"

Hayley thought for a second and said, "I guess there were assumed rules. I knew, for example, that it was wrong to take food without asking, so I guess I just applied that to everything."

"I have another question," Obadiah said. "How did you know it wasn't wrong to play dress up or to draw on paper?"

Scrunching her forehead, Hayley responded, "I'm not sure. Those things just didn't get me into trouble, so I knew they were okay."

"Living your dream is kind of like that," Obadiah said. "As you get close to the Spirit and His heart, you begin to perceive the things that are harmful, or 'wrong,' and the things that are 'good' or beneficial. In the same way that you learned what your parents allowed as acceptable as you grew to know them better, when you grow in your relationship with Christ you learn that He gives you good dreams, and you learn to distinguish those from your own fleshly desires. In the dream stage, when you're full of hope, you test the desires of your heart, and when you find they don't contradict the character and nature of God, you move forward. So when you hit the distress stage, you have to remember what was right about your dream and not analyze your way away from what Christ is leading you to do."

"That makes a lot of sense," Hayley said, "Thanks, Obadiah." The two shared a smile.

Turning back to the rest of us, Obadiah asked, "How do you think then, after hearing about these five stages of dream, distress, develop, demonstrate, death, that impatience jeopardizes the prophetic calling? How does the root cause of impatience, which we said was selfishness, influence our ministry?"

"It can cause us to plow forward instead of waiting for God's timing," I said, and Obadiah nodded.

"People in the church who feel 'star-quality gifted' and who have a selfish ambition to be seen may become frustrated and even give up on their calling if they aren't recognized," Mike said.

Then Maria observed, "If we're centered on ourselves instead of God, then we make ourselves, rather than what He is doing, the focus, which totally messes up our priorities."

"I feel like," Catherine added, "if I'm being selfish, I'm not showing the proper amount of love to the person I'm ministering to. Like you said, Obadiah, that foundation of love has to be there."

"Those are all true," Obadiah confirmed. "Prophetic ministry with visions of grandeur, or without a proper grasp of the miniscule blip we are on the timeline of eternity, can lead to selfish ambition. Don't get me wrong; there's nothing wrong with ambition. We want to be ambitious to have dreams and see God's kingdom advance and experience supernatural transformation in our own and in others' lives. But selfish ambition leads to impatience. Specifically in prophecy, selfish ambition leads prophets to be vague so they're never exactly wrong or so they can take action on their own to make things come to pass. This calls back to my earlier example of the prophet standing in front of a group of people who are all expecting something to happen; if that prophet doesn't receive a word from the Lord, he or she can be tempted to say something vague from what can be deduced about the person. A person who is trying to promote him or herself will say things that are generally comforting or generally encouraging but that don't speak specifically to a person. Let me warn all of you to never speak a word for the Lord that He hasn't given to you."

It was funny, I thought, that I would never dream of falsely speaking for the Lord, yet I identified immediately with the rationale of standing in front of a group and just wanting to share something. I was so glad I had Obadiah and the rest of the group to encourage me in these early stages so I didn't get wrapped up in myself and miss my greater calling.

"...and then next week we'll be covering faithfulness," Obadiah was saying when I snapped out of my thoughts.

"Shoot!" I whispered to Andre. "I just missed that last part. Did he say anything important?"

Andre chuckled a little. "No, just be patient, man. You'll learn everything you need to learn." With that, Andre stood up, grabbed his things, and headed for the door.

Another week over and I still had so much to learn!

I repeated Andre's words in my head, Just be patient, man.

If only it were that easy.

CHAPTER NINE: FAITHFULNESS & PEACE

IMPATIENT

Because I'd been the last person to show up for two weeks, I made a point of being early this week. When I pulled into the parking lot, I saw that Jerry had beaten me. I hurried down the path and into the cave and found Jerry sitting alone in the middle of the room, intently staring into the open room.

"Hey, Jerry," I said tentatively. "Everything okay?"

"Huh?" Jerry turned to look at me. "Oh, yeah. Hi, Jason." He went back to looking towards the wall, so I put my stuff down and took a seat.

After a few minutes of silence, I ventured, "So did you catch the game last night? I couldn't believe when—"

"I don't really follow sports," Jerry interrupted.

I closed my mouth and sat back. Then I tried, "Jerr—"

"I'm sorry, Jason," Jerry said, adjusting his seat to face mine. "I just came early because I thought this would be a good place to do some quiet processing." I nodded but still felt confused, so I was glad when he continued. "We were working on our patience this week, you know, and I've always considered myself pretty patient. I have a slow pace of life, and I usually don't care when things take a longer time than expected because it gives me time to chat with the other people around me. But I've been mentoring this one guy from my church for five years now, and I'm just not seeing him making progress. He'll listen to my advice, agree, and then do whatever he feels like doing. He may make an outward change in his behavior for a while, but he always seems to drift back to where he began. He is not making the inward change. I saw it happen again this week. I was simultaneously so discouraged and so frustrated that I really lashed out. About halfway through my rant, I realized I was only annoyed because he wasn't progressing according to my timeline. If God is still giving him time to begin making real choices, then I need to be patient, too. I apologized to him, but then for the rest of the week I kept noticing my impatience with other little things like the cashier taking too long to make change or the girl who works in the office at church not having my volunteer work ready for me when I arrived. Jason, I thought I had a handle on some of this stuff, but now I realize that as I get older, the more impatient I become. I want to see God's kingdom now, and I don't quite know how to balance knowing that it's coming but it's not here yet and I can't force it to be."

Jerry signaled that the conversation was over by turning back to the wall, but I wasn't ready for it to be over.

"You know, Jerry," I began. "I've realized through these sessions that I'm not exactly a saint either. I think it's okay to admit to ourselves that we've dropped the ball. That teaches us humility, and it gives God the chance to improve on areas where we're lacking a certain capacity or ability."

"I know those things mentally," Jerry said. "I just have to become aware of their reality when it comes to patience. I want to live according to God's timing and not my own."

Just then Mike and Catherine entered and wished us both a, "Good morning!"

"Morning," Jerry replied; he picked up his Bible and flipped to a marked page as Catherine and Michael put their things down.

"Hi, guys," I said. Catherine went toward the restrooms, and Michael went to make himself some hot tea. Left alone, I considered how each of us in the group was growing. Even wise Jerry still had some struggles. I was encouraged to see that God wasn't done with us yet.

Just this week, I'd chewed out the administrative assistant at work for scheduling two meetings at the same time. She never made mistakes, and I hadn't even asked if something was going on in her life that might have led to this oversight. I felt like I'd fallen right back to the bottom of the totem pole, learning to love.

I checked my watch. Where was everyone? It figures everyone was late the week I was early. Finally, with one minute to go, the rest of the group, including Obadiah, came trickling in.

After everyone had gotten settled, Obadiah said, "Good morning, all. How did your week go? Did any of you notice moments this week when you were being impatient and trying to accelerate God's timing? How did you handle them?"

No one responded right away, so I offered, "Well, I was feeling pretty impatient waiting for you all to get here today."

"We were on time!" Maria defended the group.

"I know, Maria. I'm just kidding," I said, raising my hands in a gesture of innocence.

She laughed and said, "You better be! I've felt like I was running late all week, and of course, as God is working with me on patience, I got stuck in every long line imaginable. I thought I was going to go crazy!"

"But you didn't go crazy," Andre reminded. "I think you're lucky to just have dealt with long lines. I realized this week that I'm feeling very impatient about my career timeline. Things just aren't moving along the way I'd hoped."

Mike agreed, "Yeah. After all the favor I received a few weeks ago, I feel like I'm at a standstill at work too. I have to admit I felt a little angry with God for not moving me forward, which I then felt ridiculous about. Why is it so hard to accept His timing?"

"I found timing difficult to deal with this week as well," Jerry said, clearly not wanting to say any more.

Obadiah waited a few moments before joining the conversation. "It's not easy to see with a godly perspective when things aren't happening the way we think they should. But there is purpose to God's timing. Sometimes He takes time to develop something in us so we can mature and prepare for whatever is coming our way."

"I was also wondering if the delay might be for the benefit of someone else," Hayley ventured. "I was supposed to have dinner with my grandpa this week, and I was praying about how to talk to Him about Jesus. I was really looking forward to the evening, but then he canceled on me at the last minute. I questioned God as to why He would allow that to happen when I felt so prepared, and then I realized Christ might have other work He wanted to do on my grandfather's heart before he would be receptive to what I wanted to share."

"You're wise beyond your years, Hayley," Jerry encouraged her.

"You're exactly right, Hayley. Sometimes things don't happen because all the elements aren't in alignment yet, and we can't control the spiritual journeys of others. As it sounds like you've all discovered, the best way to miss God's purposes is to cover them with our own agenda," Obadiah explained. "The true way to accelerate the pace of breakthrough or change is to embrace the Lord's timing and cooperate with what He's doing. Many times once we agree to follow God's timing, we find that He suddenly accelerates the process."

"How do we embrace God's timing?" Hayley asked.

Obadiah responded, "I'm glad you asked, Hayley, because your answer is intertwined with our main subject for this week, faithfulness."

FAITHFULNESS

I began writing the word "faithfulness" in my journal, and Obadiah launched right in, "I'm going to ask us to work out a definition for 'faithfulness,' but before I do, I want to take a moment to explain why I always incorporate this exercise, because I know a couple of you are wondering." Hayley dropped her head to her notebook, and I smiled at Obadiah. He said, "When I ask us to take time to define a word, one of my objectives is to break away from the traditional ways we've defined a term so we can really understand what it means. The church has a litany of words and phrases that are used so frequently that most people can't tell you in any depth what they even mean. We use words as shortcuts for broader ideas, but sometimes a word I use might mean something very different to me than it does to you. This can be based on my background, my experiences, and even ways I've heard other people use the word. So when I say something like, "being faithful," my connotations might be a little different than yours.

"I want us all to be on the same page concerning what we're talking about in these sessions, so that's why I try to avoid using well-known phrases without breaking them down into clear definitions. Okay, so 'faithfulness' is a very important aspect of being a follower of Jesus and therefore of being a prophet. Hebrews 11 says that faith is the essence of things unseen. Once something is seen in the natural, it no longer requires faith. Prophets look into that unseen world and bring what they see into the natural realm. In this way, faithfulness is the realm of the prophetic.

"The fruit of the Spirit are so intertwined we often confuse them or define them using each other, but it's essential to distinguish among them, so when we talk about faithfulness, let's be careful to give a separate, precise definition. With that in mind, how might we define 'faithfulness'?"

Mike was ready with his dictionary answer, "I have that it is to be 'moral, steady, and trustworthy.'"

"Loyalty isn't a fruit of the Spirit," Maria said, "so I'm going to say that faithfulness is being loyal."

Catherine grinned, "Leave it to Maria to tread the line on the rules." Maria laughed and shrugged her shoulders, and Catherine continued, "I think of marriage when I think of being faithful, so I'd say it has to do with committing to something and not wavering in that commitment."

"Catherine might think of marriage," Andre said, "but I think of dogs." We all laughed. "So I guess I think of faithfulness as blind trust."

"Permanent and steadfast blind trust," Catherine jokingly corrected.

"All right, all right, you all make some good points here," Obadiah said, bringing us back around. "Based on what I mentioned earlier, I'm going to give you some very specific wording today concerning 'faithfulness'. The '-ness' part means 'characteristic of,' so 'faithfulness,' means 'the characteristic of being faithful.' The definition I like to use for 'being faithful' is 'having constant certainty of the unwavering truthfulness of God.'"

I was writing as fast as I could but didn't make it to the end of the definition. When I looked up, I saw Hayley and a couple others looking lost as well. Obadiah smiled and repeated his sentence, and I copied it all down.

"That's a hundred dollar definition!" Maria said.

"That's true, but I think it covers everything you all mentioned in your discussion about faithfulness. Let's break it down and talk about it a little," Obadiah said. "So what does it mean to be 'constant' or what is 'certainty' or 'unwavering truthfulness'?"

Mike suggested, "I think that certainty comes from knowing about God's character and knowing He will consistently respond in that same character."

"Yes," Catherine agreed. "It comes from believing that God will fulfill His promises."

"This makes me think of Roman armor," Jerry ventured.

"Well, you lost me," Andre said to Jerry, dramatically throwing his hands in the air.

Jerry smiled and said, "Roman soldiers had spikes in their shoes—kind of like our soccer cleats today—so they could dig into the ground. We have that same certainty of standing firm in Christ. That connects to the 'unwavering truthfulness' part of your definition as well, Obadiah. In 1 Corinthians 4:1–2 Paul says we are to be 'stewards of the mysteries of God' and that as stewards, we must be found faithful.'"

"Good, Jerry," Obadiah confirmed. "Yes, those mysteries of God are wrapped up in the unwavering truthfulness of God. There are aspects of God's truthfulness that are difficult to understand, but we must be faithful to believe in and guard them. Stewardship and faithfulness connect knowing the mysteries of God and being able to release them. Let's go a little deeper with that. How can we explain 'stewarding the mysteries of God' in more detail? What is a 'steward,' what are 'mysteries'?" Obadiah paused for a moment until it became clear to him that we were all poised and waiting for his answer instead of ours. "Well, a 'steward' is like an agent—one who acts on behalf of another person. So another way of phrasing 1 Corinthians 4:1 is that we are 'an agent of the things of God that cannot be explained.'"

"As prophets," Obadiah continued, "we'll receive words from God, but we may not be meant to release them at that time. It's a mystery of God that oftentimes people are not yet ready to hear the word we've received for them, and we must steward those mysteries, no matter the consequences. Many of the mysteries of God in history that were finally released at the right time came at the cost of the lives of those who had held them. Consider the first-century Church who was tasked with spreading the message of Jesus. Most of them who took up stewardship of that message ended up being put to death as a result.

"Or, we may receive promises from God twenty to thirty years before they come to pass. A well-known prophet from a couple of years back named Bob Jones was told about a coming harvest decades away, and he was told he would see the beginnings of it just before his death. He had to wait all those years, but the Lord delivered."

"Why would the Lord show us things twenty to thirty years in advance?" Hayley asked.

"Yeah," Maria agreed. "I'm the type who wouldn't realize it was for thirty years later until the big reveal thirty years later when I would be like, 'Oh, so that's what God was doing.'" She laughed and I couldn't help but smile. We could always count on Maria to see the humor in a situation. "But seriously, why wouldn't He just tell me what He was doing closer to the date?"

"I think partially it's to develop faith," Mike offered.

"Or to develop peace," Catherine suggested.

"Maybe it's like a not-so-hidden treasure," I said. "God gives us the map and the opportunity to seek it out and learn about it so we're ready when He reveals it."

"I agree with Jason," Jerry said. "The greater the calling, the more difficult it is to have or to be worthy of that calling. Knowing the promises in advance can help us through the difficulties."

I had a moment of wondering if that's actually what I'd just said or if Jerry had made it far more eloquent. It was always nice having someone in the group who could make your points better than you could.

"It sounds like you're all saying very similar things," Obadiah said. "Sometimes God immediately reveals everything we need to know to us, but more often He provides us with a glimpse of His plan and with the tools we need to delve deeper into His purposes and our relationship with Him. Remember that Paul isn't talking about faithfulness in the context of being faithful to show up to church; he's talking about being a faithful steward of the mysteries of God. Sometimes God will reveal something to us as a sort of test. Are we the types of individuals who will ponder the mystery in our hearts until it's time, or do we go blabbing, exposing it before its time? We must be proven faithful in the smaller mysteries in order to be trusted with the larger, deeper mysteries. We must learn to hold the mysteries until the appropriate time to reveal them, when they'll bring real transformation."

While Obadiah was speaking, Catherine had been nudging Michael with increasing vigor. Finally he said, "Okay, okay. Around twenty years ago now, the Lord gave me a dream and I had no clue what it meant. When we moved to this town, however, all the pieces started falling into place. Now I know why he gave us that vision back then, but I'll tell you—I thought long and hard about that dream and couldn't sort it out. But now, after everything converged, it all makes perfect sense. And Catherine and I are both so glad God prepared us for this next step by opening our hearts to the idea for over twenty years."

"That's so encouraging," Hayley said. "Because I'm younger, I often feel I'm sitting on a lot of promises, just waiting for them to be fulfilled. It's good to remember that God is always on time for His purposes and that He won't let me miss what He's doing."

"Remember, Hayley, we have a very limited view of eternity. God will be faithful to use you for His purposes, but you have to be faithful to wait and to learn from Him," Obadiah said, and Hayley nodded with a serious look on her face. Obadiah continued, "Now that we've nailed down a basic definition for faithfulness, let's look at what the Bible says is the source of faithfulness. Romans 10:17 says, 'Faith comes from hearing, and hearing by the word of Christ.'"

Obadiah paused to let us write and then continued, "The two most important questions that must be answered in relation to producing the fruit of faithfulness in our lives are first, where does it come from, and second, how do we cooperate with God to obtain and develop it. We often talk about hearing from the Lord as the source of faith, but we rarely strip the religious jargon away and consider what that means. Looking at the meanings of the original Greek terms, I've come up with a translation, which is 'Faith comes through perceiving the rhema, or water-like flow, of the utterance of God.' The phrase 'water-like flow' is important; God is constantly speaking, and we have to find the flow of what He's saying and step into it. Often when people talk about hearing the Word of the Lord, they're talking about hearing Scripture. While we can gain faith from biblical stories, we must also consider people like Abraham who were called faithful yet who existed prior to a written Scripture. So reading the Bible isn't what hearing the Word means.

"To rephrase both our definition of faithfulness and how we get it then, it all boils down to this. 'The characteristic of being constantly certain of the unwavering truthfulness of the mysteries of God [which is faith] comes through a sustained, relational conversation [which is hearing] with the One from whom utterances flow like water [which is the Word].' Take a second to get that down and meditate on it," Obadiah said, pausing as we thought over his definition. "Now to simplify it. 'The key to faithfulness is abiding in God.' It all stems from a close, relational, sustained conversation with Him."

I could tell I was going to have some homework this week just sorting out Obadiah's definition. On top of that, I felt the Spirit urging me toward a closer relationship with Him and felt eager to step into that "water-like flow" of God's Word.

OVERLAP

"Do any of you need a break?" Obadiah asked. No one stirred, so he continued. "Let's look then at how faithfulness relates to last week's topic of patience. Where in Scripture do we read about the two? We could refer back to Hebrews 11 where it talks about the heroes of the faith who all waited in expectation for what they'd worked for, and they're still waiting today."

"Hearing God's Word isn't all there is to faithfulness then, right?" Andre asked. "There must have to be some sort of agreement to it."

"Yes, that's right; there is some back-and-forth," Obadiah confirmed. "The heroes of the faith responded to what God told them and took steps to live according to God's promises. Again, when you have a sustained relational conversation with God, you can hear the rhema Word of God. Anyone can tap into that water-like flow; in fact, that's how we become believers in the first place. We come across that utterance of God's truth, and we step into the flow and begin listening to God and following Christ. Remaining full of that inner constancy and certainty, however, is a choice. You decide to either stick with the rhema or not. You hear the Word, and you have to then choose to believe it."

"Can you define the word 'hearing'?" Catherine asked. "I'm not sure I understand the full concept of it."

Obadiah responded, "That's why I often use the word 'perceiving' instead of 'hearing.' When you hear from God, it's not always audible. Sometimes you perceive God speaking to you. Jesus says in John 10:27, "My sheep hear my voice, and I know them, and they follow me." This can be taken literally, but you don't always hear God's voice through sound waves. 'Knowing God's voice' also mean you understand the way God communicates. You, as a being living in God's flow, perceive His purposes and His instructions."

"All right," I said, "I've got a question: what exactly do you mean when you say 'water-like flow'?"

"I guess it means that there's no blockage," Catherine said. "I think of smooth water flowing constantly down a river."

"God is constantly communicating, and in that way, Catherine is right, there are no obstacles to the flow," Obadiah said. "Of course, that doesn't mean we're always drinking it in. God is always, on a supernatural level, releasing His mysteries through this flow that are ready to be released. Prophecy, then, is perceiving that quantum-field potential through spending time with God. When we perceive that potential and speak it forth, then it comes into reality, which brings about transformation. In other words, faithfulness comes from perceiving the will of God in the quantum field and speaking it as an expression of Jesus, who is the

Word. When we perceive where God is moving in the quantum field, we 'hear' the rhema Word."

Seeing us nodding and following along, Obadiah continued. "Now, let's get back to our discussion to the relationship between faithfulness and patience. In fact, we can also add in peace, because patience, peace, and faithfulness are all related."

Back to the whiteboard Obadiah went, this time drawing a Venn diagram consisting of three overlapping circles. He labeled the circle on the left "Peace," the circle on the right "Patience," and the middle circle overlapping the others "Faithfulness." To help distinguish the sections, he shaded the overlapping areas. His finished diagram looked like this:

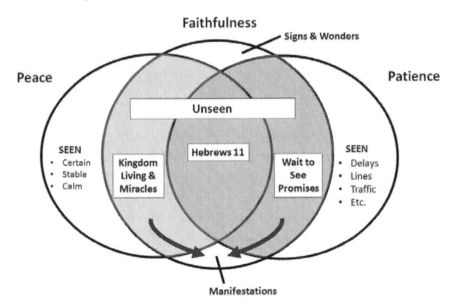

"In the space solely in the realm of patience, I'm listing the day-in, day-out struggles we have to be patient in the seen world," Obadiah explained, citing things like getting stuck in traffic, waiting in line at the store, and having a delayed flight. Then he pointed to the area where patience and faithfulness overlapped. "Where patience overlaps with faithfulness is part of the unseen world. Remember when we talked about moving up the tiers of the Spirit 'fruitcake' and I said that faith isn't needed when you see a miracle but is needed when you are believing for or in a miracle you can't yet see? Faithfulness involves believing in the promises and the potential in the unseen realm. As I mentioned earlier, it is the unseen realm that the prophet peers into and speaks what he or she perceives. The overlap of patience and faithfulness are things God has promised us that have not yet happened and that we're waiting to see.

"Then, the third area is the sweet spot where patience, faithfulness, and peace overlap. I should note, however, that for those who are living in this area, it doesn't always seem so sweet. This is the Hebrews 11 area where you're waiting on the promises of God that you may not see in your lifetime. The intersection of patience, faithfulness, and peace is where you have such a constancy of the inward certainty of the truthfulness of God, that even if you never see God's promises fulfilled here on earth, you are still trusting and living in expectation of being part of the cloud of witnesses who get to see all God's promises come to pass.

"To the left of that, where just faithfulness and peace intersect is the area of kingdom living and the place of miracles. We live in the natural world, which is out of alignment with the supernatural, but because of the knowledge of the unseen promises of God, we can live as if the kingdom of heaven is here now. Because of this inward certainty and an insistence on living in God's kingdom, miracles happen. Because you are not bound by physical laws, you see God work in supernatural, miraculous ways. This is what Jesus did. Miracles followed Him everywhere. He constantly declared that the kingdom of heaven is at hand. He lived in that kingdom while on earth, and the miracles came out of that place.

"Signs and wonders are part of the area of the faithfulness circle that doesn't overlap with either peace or patience. These occur when you haven't received a promise of God in advance but in the moment you simultaneously receive the promise and see its supernatural delivery. An example of this would be when Peter and John were going up to the temple in Acts 3. A man asked them for alms and Peter replied to him that they did not have silver or gold. Then he spoke to the man to be healed and he was. No one anticipated this happening. It was simply the need of the moment.

"This is also where you see the results of your patience as the things you've been promised and have been waiting for become part of the natural world. A very small part of faithfulness takes part in the seen world, but signs and wonders are ways God increases our faithfulness in the unseen realm.

"The last area is where peace is visible in the seen realm. Peace here helps you be certain in uncertain situations, stable in shaky situations, and calm in the midst of chaos. Peace in the seen realm is a visible manifestation of where you are in the Spirit. While God works on your inner peace in trusting Him to deliver on His promises, other people see your outer peace as you remain calm and collected during trials. But we'll cover more about peace next week.

"Okay, so now that we better understand the distinctions and the intersections of peace, patience, and faithfulness, how do you think we apply faithfulness in the life of the prophet?"

"I'm thinking about the water-like flow of God you mentioned," Michael said. "If a prophet is in that flow and is hearing what God is saying, he can't just say something completely different; he has to be faithful to trust God's word and wait to see it through."

Obadiah nodded, "When you're living in patience and faithfulness, you see a promise of God and choose to wait on it rather than trying to make it happen on your own. This is where it's so important to stay away from selfish ambition. You might perceive a promise of God but recognize that it is not the time to release it. You may even recognize that the timing is such that you might not live to see the promise come about. Trying to make things happen indicates a lack of constancy in the unwavering truthfulness of God. Selfish ambition is a departure from the sustained relationship with God, and it's poor stewardship of His mysteries. It's your responsibility to care for God's mysteries and to reveal them in the proper time—not to try to use them for selfish gain or acclaim.

"Now that we have a good idea of what hinders faithfulness, what do you think being faithful looks like?"

Jerry immediately referenced, "Galatians 5:5–7 tells us to 'wait for the hope of righteousness and run the race well.'"

"It's funny you mentioned that, Jerry," Maria said, "because I was thinking of a similar verse. In 2 Corinthians 1:24, Paul talks about 'fighting the good fight.'"

I picked up the conversation thread with, "What about that verse in Luke where Jesus talks about moving mountains with faith the size of a mustard seed? I've always wondered if being faithful literally involved moving mountains."

"It might," Obadiah said. "That verse can be taken both ways. But the point Jesus was making there was that even with small faith, we can expect God to move in big ways. Note that Jesus points out that the only thing that can defeat faith, of any size, is doubt. When we perceive ourselves as not having enough faith, we are really dealing with too much doubt. You don't combat doubt by adding more faith. You combat doubt by having less doubt, and that is the essence of having a constant certainty. Transformational prophecy requires consistency and a constant faith connected to God's rhema."

"That's like all the Hebrews 11 stuff we were talking about before," Catherine said. "All those saints persevered without ever seeing what they were waiting for. They had hope and ran the race and stayed faithful, and they're still watching for the revelation of the promise. They remained constant and never doubted His promises."

Obadiah picked up, "That's a good way of phrasing it, Catherine. In a word, faithful prophets are overcomers. Hebrews 11:1 says, 'Faith is the essence of things not seen and the substance of things hoped for.' That means faith only happens when there is no visible evidence in the natural to support the idea or hope. In Scripture, faith is not specifically tied to signs and wonders and miracles, but it is consistently associated with staying a course regardless of the circumstances or physical evidence. All miracles come from a combination of peace and faith, not just of faith.

"Having faith means that the unseen realm is more real to you than what you see in the natural. This is the realm of the prophetic. Prophets so clearly see what's going on in the supernatural that they can mix up whether something happened in the natural or the spiritual realm. They forget whether it's something they perceived in the Spirit or something they saw physically. Faith is about living in that unseen realm and having confidence in the truth of God. Staying in that place allows us to overcome everything that comes against us. We become overcomers. As prophets overcome, they show they can be trusted with power. Overcoming fosters peace and produces self-control, which enables us to access God's power to make things happen."

Obadiah looked up at the clock. "Speaking of getting caught up in the supernatural world, all our musing about faithfulness and patience has drained our time in the natural world." I was shocked to follow his eyes to the clock and discover we were over time. I secretly hoped that this session had felt so fast because I'd somehow become incredibly patient.

"Before we go," Obadiah continued, "I want to challenge all of you to enter further into the supernatural world this week. Ask the Holy Spirit to show you the unseen realities behind physical events. Pay attention to your responses and your attitude this week, and pray to have a constancy in the inward certainty of the unwavering truthfulness of God."

I immediately thought back to the second week when I'd seen the glass fall from the table and the child run into the road before either of those things had actually happened. I had a feeling my "faithfulness week" was going to look even more surreal, and I couldn't wait to see how God would grow my faith. I just hoped He didn't make me have too much patience—I was excited to see what was next.

CHAPTER TEN: PEACE

FLOWING

It took a few days to realize that God really was constantly speaking to me. Every word He spoke at every instant was a promise of His love and care for me. After our class's introduction to sitting in the Lord's presence a few weeks ago, I'd been practicing every day—well, almost every day. The practice of "beholding" allowed me to deliberately set time aside to hear what God was saying. Around Monday, I realized the things He was speaking to me in our time together each morning were then repeated many times throughout the day, almost as if each day had its own theme. On Wednesday it occurred to me that what He was telling me in the morning was a prophecy indicating what would happen during the day. You can imagine my surprise when I realized that the Lord Himself was prophesying to me each day!

Instead of disregarding what He said and hoping things would work out, my challenge was to believe the prophecy and walk it out. On Thursday, God told me to begin prophesying to my day according to what I was hearing from Him. I was a little hesitant at first. I didn't know what He meant by "prophesy to my day." But shortly before noon, I decided that He meant exactly what He said; He wanted me to prophesy, or speak, to the day. He was telling me to speak to my schedule—speak to my interactions. He wanted me to speak to my emotions and circumstances and speak according to what He spoke in our time together. So I decided to do exactly that and started commanding my afternoon. Although I was at work, I spoke out loud and commanded my schedule to come into order. Within minutes, a mandatory meeting that conflicted with two other calls was cancelled. This was especially beneficial because, while the mandatory meeting was not for anything important to the success of my company, the other two were very important calls. One concerned a new marketing initiative and the other was in regards to a new software package that will change how our company works with our clients. I thanked God for working out my schedule for me and moved forward.

By the end of the week, I was in the practice of speaking to my entire day. On Friday morning, I sat in the presence of Jesus and rehearsed what was to happen over the next twenty-four hours. It was as if Jesus was providing counsel to me, and I was coming into agreement with it. He would speak something that needed to happen, and I would prophesy it back. Like this, Jesus and I discussed who needed to meet with me to resolve a few outstanding issues and get some funding. We talked about what projects I should give time to during the day, and we considered the qualities that were needed from potential hiring candidates for an open position. After Jesus and I worked out the details, I spoke out loud and commanded my day. I declared that I would meet the person who could resolve the outstanding issue, and I spoke what decision would be made. I declared that the funding for the new software would be approved for the amount needed. I spoke out loud the qualities of the new candidate and told the day that the person with those qualifications would walk into the office and submit a résumé. Then I described what my day's schedule would look like, and I called out all the projects I would work on and what would be accomplished on each.

It was incredible how closely the day followed what I'd spoken. The outstanding issue was resolved, and the funding approval was sent to purchasing. While the candidate did not walk into the office, I did receive an email containing the ideal résumé, and I followed up with the sender, who seemed to be exactly the person we need. I was able to work on each of the projects I spoke about, and I even ended with extra time in the afternoon and was able to work on some additional projects.

Once I realized what I was supposed to do, finding the flow of the utterance of God and stepping into it made a significant difference in my day. I was glad to have more relaxed conversations with Jesus about what He would have me accomplish over the weekend, and I could hardly wait for Monday morning when Jesus and I would once again tackle my work week.

Pulling into the parking area early again this week, I noticed a car in the lot I didn't recognize. Thinking we might have a guest speaker, I hurried down the path. When I walked through the entrance, I saw Jerry sitting in the space where Maria usually sat, reading his Bible and drinking coffee.

"Hey, Jerry," I said and he looked up at me and smiled. "New car?"

"You could say that," Jerry said enigmatically and looked back down at his Bible.

I shrugged and went to grab myself a cup of coffee. Having a little extra quiet time was nice, and I used it to sit in the Lord's presence, asking Him to prepare my mind to fully grasp the day's lesson.

As everyone else trickled in, Jerry remained stoic. I watched him out of the corner of my eye, having flashbacks to our conversation the week before and wondering if something had developed with his friend.

When we were all settled, I spoke before Obadiah and said, "I'm sorry everyone, but I really haven't nailed down this patience thing yet, and I can't wait to hear about Jerry's week."

Jerry looked at me with a gleam in his eyes. "It was a good week," he said.

"Well, out with the story then!" Maria encouraged.

After marking his spot and carefully closing his Bible, Jerry smiled and began, "The bad news is that my old car, which was about ten years old, was hit by a large delivery truck early this week." A collective gasp went up from the room, and Jerry immediately waved both of his hands and said, "It's okay. My car was parked outside and I was in my house, and the delivery driver was also unharmed." Catherine let out a huge sigh. I knew how she felt. Jerry continued, "Unfortunately, my car was totaled, and because it was so old, my insurance wouldn't pay me enough to buy a new car, and I certainly didn't have the money to buy a replacement or finance a new car." I nodded. Having gone through a couple of similar experiences in my younger years, I knew it wasn't easy to find money for a car.

"Did the insurance money help at all?" Maria asked.

"Yes," Jerry said, "my insurance gave me just enough for a down payment on a modest new vehicle, but I wasn't sure if I should take that leap because I didn't know if I'd be able to make payments. I asked the Lord what to do, and He reminded me of Psalm 37:25 which says that the Lord doesn't forsake the righteous or leave them begging for bread. I felt this was God's promise for my situation, and I chose to step into the flow of God concerning the situation. The very next day, I asked a friend to take me to a car dealer to look for a replacement. As expected in the natural realm, there were no amazing deals available. We tried three more car dealers and found the same thing. I'm speaking conservatively when I say I was disappointed.

"But then it was as if a lightbulb came on in my head. I recognize now that it was the voice of God speaking to me and telling me to declare the type of car I wanted and the price I wanted to pay. So I spent the next two days doing exactly that. On Thursday, my friend and I went back to one of the dealerships we'd already visited. As we drove onto the lot, I noticed a car that hadn't been there before, and it was exactly the type of car I'd been declaring I wanted. I didn't even bother walking over to look at it; I walked right into the shop and asked for a salesperson. The dealer was confused when I told him I wasn't interested in test-driving the car because I knew it was the one for me. He urged me to check out a few of the cars on the lot, but I told him to write up the deal. When the paperwork came back, however, the final price was three times what I could afford. I stood on the fact that I had prayed for that car in the Spirit and that God would not abandon me in the middle of a deal, so I wrote a check for the amount that I had and asked the dealer to hold the car for me while I acquired the remaining funds." Jerry broke out of the story and reminded us, "I was fully aware as I made that promise that in the natural world, I had no way of procuring that kind of money." Andre winked at me as we both anticipated the upcoming miracle.

As he continued, Jerry became more and more animated. "When I got home from the dealership, there was a message on my answering machine. It was from the insurance company of the delivery truck driver, and they said they had a check waiting for me. Any guesses on the amount?" Jerry asked.

"I have one," I said. "Was it the exact amount you needed?"

His eyes twinkling, Jerry said, "Better than that. It was twice the amount I needed! I called my friend, and we went right back to the dealership where I asked if they had the same vehicle in a newer model."

Andre held up a hand as if to stop the story. "I see where this is going. So is that your new Porsche out in the parking lot?" He teased.

Chuckling, Jerry said, "No, but I guess I should have specified a better car in my declarations in the Spirit." We all laughed. "At any rate, I was able to pay for a very nice replacement, and I even had money left over. I learned my lesson to always step into God's (rhema) before even thinking about making a decision." Jerry pulled out a set of car keys on a worn key chain and began walking toward the trophy shelf. "I thought I might place these keys to my old car on the shelf as a reminder of His faithfulness toward us."

"That's incredible, Jerry," Mike said. "I've heard a lot of stories about God blessing people with the exact amount of money they need right when they need it, but I love how you point out that sometimes we dream too small when we're asking God for a blessing. I'm always blown away by how generous He is with us."

Thinking of all I'd learned the past week, I said, "I agree, Michael. This week God challenged me to meet with Him every morning to plan my days and then to verbally declare what was going to happen. The results were miraculous. I can't believe it took me this long to truly experience 'beholding God'."

Others in the room murmured their agreement, and Obadiah, who had been leaning back in his chair and allowing us to speak, leaned forward and said, "I think it's time we move on to the next level. Everyone ready?"

PEACE

The feeling in the room shifted, moving from celebration of what God was doing in our lives to learning how to know Him more. I couldn't wait to share all I was learning with my friends and family.

"Peace," Obadiah began, and Maria immediately made a peace sign at him. He good-naturedly copied her gesture and continued, "Peace is the result of a congruence of patience and faithfulness. When I talked to you several weeks ago about congruence, I mentioned the interconnection of mind, emotions, and will and the necessity of bringing them into harmony. We didn't delve into each of those words at the time, but now I want to explain how they relate to our topics of peace, patience, and faithfulness. Patience is the "mind" aspect as it involves aligning yourself with God's viewpoint—having a larger concept of eternity and reconciling your state with God's state. Faithfulness—that constancy in the inward certainty of the unwavering truthfulness of God—is the internal, emotional drive that allows us to stay on course and to overcome. Just as the mind and emotions drive the will, or the intent, when patience and faithfulness are reconciled, they result in peace. And peace determines how we respond, how we maintain our convictions, and how we declare how our days will go. You can't align with God until you're reconciled with eternity, which is patience. You can't align inwardly with God until you're maintaining certainty of the truthfulness of God, which is faithfulness. Peace then is an inward alignment of the quantum vibrations of God, regardless of what is happening externally.

"The peace Jesus spoke of is a combination of hope, trust, and quiet in the mind and soul, which is brought about by reconciliation with God. Sometimes people have an incorrect definition of peace—saying they don't have peace because the road ahead looks too difficult. But since peace is driven by patience and faithfulness, when we maintain our understanding of our place in eternity and of the truthfulness of God, we can find peace in any situation."

"Jesus is called the Prince of Peace. Princes rule over kingdoms, so that means there is a kingdom of peace where you can abide. It's important to realize that having a moment of peace is not the same as living in a sustained place of peace. When your spirit is truly at peace, you can walk through turbulent circumstances while outwardly manifesting peace."

Here Obadiah gestured toward Jerry, who sat a little straighter in his chair. "Jerry experienced peace despite trials this week. After his car was totaled and he didn't have an adequate amount to replace it, he didn't immediately try to make anything happen. He may have made some queries to see what he had to contend with, but he didn't try to force a solution. Instead, he was patient to wait for the Lord to speak. Then when he heard from the Lord, he moved in faithfulness to overcome what was in front of him. Patience and faithfulness combined to keep him in a place of peace, which resulted in a miracle."

I thought to myself that before this training, I'd been accustomed to thinking of miracles in terms of signs and wonders. It was still a small challenge to think of an insurance settlement coming through as a miracle.

"Some of you may be questioning my use of the term 'miracle,'" Obadiah said, looking right at me. "Yes, it was a legal obligation for the delivery truck driver's insurance company to pay Jerry for the damage. However, Jerry was not obligated to declare the type of car he wanted. And that exact car was not obligated to be on the lot when it had not been the day before. And for the settlement money to come through that quickly? I'd say the combination of those things were the miracle that resulted from Jerry's place of peace in the Lord."

Slowly nodding, I looked back at Obadiah. He was right. When we pray specifically, God answers specifically, and that can't be attributed to random coincidence. I was confident I'd seen my own "everyday" miracles of God firsthand on Friday.

"Let's recap," Obadiah said. "What is peace? It may be easiest to arrive at a definition of peace by explaining what peace is not. I've identified four major ways people get out of alignment with the quantum vibrations of God. The first one is fear and anxiety. There are four big fears that are the most common. The first is "fear of man," or what happens when we start worrying about how people perceive us. The pandemic form of fear of man in society today is political correctness. Fear of man intimidates us from being fully honest with others." Here Obadiah gave an aside, "While there's certainly room for speaking with kindness and gentleness, the truth of our message should never be compromised." He continued, "John 12:42 says, 'Yet at the same time many even among the leaders believed in him. But because of the Pharisees they would not openly acknowledge their faith for fear they would be put out of the synagogue.' This shows that leaders and rulers are especially prone to fear of man because they care how the people they govern will react."

"John 19:38 echoes that same message," Jerry said, flipping open his Bible and turning the pages. In a matter of seconds, he began reading, "'Later, Joseph of Arimathea asked Pilate for the body of Jesus. Now Joseph was a disciple of Jesus, but secretly because he feared the Jewish leaders. With Pilate's permission, he came and took the body away.' It seems to me that although Joseph's heart was in the right place, he was held back from publicly following Jesus because he was concerned about what the Jewish leaders would think and do."

"I think I understand Joseph here," Maria spoke up. "I often feel overwhelmed by the expectations of others on my life. It seems as if everyone wants me to act a certain way or be interested in certain things, and it makes me anxious. Is that fear of man?"

"Yes, that's also a type of fear of man. Although it can be challenging, we have to realize that our expectations of others and their expectations of us are meaningless; the only expectations that matter are God's expectations," Obadiah said.

"Easier said than practiced!" Maria exclaimed.

"That's true," Obadiah said kindly. "You're well on your way though, Maria. When you have a right understanding of your place in eternity, you also gain perspective concerning the place of others in your life. When you are at peace, you will be freed from fear of man."

Maria inhaled deeply, and nodded. Obadiah continued, "The second fear is the universal fear of death. Fear of death tends to result in hypocrisy, as Jesus tells us in Luke 12:1–5. This fear leads us to compromise not only our message but also our entire life. We're warned in Revelation 2:10–11 that faithfulness may have to be maintained through death. In both the Luke and the Revelation passages I mentioned, we're told not to fear physical death but to fear the eternal death that comes when we're separated from God. Fear of death focuses on the temporal instead of the larger concept of eternity, and this throws us out of quantum alignment with God. With this in mind, how do you think fear can impact the life of a prophet?"

"It seems to me that being fearful of saying something others don't appreciate or agree with and being fearful they might retaliate with violence could silence a prophet, which would render him completely ineffective," I said, shuddering at the possibility.

"On a less severe level," Catherine said, "a prophet might edit her words out of fear that the message won't be heard or will be rejected. No one wants to be ridiculed."

Andre agreed. "Or a prophet may not even go into a situation where love and hope need to be spoken out of fear. Like what if God told a prophet a volcano was going to wipe out his town? It would be tempting to flee the area and escape death rather than stay to warn the others."

"Yes," Obadiah said. "Those are some extreme examples, but I think you all understand the principles that can hold prophets back from speaking God's truth in a situation."

Obadiah wrote "1. Fear and Anxiety" on the whiteboard. "The third fear is around finances. Do any examples come to mind of biblical examples of financial anxiety?"

Andre pulled out his tablet, and I saw him open his Bible search function. "Hey! No cheating," I said with a smile.

Pushing me back toward my seat, Andre responded with a laugh, "Obadiah just asked for examples. He didn't say we had to pull them from memory."

Obadiah nodded to confirm, and Andre continued, "At any rate, I have one. Matthew 13:22 talks about how financial worry can steal away what God has for us. It says, 'The seed falling among the thorns refers to someone who hears the word, but the worries of this life and the deceitfulness of wealth choke the word, making it unfruitful.' I think the 'deceitfulness of wealth' is the term they used back in the day for financial anxiety. This verse says it can choke out what God has spoken and make it unfruitful."

"That's a powerful way of phrasing that, Andre," Hayley added. "And I was thinking of later in Matthew, in 6:24–34, where Jesus reminds us that worrying about our needs and our possessions won't add anything to our lives. Specifically God gives us a promise in verses 30 and 33, 'If that is how God clothes the grass of the field, which is here today and tomorrow is thrown into the fire, will he not much more clothe you—you of little faith?... Seek first his kingdom and his righteousness, and all these things will be given to you as well.'"

Mike added, "That same story is repeated in Luke 12:22–34, and here Jesus gives His followers a cure for financial anxiety. He says to sell everything and wear an eternal money belt, so to speak."

"That's a good connection, Mike," Obadiah said. "I do want to emphasize, however, that what you're pointing out is a cure for financial anxiety. For many of us, getting rid of everything would create financial anxiety. But if you are anxious about whether or not you will have enough money in the future, the cure is to begin giving money away. I can't go into detail about this right now, but I'll hang around after class if you'd like to talk more." Mike whispered something to Catherine and she nodded.

"Any other examples?" Obadiah asked. No one volunteered, so Obadiah said, "Okay, the final type of fear or anxiety is over safety. Mark 13:11 and Luke 12:11–12 are identical accounts that address the topic of anxiety about safety. In these verses, Jesus talks about how His followers will be dragged before authorities and ordered to defend themselves. He tells His followers not to worry about what to say and then gives them a promise from God that the Holy Spirit will give them—as He will give us—the inspired words to answer those authorities. We see in the book of Acts that what He promised was true, though they still ended up being beaten or imprisoned. Here we see that the worry is over physical pain and suffering, and this can disturb prophets as well. Just as it can be tempting to compromise a word from God to please others or to receive monetary thanks, it can be scary to share the whole truth of God for fear the listeners will be hostile to the message. Prophets may be mocked and rejected on a public scale, which can be painful and even heartbreaking."

"Heartbreak can certainly rob you of peace too," Catherine quipped.

"Yes, there's a self-feeding cycle here," Obadiah agreed. "Depression in any form, including heartbreak, can rob you of peace." He wrote "2. Depression" on the whiteboard. "When you're depressed, you're out of alignment with God. The ultimate source of depression is loss of hope. Proverbs 13:12 says, 'Hope deferred makes the heart sick, but a longing fulfilled is a tree of life.' A heart gets sick when emotions atrophy and the congruence among mind, emotions, and will is lost. For example, say you hear something from the Lord and prepare your mind for it and hope for it, but the promise takes forever to arrive and seems to keep getting delayed. Because you may not have patience from properly developing your concept of eternity, you may lose hope. You may understand something in your mind but not accept its reality in your heart and therefore direct your will to act halfheartedly or not at all.

"An early warning form of this same thing is frustration. This happens when external interruptions or distractions seem to keep getting in the way of the thing hoped for. Circumstances seem to be working against you. Eventually, enough frustration can lead to depression because both have to do with hope deferred. It is important to take action to end the frustration as soon as you encounter it so that it doesn't metastasize into depression.

"Hopelessness is combatted, then, by rehearsing the promises of God. In other words, search Scripture for promises relating to your situation and repeat them to yourself. You may even find a specific passage that has deep symbolic significance for your situation. An effective exercise is to repeat the verses verbally. Faith comes by hearing the word of Lord, and hearing your own voice speaking God's word counts. You can even combat frustration by repeating those promises to the circumstances, and commanding the circumstances to align with His promises."

"Question," Andre said. "I often hear about looking for God's promises in Scripture. Can we receive His promises from anywhere else?"

"Excellent question, Andre," Obadiah said. "Promises of God can also come through prophetic words. When you receive prophetic ministry and a word comes to you that you had not previously identified as a desire in your own heart, treat it as a promise of God. Consider it, and ask the Lord how it applies. Through such words and through trusting God's promises, we fend off hopelessness. Frequently remind yourself of God's promises—especially when you don't feel like it. Even if the depression gets severe, keep praying."

"I can testify to that one," Andre agreed. "I've been in some dark situations, and I know that I only made it through them because others were praying God's promises over my life, even when I couldn't believe them."

"It's a huge blessing to have friends who will agree with you in prayer concerning God's promises," Obadiah said, looking at each of us in turn. Then he continued, "Another alignment-breaker," he said, stepping back toward the whiteboard and writing as he spoke, "is '3. Discouragement.' Discouragement typically comes from two sources. The first is words of opposition. There is power in the spoken word, including words that aren't from God. For example, when Nehemiah was doing what God had called him to do and was rebuilding the wall of Jerusalem, many spoke and prophesied against him, but he refused to be discouraged. Nehemiah 6:9 says, 'They were all trying to frighten us, thinking, "Their hands will get too weak for the work, and it will not be completed." But I prayed, "Now strengthen my hands."' There was also opposition to the rebuilding of the temple, as Ezra 4:4 records, 'The peoples around them set out to discourage the people of Judah and make them afraid to go on building.' In both of these examples, the plan of the enemy was to use words to intimidate the people who were doing God's restorative work. Over and over, the lie that the work couldn't be done was repeated in order to discourage the workers; since God had never spoken that word, it wasn't true.

"Take note: when something significant is being built in your life, the enemy will put people in your path who will speak words of opposition. You need to surround yourself with people who are in alignment with God and who will speak truth to you, especially during times of spiritual advancement. This is why agreement, or multiple people speaking the same truths, is a reoccurring theme in Scripture. Jesus says in Matthew 18:19, 'If two of you agree on earth about anything that they may ask, it shall be done for them by My Father who is in heaven.' Deuteronomy 32:30 talks about one man making one thousand flee but two men making ten thousand flee. Ecclesiastes 4:12 says, 'A cord of three strands is not quickly broken.' Agreement with others helps you stay aligned with God. Working in a five-fold ministry team can help alleviate much of the causes of discouragement."

I looked around the room and wondered what Obadiah might be thinking about our motley group.

"Another source of discouragement is sickness," Obadiah said. "Not only does sickness wear down the physical body, which can erode the strength needed to fight in the Spirit, it begins to whisper fear of pain and fear of death to the person who is suffering. This fear, combined with physical brokenness, can lead to hopelessness and even to depression. In Matthew 9:2 and 9:22 we see two different people healed of chronic sickness. In both cases, Jesus's first words to the sufferer were, 'Take heart!' Jesus spoke first to the discouragement He perceived in their spirits in order to ensure the healing would persist. Only after that did He speak words of healing to them. Many times people lose their healing because their discouragement wasn't dealt with and they allow fear of a relapse to bring another sickness on them."

Obadiah paused and looked around the room. Then he asked, "Where in your life has discouragement come to you through external words or through sickness, and how did you combat it?"

"When I was little," Catherine began, "I wanted to be a ballerina. I wasn't naturally gifted, but I practiced for hours and hours on end. One day I heard some of the older girls in the class making fun of my form and I was devastated. For weeks I refused to go to my classes. When my teacher figured out what had happened, she insisted that I come in for private lessons to get caught up. I didn't become a dancer, but I learned a lot about grace and stage presence in those classes. Most importantly, my teacher helped me break out of my discouragement by speaking affirming words to me. I try to do the same thing for my son now, reminding him of who he is to God."

"It's great that you do that for your son, Catherine," Andre said. "I never would have gotten out of my situation had it not been for this awesome old guy from one of the local churches who, whenever he saw me, would tell me, 'Andre, God made you on purpose and for a purpose.' When I hit my low, I didn't believe God could make anything out of me, but I remember thinking that if that old guy saw something in me, then maybe there was still hope."

"We all hope to be that hope to others," I said, patting Andre on the back.

Hayley said, "When my grandma was in the hospital, she shared a room with an elderly lady who had just broken her hip.

That lady complained day in and day out about how useless she was until one day my grandma said, 'There's a reason God has kept you alive this long, and you'd better spend your days figuring out what that reason is instead of wasting your time being miserable.'"

"Ouch! Tough love," Maria interjected.

"It was," Hayley agreed. "But a week later that lady called my grandma and thanked her for reminding her that she was still worth something. She had called up every living member of her family and had asked them if they knew Jesus. She'd even reconciled with one of her sons whom she hadn't spoken to in years. Long story short, today two more of her children, eight of her grandchildren, and one of her neighbors are following Christ. If that doesn't inspire hope, I don't know what does!"

"I love that story, Hayley," Obadiah said. "We are never too young or too old to be used by God. You all might notice that in each of those stories, someone else helped speak truth to the person who was discouraged. That's why it is so essential to surround ourselves with others who trust in the power of God's word."

Obadiah wrote "4. Disorientation" on the board and said, "The last disruptor of alignment with God is disorientation. As with the two previous points, there is a verbal component. We get disoriented when we take input from too many sources that control our thoughts and subvert truth. We talked a few weeks ago about the current cultural deception being perpetrated through media and entertainment outlets. The enemy is using unwitting people to use words to divert our attention from what God is doing and focus it on man. The bad news we hear every day changes our orientation, causing us to focus on danger, threats, failure, and sin rather than on the encouraging, eternal word of God. I'm not saying we should never watch television. In fact it's helpful for prophets to watch the news in order to understand our current time, but it's important to exercise caution so we don't get inundated with negative material and begin questioning the promises of God."

"Another source of disorientation is lack of communication with other believers. Just as a lion will single out a weak gazelle from the herd to track and kill it, the devil, referred to as a 'roaring lion' in 1 Peter, will seek to isolate us from others so he can destroy us. Disconnection and isolation—even just the perception of isolation—robs us of our place in the body of Christ. Never underestimate the cleverness of the enemy. While he may not physically isolate us, he might, for example, disrupt or even break the flow of communication between leaders of an organization. When things begin to fall apart, it's generally preceded by a communication breakdown. Communication is key. When the descendants of Noah united to build a tower that would reach to the heavens and make them like gods, God chose to humble them from their proud sin by giving them different languages and dispersing them. This disruption of their communication made it impossible for them to move forward."

"Clear and frequent communication with each other keeps people focused on the vision and path needed to get there. It leaves no room for disorientation. We see in 1 Corinthians 14:31–33 that God is 'not a God of disorder but of peace'; He is not an author of confusion. In these verses, Paul explains that if everyone tries to speak prophetically at the same time and with no interpretation, no message will get across. He speaks practical order into the situation so proper exhortation and encouragement can occur. If you're in a situation where everyone is talking at one another and not listening and there is disaccord, you should bring the peace of the Lord into the room through calling things to order."

"Now that we've covered the five major peace-stealers—fear, anxiety, depression, discouragement, and disorientation—I want each of you to take a moment and write down a couple you struggle with. Once you've done that, get into a group of two or three and share what you wrote down. Then take turns speaking to one another about those things with declarations of God's promises and specific encouragement."

I looked at Andre and made an exaggeratedly nervous face, and he returned the expression. Looking back and forth from my blank piece of paper to the words on the board, I couldn't decide which ones I struggled with the most. I felt as if my peace had been taken from me by all of them at one point or another. Finally I wrote down "Fear: work" and "Disorientation: baby news." When Andre was done writing, I explained to him how much I struggled with wanting to please my bosses at work, even to the point of lying about how much work I was able to complete in a forty-hour workweek. "I'm letting my fear of man rob me of my family time and many ministry opportunities instead of standing on God's word," I explained. "And I'm also struggling with disorientation. My wife and I have been wanting to have a baby for a while. We received a prophetic word a few months ago that my wife would conceive and have a healthy baby boy this year. But then I started reading all these articles about getting pregnant when you're older and the health risks involved and the probabilities that the baby will be born with some sort of defect, and I have to confess that I'm scared. I've been doubting God's promise." Andre put a hand on my shoulder, and we prayed together, proclaiming that I would trust the prophecy that God had given me and that my wife would be like Sarah, full of faith and vitality. We thanked God for His word that the baby would be healthy. Then we declared that I would work for the Lord and not for man. Andre then prayed Psalm 147:2–3 over me, inserting my name into the verse, "'In vain Jason rises early and stays up late, toiling for food to eat—for God grants sleep to those he loves. Children are a heritage from the Lord, offspring a reward from him.'" When he finished, I was in tears. He handed me a tissue. "Thanks for speaking God's promises to me. I actually felt something lift off of me as you prayed and declared," I said. Before we had a chance to discuss his list, Obadiah called us back together.

"I'll pray with you after this session," I whispered to Andre and he nodded.

"We are running close on time, but would two of you mind sharing something from your session?" Obadiah asked.

I briefly explained how I'd been struggling with fear of man and with disorientation and how Andre had spoken a verse over me that had completely reoriented me, reminded me what I was living for, and broke something off my spirit. Everyone smiled at me, several with tears in their eyes.

Then Maria said, "I feel rejuvenated as well. As I alluded to earlier, I've struggled with anxiety for many years. I'm not very worried about my finances, but I'm constantly afraid that someone is going to try to hurt me. I have a hard time believing that God will protect me, and actually I've found it difficult even to admit that because I'm afraid I'll be punished for my fear. Jerry reminded me of Romans 8:31 that says, 'If God is for us, who can be against us?' Then he encouraged me to repeat Hebrews 13:6 aloud to myself. I feel like God has restored His warrior spirit within me. I'm going to be saying, 'The Lord is my helper; I will not be afraid. What can mere mortals do to me?' all day every day now! I'm so glad we did this exercise."

"I'm glad you're all realizing the impact of encouraging others. That's a practice that will serve you well. I know each of you could share a powerful story from that exercise. Since we have limited time in class, we're not all going to share now, but I want you to write down your story and what you heard from the Lord today to encourage you in your time of need."

Hayley immediately bent over her notebook, and I noticed others taking a few notes as well.

"Let's take a quick, two-minute break and then get right back into it," Obadiah said. Catherine and Michael immediately went into prayer. I told Andre I wanted to hear his story but really had to go to the bathroom and he motioned me on.

When I got back to my seat, Obadiah was already beginning the next section. "You all remember the levels of prophetic maturity, right?" he asked.

"The fruitcake?" Maria asked.

"Yes, the Prophetic Fruitcake," Obadiah said smiling. "On that cake, we said that miracles appear when we reach the peace stage. Now that we're talking about peace, then, we better define what we mean by the term 'miracle.'"

Feeling like I had the answer for this one, I immediately spoke up. "Miracles are supernatural occurrences involving the intervention of God," I said.

"That's a common phrase in churches, but I want to challenge that definition," Obadiah said, and I sat back in my seat.

So much for Sunday school answers, I thought. "Here's the definition of 'miracle' I want to use in this class: an event that appears to contradict the laws of nature and that is regarded as an act of God."

"I hate to sound stupid," Maria said, "but that sounds awfully similar to what Jason just said." She winked at me, and I smiled back.

Obadiah laughed. "Yes, it does. I'm trying to emphasize that while miracles appear to contradict the laws of nature, they're actually events that apply laws of nature we have not yet discovered. Miracles aren't about what happens; they're about the ability to access a law of nature prior to its discovery by scientists."

Maria cut in, "To remind you all of my love for science fiction and to reinforce Obadiah's argument, I want to point out that there's an ongoing sci-fi theme that civilizations with advanced technology will appear to more primitive civilization to be gods working miracles."

"Yes," Hayley agreed, "That makes me think of Mark Twain's book A Connecticut Yankee in King Arthur's Court in which a modern-day person was somehow transported back to the days of King Arthur. His ability to build things that had not yet been invented made people believe he was a wizard."

"Thanks for those examples, ladies," Obadiah said. "So outside the church, it's commonly accepted principle that 'miracles' might just be things that haven't been discovered yet. If we adjust our definition of a miracle inside the church then, it explains, for example, why the magicians in Pharaoh's court were able to reproduce many of the miracles of Moses; they were accessing the same undiscovered laws of nature. Our medicine today performs what would have been considered miracles three hundred years ago. The 'miracle' part involves accessing the law— knowing its existence through peace before it is known in the natural realm, and there are plenty of things we have not yet discovered. For example, there are laws that allow a disease that has taken over a body to completely disintegrate and disappear. We see this often when we pray for healing. Some day we may identify the science of how this occurs, but that doesn't make it any less of a miracle now. Although imposters may be able to access miracles, true miracles are expressions of God's saving love as well as of His holy justice. True miracles will always point to and exalt the character of Jesus, and the test of a true miracle of God is the lasting fruit."

"To tackle the second part of Jason's definition then," Obadiah said, and I cringed for comedic effect, "miracles are not actually 'interventions by God' as they require someone speaking for God to initiate them. If they were sovereign interventions, then when someone was saved miraculously in a disaster and others were not, it would imply that God loved that person more than the others, which we know isn't true. Miracles then are an expression of God's love by those expressing His kingdom on earth."

"Can you explain what distinguishes signs and wonders from miracles again?" Catherine asked.

"Sure," Obadiah said. "Signs and wonders are a subset of miracles that authenticate that a message is from God. They validate both the messenger and God's message. In the first century, the use of signs and wonders by one who was only pretending to be authentic brought severe consequences. Take for example Elymas the sorcerer who is referenced in Acts 13:8–12. He tried to use 'magic,' or the supernatural laws of physics, for personal gain, but Paul declared, "You are full of all kinds of deceit and trickery," and Elymas was struck blind. Authentic signs and wonders then are miracles that indicate that what is being said is true."

"I think I understand," Catherine said. "Thank you!"

Obadiah nodded at her and then asked, "Now that we have a better definition of miracles, let's put the whole thing together. Why do you think peace is necessary in order see consistent and sustained miracles?"

We all thought for a couple moments. When no one spoke up, Obadiah continued, "Miracles are an expected manifestation of a life at peace with God. When we're aligned with God, we have access to His laws—even the ones that appear to be contrary to the laws of nature. As we enter into true peace, we tune into the vibrations of God in the quantum field, understand supernatural truths, and miracles begin manifesting in the physical realm. Each of us carries an embassy with us. In 2 Corinthians 5:20, we're called 'ambassadors for Christ.' Our spirits dwell in the kingdom of heaven, so we carry it around with us, and the kingdom of heaven meets the natural world."

Surprised I'd never thought of that blending of the two worlds before, I considered its implications. Being an ambassador for Christ means that this world is not my home but is my responsibility. That must be a little how Jesus felt when He performed supernatural miracles in front of an audience who had not yet been trained to understand what they were witnessing. "Wow," I said under my breath.

Obadiah continued, "If peace is required to move prolifically in miracles, we need to learn how to practice peace. Romans 12:8 encourages us to, 'be at peace with all men.' This verse encourages us to avoid elitism, sectarianism, and revenge. Being at peace with everyone involves being open and inclusive to anyone who might come to Jesus. You see, peace within us is an appreciation of God's ways. We are working to bring God's kingdom into the world, walking along with those who walk in the name of the Lord.

"Peace is vital to the life of the prophet. Prophesying without peace results in pressure and possible coercion. A prophet who is not at peace will try to make things happen, perhaps out of fear of man or of death. Being at peace, however, allows prophets to move into stage three and beyond.

"When you find yourself needing a miracle because there's no way something can happen according to natural laws, find a place of peace. Work to identify the promise of God to have patience and then bring it into congruence with your faithfulness. Finding peace is up to you, but once you're at peace, the miracle will flow naturally."

"This might be an odd question," Maria said, "but how do I know if I need peace or patience?"

"Peace has to do with your relationship with God and others, whereas patience has to do with circumstances and externals. When you feel like time is running out, you need patience so you tap into God's eternal timing. When you are expecting something from God or other people or for yourself, you need peace to accept your situation and the outcome.

"Did you know you can carry peace with you? In John 14:27, Jesus says, 'Peace I leave with you; my peace I give you.' In other words, Jesus has given us peace, and we need to accept the gift. Matthew 10:13 says, 'If the household is worthy, let your peace come upon it.' This indicates that in addition to being able to carry your own peace, you can release it to others. Luke 10:5-6 says, 'When you enter a house, first say, "Peace to this house." If someone who promotes peace is there, your peace will rest on them; if not, it will return to you.' Luke tells us how to do what

Matthew said we could do. To release peace on a house, all you have to do is speak it. If it is a peaceful house, peace will rest there."

Mike interrupted, "So to give peace to someone, all I have to do is speak it to them?"

Obadiah responded, "Yes. Peace isn't imparted by the laying on of hands. It doesn't need to be. You see, peace is contagious. As I mentioned earlier, you carry an embassy of the kingdom of God with you. You can extend that embassy into places of unrest and allow the peace you carry to calm them."

For the last couple of minutes, as Obadiah had been talking, a calmness had come over the room. I hadn't recognized it at first, but now that it had settled in, it was as if we were all breathing in unison. All the things that had been running through my mind about what I was learning and what I needed to do this afternoon had ceased churning around in my head, and I felt calm. Looking around the room, I noticed everyone was sitting back in their chairs and looking relaxed. Andre's hands dangled to either side of him. Hayley had uncrossed her arms, and her hands were resting in her lap. Even Catherine, who usually sat upright on the edge of her seat, was leaning into Mike with a smile on her face. I realized that as Obadiah had been talking about releasing peace to others, he had done exactly that to us.

"Peace isn't subject to circumstances," Obadiah was saying. "You don't acquire peace because something happens; it's actually the inverse: things happen because you are at peace."

With Obadiah's final words, the room lightened again, and the shift was visibly noticeable. We all sat back up and began packing our things, and I noticed my list of things to do was reemerging in my mind. "Holy Spirit," I prayed to myself, "I want to keep your peace." Immediately I was calm once more, and I maintained my peace as I walked up the path and got into my car.

"Have a good week!" Mike called, waving. "Remember, things happen when you're at peace!"

"Peace to you too then, Mike!" I said smiling, ready for another week with Jesus.

CHAPTER ELEVEN: SELF-CONTROL

LIVING THE FRUIT

On my way to the meeting this week, I began to review all of the fruit of the Spirit we had studied. The order in which Obadiah had chosen to introduce the fruit was starting to make sense. The more I studied and tried to live out all the fruit, the more I saw a pattern emerging. The first three tiers are focused on how we relate with others. We begin by loving them, even if we don't like them. Then we express goodness and joy to other people, delivering it with kindness and gentleness. These three tiers have internal aspects and are all behavioral in nature, especially as it pertains to others. We have to love. We have to walk in goodness and manage our state to live in joy. We have to treat others with kindness and gentleness. All of these are things that people will be able to see in us and will respond to.

The next three tiers are more about how we approach God and what He is doing in us. Patience is how we view eternity and God's timing. Faithfulness is how we stand on the promises of God regardless of circumstances. Peace has to do with the internal alignment with God's timing and His promises and sets the tone for our lives. All of these have external signs and behaviors, but they are rooted in how we engage with God and what He is doing.

I was able to experience the harmony of all these fruit this past week and appreciated how important they all are to each other. When I found myself getting agitated or fearful or losing my grip on an aspect of peace, I would ask the Lord which fruit was out of kilter, and He always graciously showed me so I could make an adjustment.

One of the challenges I faced this week involved a bank account error. I noticed that too much money had been withdrawn for one of my bills; the bank had accidentally double charged the payment. When I caught the error, I called customer service, but the person wasn't able—or didn't want—to help me. After talking to what felt like every person in the office, I was finally connected to a manger who then connected me to one of the branch managers to resolve the issue. It turned out the payee had initiated the payment twice, which is why the bank hadn't caught it as a duplicate payment. The bank finally refunded the double withdrawal and the service fee I'd been charged. Anyway, throughout the length of this engagement, I had to treat several people with kindness and goodness. I had to love the unhelpful customer service representative. On top of that, I had a fear of financial harm that agitated my peace. I needed patience to wait for the research to be completed and for the documents to be processed to set everything right. I learned that walking in the fruit of the Spirit involves a delicate balance of all the ingredients, and low peace indicates that something is out of whack. I was thankful that through the entire experience, God had lovingly pointed out where I was in danger of getting out of alignment with Him and had guided me back to a place of peace.

I pulled into the lot right behind Michael and Catherine. They waved and waited for me. And as we walked down from the lot together, I learned that they had discovered much of the same thing about the fruit as me.

After our greetings, Mike seemed to be bursting with a story.

"Out with it," I said. "What happened this week?"

Mike hesitated and dipped his head but then obliged me and explained, "One of my employees made an error in sales figures to a potential large client we were hoping to close a deal with, and it nearly cost us the account. The client was not happy, and it looked like they were going to take their business elsewhere. The thing is—I had heard from the Lord that this client would work with me personally and that the deal would result in enough bonus commission to fund a mission trip I'm planning in three months. When I remembered that specific promise, I decided to rest in peace and work with the customer to recover the business. I put on my best 'joy face'"—here Catherine and I smiled knowingly—"and visited the client to discuss the error. The Lord showed me tremendous favor, and long story short, the CEO said he wanted their company to work personally with me on the deal, which was the exact terminology the Lord had given me in His promise."

"That's incredible, Mike," I said, exercising my own, natural joy face.

"Of course," Mike continued, "it wasn't all easy. After returning from sealing the deal, I had to exercise a great deal of gentleness in correcting the training issue that had caused my employee to almost lose us the deal."

"I learned a little something of that kind of patience this week after a bank error," I said, feeling like I understood where Mike was coming from.

"We're all certainly growing in the fruit, aren't we?" Catherine asked. "It's not easy, but it's definitely good."

Mike and I agreed, and we all stepped through the opening into the cave. After grabbing some coffee, I took my seat and saw that Maria and Jerry and Mike were all leaning toward Catherine, seemingly enthralled with her story.

"Hey!" I called. "Speak up so all of us can hear!"

Catherine smiled and graciously started over at the beginning of her story. "I was just telling these guys something that has developed with my art through this whole process of living out the fruit of the Spirit."

I scooted my chair closer, and Catherine continued, "I've always been able to find peace in my art. Spending time with the paint and the canvas helps to calm me, and I feel like I draw strength from the painting. This week, however, I decided to try something different. I decided to sit with the Lord until I found peace. This was incredibly challenging, as it meant I had to go through every fear, anxiety, doubt, and agitation in my spirit and apply patience, faithfulness, or one of the other fruit until I found a place of alignment with God. Once the fear and doubt and all were removed, I began painting. I was surprised by how different my work was. Not only did it seem to flow easier, it spoke to me more deeply than my other pieces. I realized that I had been painting my lack of peace onto the canvas. The old works took my agitation and brought resolution to it, but the new stuff this week didn't need to. It had no agitation to resolve. There was only peace in my color, texture, and lines. At first I thought I must just be inventing things because I knew I was in a state of peace when I did the work, so I asked Mike about it one day."

Mike said, "I just looked at it and said it looked like peace."

"Yes," Catherine said, beaming. "He didn't say it looked peaceful. He said it looked like peace."

Hayley had entered about halfway through the story, but she had clearly caught the gist. She said to Catherine, "I love how you discovered a new level in the Spirit. I've been surprised too in my writing with how He makes everything—my perspective and my skill included—better. It's not that I couldn't write good pieces before, but now that I'm making an effort to live in the fruit of the Spirit, it's as if my words have new life."

"Exactly, new life," Catherine agreed. "I made a small print of the 'peace' painting to put up on the trophy shelf. Do you think it will be okay to put it up there?" She held up a small print with many colors brushed, blended, and swirled—I could see Catherine's gift for creativity and even in the small print, I could feel the peace she spoke about in her painting. Everyone agreed it was a great idea.

As Catherine placed the print on the shelf just right, as only an artist can do, I sat back to consider how these same principles were playing out in my workplace and realized that Obadiah and Andre had entered the room. Moving my chair back into the circle, I greeted them.

SELF-CONTROL

"Good morning, everyone," Obadiah said as he took his seat, and a sense of calm permeated the room. "It sounds like you've had some good experiences this week practicing peace in the Spirit. This week we're going to round out your fruit and talk about the final tier of prophetic maturity, self-control. We've been discussing what it means to step into the rhema word of God and to follow the leading of the Holy Spirit. So why, if we're led by the Spirit, does Paul encourage us to develop self-control?"

Obadiah turned to look at Michael who looked surprised and then said, "If we were fully controlled by the Spirit, that would reverse the free will choice that God has given us. While the Spirit of God calls us to what He wants us to do and while there are other spirits that woo us, we have free will choice to make our own decision. God receives greater glory from a vessel that can choose not to serve him, and even following the Spirit is in act of our self-control."

Nodding, Obadiah said, "That's a great way to put it, Michael. Self-control gives us the opportunity to walk in the Spirit and grow closer to the Lord. Walking in the fruit of the Spirit requires our participation, but we should also remember that it's not a man-made effort, because that would be striving. Rather than striving not to sin, our desire not to sin should naturally arise out of being with the Lord. So how do we practice self-control without walking in legalism? How do we do it so it isn't just a set of rules?"

Mike, gaining confidence, said, "Choices. The reason self-control is a fruit of the Spirit is because the Holy Spirit counsels us regarding the choices before us. We walk in self-control instead of legalism because it's about life choices, not legal choices. We can choose to give a flash response—the one that feels good now—or a Holy Spirit response—the one that will bring about the greater good."

"Very good," Obadiah said. "Self-control is choosing to walk in the Spirit. Instead of the Holy Spirit restraining you, He is transforming you to resist sin. That's what grace is all about. Grace doesn't forgive us of sin; it keeps us from sinning. We live under grace, which means we have the power to fail and make better choices later. That said, I'm sure you've heard the expression 'living under grace' used as an excuse to head toward sin. Even in the first-century church, some used the excuse that it's okay to sin because there is grace for it, but the fact that they wanted to sin means they were not living in grace. What grace actually does is empower us to make the choice the Holy Spirit is counseling us to make."

Andre spoke up, "I have a question. You said that grace isn't the thing that forgives us of sin but the thing that allows us not to sin, yet I've always heard that we're 'saved by grace.'"

Obadiah titled his head slightly and responded, "Yes, we are saved by grace. But the blood of Jesus is what washes us clean and forgives us of our sin. Grace then is the empowerment we get through His blood to be saved from future sin. When we're under grace, we don't have to live that life of sin anymore and we're freed from the bondage of it."

Looking off to a corner as he pieced his thoughts together, Andre responded, "Oh, so Jesus saves us and grace maintains our saved state?"

Obadiah responded, "It's more complex than that, but essentially, yes. Now I have another question for all of you: what other verses in the Bible aside from the list in Galatians 5 talk about self-control?"

Since we were only one week away from our last class, I'd put a little extra effort into my preparation for the week and had come prepared with a list of verses. "Proverbs 16:32," I began, "says 'Better a patient person than a warrior, one with self-control than one who takes a city.'"

"That's similar to Proverbs 25:28," Jerry added. He quoted the verse from memory, "'Like a city whose walls are broken through is a person who lacks self-control.'"

"Thanks Jason and Jerry. Those are two verses that talk about temper as it relates to self-control. What are some others to broaden our conversation?"

Michael had his tablet open and read, "In 1 Corinthians 9:24–27, Paul compares the Christian walk to a race and explains that self-control makes us deliberate and effective in the kingdom."

"I was just reading in Acts 24 this morning," Maria said. "In it, Paul talks about righteousness and self-control to Felix."

"Yes, good," Obadiah agreed. "The two of those— righteousness and self-control—are connected. I'll explain how in a minute, but Andre, did you have a verse to add?"

I turned to look at Andre, who was looking back and forth from Obadiah and his tablet, surprised. Obadiah had a way of bringing out everything we had to offer.

"Yeah," Andre said, still sounding suspicious. "Second Timothy 3:3 suggests that people in the last days who lack self-control should be avoided. Paul seems to be saying that we should avoid people who don't have self-control because they aren't trustworthy, which makes me think that having truth is part of gaining self-control. That seems to connect to prophets because prophets are called to hold fast to the truth."

Obadiah was clearly pleased. "Your guesses are spot on, Andre. To have self-control, it's essential to have many of the other fruit. And, interestingly, self-control is both the result of and the pathway to love. I want to break down 2 Peter 1:5–7 and look at the fruit of the Spirit, 'For this very reason, make every effort to add to your faith goodness; and to goodness, knowledge; and to knowledge, self-control; and to self-control, perseverance; and to perseverance, godliness; and to godliness, mutual affection; and to mutual affection, love.'

The fruit of the Spirit aren't listed in the same order as in Galatians 5, but if you look closely, they're all there. When you're practicing moral excellence, which is goodness, you develop knowledge about your faith. You begin to know what is right and moral to do. When you have that knowledge, you will need self-control to apply it in all circumstances. Then self-control leads to perseverance, which is like overcoming, or faithfulness. Perseverance leads to godliness. And then godliness leads to kindness. And finally love is added to kindness.

"This means that as you learn more about God and His ways, the more you'll be required to make choices using self-control. Self-control is built upon knowledge, because, to state the obvious, you cannot make a good choice without knowing your options. Once you know what your options are, you can utilize self-control, with the Holy Spirit, to choose your path. Then you have to persevere in that choice, which helps you reach godliness, and then kindness and love are added. In other words, getting to perfect love requires a lifestyle of self-control. Love is the foundation that gets us to self-control where we can speak words that do things. Self-control is the starting point that takes us back to love. Love isn't just where you start— it's also your goal."

Because we'd had so many weeks sitting in the fruit of the Spirit, this made total sense to me. I'd seen how each of the fruit strengthened the others and saw how love was what allowed the others to grow and also what was the end result of being kind, gentle, and peaceful, etc.

"Let's write some more verses regarding self-control on the whiteboard," Obadiah said.

We each took turns, and when we finished, we had this collection:

"Submit yourself to God, resist the devil, and he will flee from you."

"Guard your heart with all diligence." As Maria wrote this point, Obadiah explained, "This connects stewardship to self-control. We are like gatekeepers who decide what goes in and what goes out of my heart."

2 Cor. 10:5: "We take captive every thought to make it obedient to Christ." Obadiah explained, "This is a process of making choices. Taking your thoughts captive means evaluating them according to the thoughts of the Lord. As you bring each thought in, you study it, determine if it's good or bad—or if it reflects God or not—and after evaluation, you choose whether to accept it or let it go."

1 Cor. 10: 14: "Therefore, my dear friends, flee from idolatry." Obadiah wrote this verse and then explained, "Self-control involves living in the Spirit and turning away from idols."

1 Tim. 6:11: "But you, man of God, flee from all this, and pursue righteousness, godliness, faith, love, endurance, and gentleness."

After we'd finished our list, Obadiah said, "All these verses talk about not even going near the opportunity for sins in the flesh. Self-control doesn't mean choosing not to sin when tempted by the flesh; it means making the choice to avoid the temptation in the first place. Paul wrote about avoiding the temptation to sin as part of self-control. Apparently the Corinthians had a problem with this because he wrote about it twice in the same letter to them."

"I know what that feels like," said Andre. "My mom used to repeat her warnings to me at least seven times just to make sure I heard them."

Obadiah smiled, "That is kind of what Paul is doing here. So I want to talk about what avoiding the temptation to sin looks like. For example, a recovering alcoholic would exercise self-control by not even attending parties at bars. We are also tempted to sin with our words. James 1:26 talks about 'bridling the tongue.' This is extremely important for the prophet because there is power in words. If you cannot control your tongue, you cannot be trusted with power. This brings me to an important point. James 3:8–12 says, 'No fountain can give forth fresh and bitter water.' It's important to choose what you're going to use your words for. People will drink from the flow of words that come from your mouth: will you use fresh words or bitter words? For example, when you swear, you train your tongue to use curse words. Then you try to say something prophetic to release life. This creates a mixed message in the Spirit and you lose a lot of authority."

Andre perked up. "Are you saying we can't swear?"

Obadiah chuckled, "No, but I'm saying you have choices to make regarding what you say. James talks about giving fresh or bitter water; there is no option to give forth both. It's up to you to decide which way you will speak. Then 1 Peter 3:10 says to, 'Keep your tongue from evil.' Since the primary tool of the prophet is speaking, prophets have to be more careful with words than others."

Maria spoke up, "You know, I'm quick to be angry and quick to laugh. Do my spontaneous emotions reflect a lack of self-control?"

Obadiah replied, "If you're depending on self-control to keep you from an emotional reaction, it's too late. Instead, you want to walk in peace so your emotions come from a place of peace and so you don't have to make a choice when it comes time to react."

Maria nodded slowly as she took a few notes. Obadiah continued, "I have another question then, why is the ability to maintain self-control important to the prophet?"

We all thought for a few moments but didn't come up with an answer. Plus, speaking personally, I wanted to hold off because I knew that if we waited long enough, Obadiah would give us his interpretation, and his answers were always more eloquent than any of mine.

After thirty seconds or so, Obadiah said, "There are three big reasons I've found self-control to be a vital fruit for the prophet. The first is that self-control is important because controlling impulses maintains influence in the quantum field. When we flee from the flesh—from the things that feel good and involve immediate satisfaction—we control our impulses.

"Let me explain. It's possible to receive an emotion from God and act on it impulsively. For example, when David killed Goliath, he had God's anger. He acted by the power of the Holy Spirit and moved in self-control. Moses, however, felt God's anger concerning the oppression of his people, yet he acted impulsively when he killed the Egyptian. Both Moses and David felt godly anger, but while David exercised self-control and acted at the right time and in the right way, Moses acted impulsively, to his own detriment."

"A second way we show self-control is through managing our thoughts. When we control our thoughts, we open the door for the fruit of the Spirit. Like I mentioned earlier, it's important to take every thought captive and then choose to either crucify the unredemptive thought or release the loving thought.

thoughts, words and impulses

"It's important to recognize that our thoughts have different origins. They can come from ourselves, from Satan, or from God. Thoughts from God are usually easy to recognize. Thoughts from Satan, however, can be hard to identify as he is the deceiver. Satan will try to make it appear as if God is doing something, but when you test the thought, you'll find that the motivation behind it is not love. Our own thoughts are even harder to identify, since we tend to think our thoughts are either from God or from Satan. We like blaming Satan for our own fleshly and selfish desires. If we want something and haven't trained ourselves to step into and receive God's rhema word, we can trick ourselves into thinking our desires are God's voice."

Hayley raised her hand, and Obadiah looked at her and continued, "Ultimately, where the word is from may not be important; what's important is what we do with it."

Obadiah looked back at Hayley who had dropped her hand and was laughing to herself and nodding. He said, "If a thought ends in love, it's either from us or from God, and we should act on it. If it isn't redemptive, we can discard it no matter where it's from. Is everyone following?"

I looked at my list. "1. Use self-control over impulses. 2. Use self-control over thoughts." I nodded at Obadiah and he continued.

"The third thing we use self-control over is our words. All words have power, and controlling those words creates supernatural release. This is crucial for the prophet. I already mentioned that coarse talk pollutes your fountain. Andre, you brought up swearing earlier. Now I want to talk about profane language, irony, and sarcasm."

When Obadiah mentioned sarcasm, Hayley and Maria gasped simultaneously and looked at each other nervously.

Andre looked at Obadiah and commented, "Well, it looks like you just made yourself the most popular person in the room."

Obadiah remained unfazed and said, "Let's make sure we're all on the same page here. I'll define the three terms I just used. Profane language is 'coarse talk" that resonates with the baser elements of our flesh and not with the Spirit of God within us. When we speak in profanity, we release those baser elements into the supernatural realm, and this pollutes our fountain. 'Irony' means to say one thing but mean the opposite, like saying, 'Nice job!' to someone who performed horribly. 'Sarcasm' is a form of teasing that uses irony with the intention to hurt someone. A player on a soccer team, for example, might yell 'Nice job!' to someone who just missed the goal, intending to remove some of that player's confidence."

"I have to ask," Maria said, glancing at Hayley for support, "is it really that important to always avoid sarcasm?"

Obadiah was quick to respond, "I'm not trying to give you a list of rules. I'm just explaining that what you speak or sow in sarcasm now may come back years later as a harvest of damage. In the moment of speaking sarcasm, you show incongruence and disbelief, which may cause you to lose authority in that area in the future. That's why this use of words can pollute the prophet's fountain. Sarcasm is dangerous as it's typically a form of anger or passive aggression and is often rooted in a place of judgment or pride. When you emotionally wound someone by treating them as inferior to yourself, it hurts them at a level that's hard to heal."

"What about good-natured teasing then?" Maria tested.

"We often use sarcastic or ironic statements in a friendly way, but we need to be careful," Obadiah said. "It's easy to injure a person even if that wasn't your intent. Keep in mind that when you're the person delivering the sarcasm, you don't get to decide whether or not it's friendly; that's up to the person on the other end."

Jerry added, "I agree, but I also have to argue that there's usually an intent in sarcasm to jab or hurt. Teasing is related to that. I read an article this week that defined teasing as 'to tear.' I think that teasing and sarcasm are related. Teasing can be friendly to a certain point, but it can quickly become evil. Over the years I've been convicted of many of my teasing words and have had to repent and ask for forgiveness from the people I've unintentionally injured with my words."

Obadiah responded, "Yes, sarcasm and teasing can cross a line based on the degree of participation of both parties. You see, this whole issue has to deal with relationship. Because self-control is a lifestyle choice, you will have to be careful and decide for yourself what degree, if any, of sarcasm is right for you. I'm not going to say you can never be sarcastic, but you do need to understand and respect the nature of sarcasm and irony. You're being called to a higher standard when it comes to your words. You can't be a prophet if you can't control what you say. If you want to speak words that do things, you need to keep your fountain clean. If you believe that every word you speak has the power to be an impactful prophetic release, it will affect what you say and how you say it."

I noticed Hayley underlining vigorously in her notebook as we all contemplated the weight of the last statement.

Sensing what we were feeling, Obadiah suggested, "Let's take a short break" The room was mostly silent as we refreshed our drinks and stretched our legs. It was as if no one wanted to speak words now that we began to understand the power behind them.

When we were all back in our seats, Obadiah continued, "A stage four or five prophet speaks words that do things. Choose your weapons wisely. When you criticize others, through sarcasm or any other means, you prophesy bad things to them and bitterness to yourself, and bitterness is a major enemy of the prophet. Bitterness imparts a corrosiveness to the words that are spoken, just like an acid, and it leaves a residue within you that will slowly eat away at your hope and your love for others, leaving cynicism and a loss of peace."

"What are the steps to get rid of bitterness then?" Andre asked.

Mike jumped in, "For me, I've learned to continuously repent and forgive others to keep from harboring bitterness."

I added, "I think it's also important to remember where we started: all of this is a choice. We have the power to take our thoughts captive and keep them from getting out of alignment with God's word. In that way, we choose whether or not we're going to be bitter."

Obadiah responded, "Ridding yourself of bitterness is a continual process of choosing to love and freeing yourself from the significant emotional events at the root of the bitterness. Often bitterness stems from a major emotional event in your past. When you feel that bitterness rising up, ask the Lord to take you back to the moment where it began. Walk through our significant emotional event exercise we did a few weeks ago and free yourself from that moment."

With this, Obadiah checked his watch. "There's a lot more to say about self-control, but I think you all have the tools to work toward this fruit on your own this week. This is the last of the fruit of the Spirit, and next week will be our final meeting together."

None of us had really thought about it, but Obadiah had told us at the beginning we would be together for twelve weeks. The time had passed so quickly. I was wondering how all that we had been learning would fit into our lives, and what we were to do next. But since there is another week left, I was certain Obadiah would explain it all next week.

We began putting away our coffee cups and straightening the room and found ourselves back on the topic of polluting the fountain.

"I'm thinking about self-directed sarcasm," Maria said. "That's like humility, right? Isn't that okay?"

"No," Obadiah said. "That's still speaking something that isn't true, and there is a 'wrongness' for a prophet to say something is true that isn't."

Catherine joined in, "But what about the Jewish midwives who lied to the Egyptians about their children, or what about Rahab who lied to save the spies and was commended for it?"

Andre added, "Or for a modern-day example, is it wrong for missionaries to Muslims to hide part of the truth about themselves or lie to maintain their lives?"

Then Michael said, "What about when God told Sarah she would have a son and she laughed and said something along the lines of, 'What, with that old man?!' regarding Abraham, but then when God addressed Abraham about what Sarah said, He left out the insult. Wasn't that less than the truth? And God did that."

Andre couldn't resist thickening the discussion, "Here's a tricky one for you. In 1 Kings 22, Micaiah the prophet told the king of Israel that God placed a lying spirit in the mouths of all of the king's prophets. Why would God have someone lie?"

Everyone stopped for a moment. Then Jerry and Haley, almost as one, stepped over to get their Bible and looked up 1 Kings 22. I was somewhat impressed that Andre knew this passage off the top of his head, though it does explain a little about why he seemed a little skeptical in our early meetings. I could tell it still bothered him a little.

Hayley sat on the arm of the sofa and said, "I don't get it. I've read the chapter twice and I still don't understand why the Lord sent a deceiving spirit to the prophets."

Jerry looked up from his Bible, "It appears that the king had already decided what he wanted to do, and simply wanted prophets to tell him what he wanted to hear. Yet, when they told him he would win in battle, he correctly recognized that they were not speaking for the Lord and inquired for a prophet who would speak for God. When that prophet, Micaiah, came and gave the same word as the others, the king called him out for not telling the truth. But when Micaiah told the king the truth, and that the battle would end in defeat and the king's death, the king was angry with him. He didn't want deception, and he didn't want the truth. He wanted his way, and he wanted his way to be God's way."

Jerry glanced down at his Bible for a few seconds before looking up again. "That is the simplest definition of lawlessness. We don't want truth, and we don't want lies. We want our desires to become the truth. We want God to be who we decide He should be and to say what we decide He should say. We see in the New

Testament that the Lord deals very severely with lawlessness. Perhaps the deceiving spirit was released as a final test of the king, to see if he was truly willing to walk in lawlessness which ultimately ended in his death."

We sat quietly for a few more moments, thinking about what Jerry had said. Finally, Jerry laughed and held both of his hands up, "You know, I don't think the church does well with discussions about lying. We try to make it very simple, black and white. But where does religion end and holiness begin? Looking at examples of moral lies like hiding Jews in Nazi Germany makes it difficult to set the ultimatum that lies are always wrong. But I think it's rarely a 'necessity' to lie."

Michael responded, "I guess it's true that when we look at Scripture, there are a few instances of lies, and we're using that as our context. If keeping our fountain pure and practicing self-control are important because we are speaking words that do things, then we are required to speak the truth. Otherwise, the lies may become true. I notice that each of the examples we found in scripture always communicated toward God's purpose. But in general we're not confronted with needing to lie to save someone's life, so our lives should be about the truth."

He put his arm around Catherine and she said, "Exactly. That's the difference between 'lying' and being 'a liar'."

Making a face, Michael said, "I'm not sure that settles our discussion, though."

I laughed a little and said, "Let's just ask Obadiah about it." As I spoke, I turned to find him and discovered he was no longer there. We all looked around us, bewildered. After a couple of moments of surprise, I said, "I have a suspicion there are some things Obadiah wants us to resolve with the Lord on our own."

CHAPTER TWELVE:
STEWARDING GOD'S MYSTERIES

WORD POWER

It all began coming together for me this week. Not that I practiced self-control flawlessly, but I was getting clarity of how everything fit together. The Christian walk—kingdom living—was really about choices. I thought about the command, "Do to others as you would have them do to you." This speaks of making a choice to exercise the amount of love, gentleness, kindness, and patience that I would want other people to have with me.

Then I thought of Romans 8:28 that says all things work together for those who love the Lord and follow His purpose, and I realized that was speaking of peace and the influence that a large concept of eternity and an inward certainty of God's promises has on that peace. When Paul says we are new creatures, he really means that we are not like other humans because we are living in both the natural and the spiritual realms, joined with the Holy Spirit. When he speaks of renewing our minds, he is talking about taking thoughts captive, focusing on God's promises, operating in love, and understanding that the spiritual realm is more real than the natural realm. There were many more scriptures that came to mind this week, and I could tie each of them back to the principles we had been taught about the fruit of the spirit. It seemed as if the whole Bible was suddenly taking on a new meaning for me. The basic doctrine was the same, but it felt more alive to me.

In the natural, however, this week was a very bad week. We received word that my company had been purchased by a larger firm and that our offices were being consolidated and relocated. Prior to these meetings, my tendency to see my whole value as being able to provide a good income for my family would have caused this news to devastate me. I would have imagined my whole world falling apart, and my value as worthless. But this week I took the situation to Jesus in my times of sitting with Him. He asked me if I was something He had created. Of course I was. He then asked me if He ever created anything worthless. Of course not. Then He told me that because I am His creation and because I am in Him and He is in me, there is value inherent in me. He finished by telling me that people will always be willing to trade something of value for the value that is in me, and my job was to be my authentic self so that that value would be evident to others. This was the promise that gave me the basis of my hope. Instead of feeling fear, anxiety, and depression, I found myself feeling true joy—even to the point of laughing out loud at the situation many times during the week. I am genuinely looking forward to what is ahead.

There was a point during the week when I began to waver in my faithfulness and my resolve. Then I received a phone call out of the blue from a man I had met almost two months ago. I had spoken with him a few minutes, and he'd told me he would like to be able to prophesy to people, but he just didn't have that gift. This happened very early after the sessions with Obadiah had begun, and I was enthusiastic about everyone's ability to prophesy at some level. I told the man that he would begin prophesying and would continue to prophesy to people for as long as he wanted to. I had forgotten about speaking to him, but he had remembered my words. He called this week to report on what had been happening. He told me that a few days after I prophesied to him, he started waking up in the middle of the night, getting words for other people. Then he would see those people within a few days and would be able to share what he had received for them. He has continued being able to do this, just as I had said. He wanted to thank me for changing his life. He was living a new reality that he had been longing after for many years. After he hung up, I was encouraged, but about fifteen minutes later it occurred to me that my words had changed reality for this man. I had spoken words that did something. With this realization that my words have the power to change reality, I was again able to find hope in the promises of God that allowed me to reenter a place of faithfulness.

I pulled into the parking lot for the last session both encouraged and saddened. Our whole group had grown a lot in such a short period, and as a result, we'd also grown close. I couldn't imagine Saturday mornings without receiving a challenge for the next week and encouragement from the others. But I knew that any good training period had to come to an end. Now we were going to be sent out.

Walking the path alone had a somber feel. I wondered if I'd ever be able to come back to the cave, and part of me was frightened that Obadiah might not be around any longer to help answer my questions. Just then the Holy Spirit reminded me that He would always be with me, and I breathed a sigh of relief and steeled myself as I entered the bright light of the cave.

This week we weren't very talkative before the session. It was as if we were all lost in thought, reflecting on what we'd learned and what was coming next. When Obadiah entered, he broke the hush over the room, startling many of us.

"I didn't mean to scare you," Obadiah said, smiling and looking around the room. "But now that I have your attention, let's get started. This is the final week we will be together. There is still so much more I would like to tell you, but our time has come to an end. After this meeting, you will be released for your real time of training. I want to talk to you about a few topics that will be very important for you as you embark on the next phase of the journey. We have a lot of ground to cover, so prepare yourselves."

Maria faked putting on a seatbelt and Andre exaggeratedly clenched the sides of his seat. I laughed with the others, but I couldn't help wondering if I was prepared.

"Before I dive into what I have prepared for this week for you, do any of you have any questions from last week or anything to share?" Obadiah said, looking in the general direction of Maria and Hayley.

Maria and Hayley exchanged a glance and then pointed at one another. Laughing nervously, Maria said, "I have something to share. As you know, Hayley and I were both taken aback by the reference to sarcasm last week. I love joking around with people, and sarcasm is a major part of my life. In fact, in my family, we've even joked that sarcasm is our love language. This week then, I had a lot of reflecting to do. I found I had an overwhelming awareness of when I was being sarcastic, and I honestly hadn't realized I'd used it that much. I never meant any of the things I said to be harmful, but I became aware of how they could be perceived that way. I'm not sure God is telling me that I need to totally give it up, but I am definitely being more careful about it and paying attention to how it might pollute my fountain."

Hayley nodded along. "Maria and I talked about this over the week, and I had a similar experience to hers. I still think irony and sarcasm involve good mental skills, which can have some benefits, but I became aware that sometimes my words were cutting, even when I didn't intend them to be. I even hurt myself this week when I made a sarcastic comment about my cooking abilities, and I had to repent and stop that negative self-speak."

"I realized I was doing something like that at work," Mike said. "God has given me so much provision over the past couple months, yet I was still speaking words of negativity about the future of my company. I discovered this week that I was polluting my fountain by focusing on the systems that I think are doomed to fail and the people who aren't doing their jobs instead of verbally affirming what is good and hopeful. I had to replace my pessimism with some of the positive promises of God."

"You discovered something important there, Michael," Obadiah said. "Sometimes it can be difficult for us to just stop doing something, but we can replace negative thoughts or habits with a positive word from the Spirit or a promise from God. Cleaning your fountain and maintaining clear water will take work, but as you commit, you'll find that your words hold more and more weight and that you can speak with more and more power."

I stared at my coffee and thought about how that must be what my soul currently looked like, but then I thought about how the more clean water that is added to coffee, the clearer it becomes, and I pictured the Holy Spirit washing my mouth and my words clean.

"As you've already partially experienced, it isn't always easy to speak in the prophetic." Here Jerry grunted and Catherine vigorously nodded. Obadiah continued, "I want to prepare you for some of the trials you can expect, so search Scripture for some examples of prophets' trials or for things that might be challenging for a prophet to endure."

Drawing my eyebrows together, I tried to appear studious as I flipped through my Bible and hoped someone else had an example ready.

None of us was surprised when Jerry spoke up first. "Hosea faithfully lived out a prophetic example with his unfaithful wife Gomer that ended up being very painful to him."

✓ That sparked a thought. I said, "Jesus says in John 15: 18 that if the world hates us, we have to remember that it hated Him before us. Nobody likes being hated, so being disliked or criticized by our culture or even by other Christians could be a major obstacle for a prophet."

"Or even if others don't hate the prophet, they might just not believe what she's saying," added Catherine. "I know I struggle when people think I'm off in my own little crazy land. I have to overcome that fear of rejection."

"We get a strong example of rejection in the life of the prophet Jeremiah," Jerry said. "There are lots of examples of prophets being persecuted and forced into isolation or exile."

"And then there's Elisha," Maria added, "who was ridiculed by a group of teenage boys and called two bears out to maul them."

"Some approaches for handling the pressure of being a prophet might be better than others," Andre quipped, and Maria laughed.

"Yes," Maria said, "I think I identify more with some like Moses. Moses saw something that was coming down the road, but the people around him couldn't see it or understand it. He was living in the physical and the spiritual realms, but everyone else was stuck in the physical. He saw the glory of God, but it had to be frustrating to not be able to translate that experience. Carrying the mysteries of God is a huge burden, especially if a prophet is called to do it alone."

Mike said, "I think it gets even more challenging when a prophet's friends or family provide bad counsel. Think of Paul who knew he was supposed to go to Rome even though he knew he would be killed there. His friends, because of their fondness for him, misunderstood the revelation and tried to keep him from going to save him. Paul must have struggled with the emotional weight of his decision."

"And worse," Andre added, "sometimes there's demonic resistance on top of everything else we've mentioned. Remember when Daniel was praying and praying and Michael had an answer but the prince of Persia resisted it coming through for some time?"

Obadiah said, "All those examples are good, and you're hitting on some important points. Remember as you grow in your gifting that you are not alone in your struggle."

I nodded at Andre and he nodded back.

"Now let's expand our discussion to include challenges you can expect just from living among other people."

"I was ready for this question," Hayley cheered. "Ephesians 4:31 tells us, 'Get rid of all bitterness, rage and anger, brawling and slander, along with every form of malice.' That means there is malice out there. We're going to have to deal with and pray for and speak to some angry, bitter people."

"A couple verses mirror the one Hayley just referenced," Jerry said. Then he quoted, "Colossians 3:8–9 says, 'But now you must also rid yourselves of all such things as these: anger, rage, malice, slander, and filthy language from your lips. Do not lie to each other, since you have taken off your old self with its practices.' And 1 Peter 2:1 says, 'Therefore, rid yourselves of all malice and all deceit, hypocrisy, envy, and slander of every kind.'"

"I'm glad you're pointing us to these verses because there's something specific about them we need to note," Obadiah said. "You see, all these scriptures were written for people who were already in the church and who had been filled with the Holy Spirit. So the people in the early church who are being told in these verses to stop manifesting malice and anger were the ones who were spreading the gospel. This is significant. Sometimes we think that when a person gets saved, he or she will instantly transform into a perfect being, but the Bible tells us that isn't true. Paul had to write to all these churches to remind them not to exhibit this bad behavior. We need to remind ourselves not to have unrealistic expectations of others, including the people we're working alongside in the church."

"Church people are the worst," Andre mumbled low enough that only I could hear him.

Obadiah continued, saying, "If we can expect malice from people in the church, just imagine what we can expect from people who are not trying to live in sync with the Spirit. How should we deal with people then?"

After letting the question sink in, Obadiah said, "We need to understand that people will be people. Let me explain. We're not surprised when dogs act like dogs or when cats act like cats. We aren't offended, for example, when cats meow to ask for food but then act like they aren't hungry because they're just being cats. We aren't offended when a dog wakes us up in the morning by jumping on us, because it's just being a dog. Similarly, we shouldn't get upset when people act like people."

"The species of people reacts in certain ways due to our sin nature. We can become a new creation and not exhibit these kind of behaviors, but we are still living among others who do. We know from Paul's list that people can be angry, malicious liars. Our expectation that people in church, and especially in church leadership, won't be like the rest of us leads to many hurts and wounds. Remember, just because you're growing in self-control, goodness, kindness, and love doesn't mean every other believer is. Your growth might make you different than others, and it will hurt you if you don't accept that others around you are still spending their time just acting like people."

"Here's what you need to accept: when you're dealing with people, you will be hurt. You won't be able to undo what they did or unsay what they said. The only thing you are able to control is how others' actions or words impact you. This is difficult, but grasping this concept will transform your Christian walk."

"We're often told not to be offended, but we don't talk about the fact that we still experience offense. If you prepare yourself with the expectation that you'll encounter people who will act like people, which means they will do offensive things, it will be easier for you not take offense."

"Let's go a little deeper. In Matthew 16:24–25, Jesus tells us to take up our cross daily. Jesus was falsely accused and was punished for wrongdoing, but He didn't say anything against the people who acted against Him and who mocked and slandered His name. Instead He forgave them and asked God to forgive them because they didn't know what they were doing—they were just acting like people. Jesus took up His cross, took responsibility for things He hadn't done, and spoke forgiveness. Jesus accepted responsibility for sins He hadn't committed, and then He died and overcame death."

"That's the principle of salvation: although Jesus committed no sin, He accepted the punishment for sin from God. Taking up your cross means that you forgive your wrongdoers, ask God to forgive them, and then don't respond in like manner. It's your responsibility to forgive them even if they haven't asked for forgiveness. Approach the situation, take responsibility for being wrong even if you're not, and ask them something like, 'How can I make this right between us?' We're not perfect people, so there is probably an area in which you are also at fault in the offense, even if it's minor. Start your conversation there and ask for forgiveness for whatever part you played. This will help bring about restoration. It's often very difficult to take the blame for a situation, but when you choose to take up your cross, you have the opportunity to be Jesus to the other person."

"When you start practicing taking up your cross in day-to-day situations, you're going to make mistakes. But as you continue walking in peace, beholding God, growing in the fruit of the Spirit, and taking every thought captive, you will become a new creation. I won't lie to you: your death is involved in taking up your cross. You'll have to die when you're in the right and the other person is in the wrong and you still take the responsibility. But taking this action is a beautiful model of Jesus."

"Okay," Maria interrupted. "But what if I do all these things and nothing still changes in the relationship?"

"Consider how Jesus treats us," Obadiah responded. "When we enter into a relationship with Him, He takes on our sin. Do we immediately stop sinning? No, and that continues to hurt our relationship. But over time, hopefully, as we behold Christ, we become more like Him and less like malicious, sinful people. In a similar way, it's not up to you to control the timing of how things develop in your relationship. You have to die to yourself and let God work on the other person's heart."

Jerry agreed, "I learned a while back to ask God for the grace to forgive before going to have those tough kinds of conversations. I ask Him in advance to keep me from my human response and to be graceful and forgiving—and, to your point, Maria, I ask him to keep me from being discouraged if the whole process takes longer than I'd like."

"None of you are going to be perfect at this right away. It's going to seem unnatural and frustrating. And you're going to respond like a person yourself until you come to terms with the fact that you are constantly dealing with people who are just people. Learn now to take your thoughts captive and crucify any negative response, and then walk with God in peace. Any questions?"

"I have a question about the offense thing," I said. "Jesus offended people at times, and then they responded with offense, but Jesus wasn't wrong. So if our goal is to be like Jesus, how do we tell if other people's offense is based on us or them being in the wrong?"

"The answer is complicated and also easy," Obadiah said. "We usually don't perceive our own emotions accurately, which means it can be hard to tell if we're wrong. Others will respond from their own nature, and their response might be obviously wrong to you. But none of this really matters. Regardless of our circumstance, it's our responsibility to ask the Lord to open our offender's eyes and ears. Even if you know you aren't in the wrong, you should still take on the responsibility of being in the wrong. That's what Jesus ultimately did by going to the cross."

"Whoa," I whispered to Andre. "This is some radical living we're gearing up for."

He looked at me with big eyes, "You're telling me. Good stuff though."

Hayley said, "You know, the first time I read the Gospels, I was surprised that God showed mercy to the Pharisees. Christ gave them time and let God work on their hearts. That was really humbling to me. I thought, if God still wanted to see the Pharisees saved, He must still want me too."

I said, "You're right, Hayley. Jesus set a good example for us with the Pharisees. Even though they were in the wrong, He showed them grace."

Obadiah, clearly pleased at how we were all at the stage of encouraging one another in our discussions, said, "We've worked through a lot in this course that will give you a strong foundation to help you with taking up your cross. You have the tools you need. You just have to work now to get yourself into the right mindset and to let go of expecting right responses from others.

"I should point out that there isn't one, singular way to deal with people. I've been simplifying all of this for the sake of our discussion, but in practice, your response to the person who offended you will depend on what your relationship with that person looks like. If you are in a close relationship with someone and there is an offense, you need to find a way to apologize. If there is an offense with someone you may never see again, however, apologize to the Lord for anything you did wrong and ask Him to forgive the other person. Exercise wisdom and good judgment in each situation. What is guaranteed is that in every situation, you will have to die to being right."

"Everything I've been talking about hinges on the fruit of the Spirit we've been studying. When we spend time beholding the Lord, we can ask Him to help the other person, which gives us hope, which helps us to grow patience, which leads us to peace. When we get to the place where we're holistically applying all the fruit of the Spirit and taking up our cross daily, then we're modeling Jesus. We're giving the world a glimpse of what Jesus did for them and of how Jesus feels about them. And when we're being Jesus to someone else, our words will have His authority."

Obadiah paused for a moment to let what he said sink in, and then continued, "I want to transition slightly from discussing handling offenses to talk about how we personally deal with harsh words and accusations."

I got ready to take notes, because this was an area in my life on which I knew I needed to work.

"Before you're released from here," Obadiah continued, "you need to learn how to live with yourself. Most negative perceptions about ourselves are due to the harsh words of others. Those words are accusations against you, and unfortunately they're likely to increase as you grow in your prophetic calling. As you grow in character, others will be envious of what they see in you, and their jealously will provoke greater accusations. If you're being accused, the good news is that you're developing character. The bad news is that it's probably going to get worse as accusation is the only weapon the enemy has against us and he uses its full force. Before we talk about the accuser's role, I'd like to hear how each of you personally handle accusations."

"I get angry," Mike said. "And I tend to accuse the person who accused me with something even bigger."

"I think I just blame other people," Maria said. "Either that or I make excuses."

I was impressed with how vulnerable and honest we'd all gotten in our responses.

"Mine's obvious," Hayley said. "I cry."

"I'm more of a sulker," Catherine admitted. "I pout when I'm upset."

"That's a good short list," Obadiah said. "You all mentioned your external reactions to accusations, and I want to point out that most of us also internalize accusations. Oddly enough, there's usually a good reason for that. You see, the truth that frees us often offends us first. There is a key way to respond to accusations, and it's a little principle I call 'don't eat the artichoke.'"

"First fruitcake, now artichokes—we're on a real culinary adventure here!" Maria teased.

Smiling, Obadiah continued, "Do you all know what an artichoke looks like?" We all nodded. "Typically we only eat the tender heart at the center of the artichoke. If you tried to swallow an entire artichoke, the spiny projections on its exterior would get stuck in your throat and choke you.

"Stay with me as I connect this to accusations. So because Satan only has the weapon of accusation, he knows how to use it well, and he presents accusations to you as truth. You see, lies that are completely false are easy to recognize. Usually the lies we internalize are the ones that have a tiny element of truth to them. In other words, the enemy will see a shortcoming or sin in you and will take that small thing and blow it out of proportion. You then see the truth at the heart of the accusation—the tender heart—but swallow the whole lie that's with it, and it hurts you.

"For example, if you mishandle a situation and get angry with someone, the enemy will misconstrue the results and tell you that you don't love people at all and that you'll never be able to walk in the fruit of the Spirit. If you believe those lies, you'll eventually believe you're a bad Christian. Whereas in reality, you had a bad moment and operated out of anger instead of love. The enemy just took that one failure and applied it to all times and all situations. He will try to make your mistakes define you as a person. Remember the artichoke. Instead of swallowing the lies, peel them back and look for the kernel of truth at the center. Recognize that you will make mistakes but that you are not defined by the mistakes.

"In Matthew 5:11–12, Jesus says, 'Blessed are you when people insult you, persecute you and falsely say all kinds of evil against you because of me. Rejoice and be glad, because great is your reward in heaven, for in the same way they persecuted the prophets who were before you.' That clause—'in the same way'—is important. The prophets before you were persecuted when others said false things about them because of their commitment to Jesus. In other words, sometimes there isn't even a heart of truth to the accusation; it can be entirely malicious and false. So when an accusation comes, look for what might be true and repent of it.

"Have you all heard the phrase, 'to push someone's buttons'?" Again, we all nodded. Obadiah continued, "People who are close to you know the specific things to say or do to push your buttons and make you immediately angry. Take a few moments and think about what some of your buttons are. What are the things others say or do that get an immediate emotional rise out of you? Write down one or two."

We all wrote for a couple minutes. On my page were "Argue with a point I made that was obviously right" and "Criticize where I went to college."

"Now," Obadiah said, "ask the Lord to show you why those things are your buttons. What happened in your past, what was said about you or to you, what behavior did you experience that caused the thought process that made you develop this reaction? Ask the Lord to show you your earliest experience with those false words that were repeated about you."

I quieted myself and invited the Holy Spirit to speak to me. At once I realized why the two things I had written down were my buttons: my dad had once told me I wasn't smart enough to make it into a top university, and he always disagreed with me over things that seemed obviously right. He challenged me relentlessly when I was young. He and I would argue for hours about something that I clearly knew was right, though I had a hard time explaining why. He just didn't seem to see it the way I did or maybe he pretended not to, but I had to explain myself over and over in different ways. Often, when we finally stopped arguing, he would comment that I would have to get better at making my points or I would never get into a top university.

I was overwhelmed. I couldn't believe I'd been allowing those two things to be my anger triggers for so many years, and I was sad to discover that I was still bothered by my father's words all those years ago.

"Ask the Lord to peel away the lies surrounding those hot button issues," Obadiah said. "The thing that causes you to get angry stems out of something you believe about yourself. Look for the kernel of truth. Most likely there was something in that first lie or those first behaviors that was true about you. It may even have been a gift from God that the enemy wrapped in lies."

I thought back and realized I have always been certain of my choices and have been able to intuit future circumstances. Because of the intuition, I had a hard time explaining my points to others, especially my dad. I would just know what was right, and he would always try to make me explain why I believed the way I did. I see now that I was using a part of a natural prophetic gifting and I didn't know how to explain it. When I took the pressure to succeed off myself and only considered growing in my gifting, I felt free. I can also look back now and realize that the hard training he put me through with the arguing grew communication skills that paved the way for me to get into the university I wanted to attend and to do well there.

"Now, since we're all comfortable with one another, I'm not going to have you partner off. I'm just going to ask a couple of you to share the causes and effects of your hot button issues with the group," Obadiah said. "When someone shares, we're going to reaffirm the kernel of truth in the accusation and reinforce what is good. Then we will call out any gifts we see, and if there's something bad in the truth, we'll pray for release and bring freedom."

"I only wrote one down," Maria shared. "I wrote down that I get angry when people don't think I handle money well. I'm an 'artsy' type, so people always assume I can't balance a checkbook, and it bothers me. Anyway, when I asked the Lord to show me what the issue actually was, He revealed to me that I have a gift of mercy. He told me that I care for others and give sacrificially. But He warned me that sometimes I over operate in the gift and fail to provide for myself before providing for others."

"That's a beautiful gift," Catherine said. Then Catherine began to speak to Maria and to make declarations. "Maria, I encourage you in that gift. I declare that you are free from feelings of financial inadequacy. I bless you with opportunities to speak into others' lives to share your gift and with wisdom and accountability to stop overextending your means."

Maria looked at Catherine and nearly shouted, "Wow! I felt some power on that!"

Then Andre shared, "I think my button is my past. Whenever someone else brings it up, I get really defensive like there's something I need to protect. When I was just sharing, the Holy Spirit showed me that I feel inferior in the church sometimes because I have this long history of very visible sin."

I immediately began declaring for Andre, "Andre, the Lord knows your true identity and He speaks that identity to you. I now declare that you are free from the wounds and shame of the past, and your story will bring about life change for others." And then I continued a little beyond myself. I spoke directly to Andre. "I will personally continue to remind you of that truth in your life, Andre, and I will remind you of who you are to God." When I finished, I saw Andre's eyes were moist.

"Thanks, man," he said.

Obadiah said, "Several of you are experiencing healing today, and the others of you will experience it this week as you work through your buttons. When you do discover the kernel of truth in the accusation, know that there are two ways to respond to it. If the kernel is a sin, repent. Stop doing the sin and start doing the right thing. If the kernel is not built around a sin but instead is built around the misuse of a gift or something else that got twisted, ask God to bring the truth and to redeem the good from the bad."

Placing the notebook he was holding aside, Obadiah said, "I think we could all use a moment to stretch and get something to drink. Meet back in five?"

Overwhelmed with the weight of the last week and all we were learning, I immediately agreed and went for more coffee. Mike met me at the coffee station and said, "Hey, Jason, if I don't get another chance to say it, I wanted to let you know how much I appreciated your insight during this class."

"Wow, thanks," I said. "I'm humbled by that comment because I didn't feel like I said much of value. I really appreciated what you offered, though." With that Mike patted me on the back and walked back to his chair, and I stood smiling, glad to have been appreciated.

Finally I made my way back to the group who all looked eager to hear what was next.

REVELATIONS OF GOD'S MYSTERIES

"In an earlier week," Obadiah said, "we talked about being stewards of the mysteries of God. As you begin to move prophetically, you're going to move to even higher levels of revelation, and your words will have even greater clarity, precision, and effect. You're suddenly going to know things about a variety of people. You're going to know what corrections need to take place, and you're going to be aware of future events. It might feel a little like information overload. So I want to talk about a biblical model for handling revelation. I've identified three different modes of revelation."

Obadiah stood and wrote this list on the white board:

1. Timing: when to give a word at the right time

2. Delivery: how to give a word so it has the most impact

3. Disclosure: who to give the word to, if at all

Then Obadiah put the marker down and said, "I want to look at some biblical examples of each of these kinds of revelations. We'll start with timing. John 6:64 tells us that Jesus knew Judas was His betrayer, yet He kept it a secret. We don't know why exactly, but perhaps Jesus was giving Judas time to overcome greed. If that's the case, it's encouraging because it means that if we're having a hard time overcoming something, God will allow us the chance to change. Do any of you have another example of timing in revelation?"

"Simeon had a prophetic word but waited to declare it until he saw Jesus," Mike said.

Jerry added, "And John was told to seal up the book of Revelation until the right time."

"Good," Obadiah said. "Those are both great examples when timing played an important role. Now let's talk about delivery. I'll start with an example again to get us rolling. Consider when Jesus stopped the crowd from stoning the woman who had been caught in adultery. In the midst of a heated situation, He stooped and wrote in the sand. No one really knows what He wrote, but we know He either wrote something important or He didn't. If it wasn't important, then He was just using time, maybe waiting to hear from God on how to respond. If it was something important, like perhaps the sins of others watching, Jesus kept from directly accusing anyone. Christ's delivery softened the revelation for the others."

"Jesus also gives us a good example with the Samaritan woman at the well," Hayley said. "He allowed her to perceive that He was a prophet, and then He shared things with her without directly stating who He was until she ultimately determined that He was the Messiah."

"Jesus did that several times in regard to people asking Him about being the Messiah," Jerry said. "When John asked Jesus if He was the Messiah, Jesus didn't respond with a simple yes answer. Instead, He responded with a list of ways He had fulfilled Old Testament prophecies about the Messiah. This was a more impactful, very personal revelation for John as it allowed him to apply the teachings he'd learned and the prophecies he himself had spoken to see for himself that yes, Christ was the Messiah."

"You barely need me to teach you anymore," Obadiah encouraged. "I'm pleased to see how quickly you're coming up with all these examples. Does anyone have anything for disclosure?"

"I do," Andre said, clearly pleased that he had a response ready. "Paul wrote an enormous body of work, yet all his letters only contained a small part of what God had revealed to him. On top of that, he waited for three years before even sharing that part, and he never revealed the entirety. That had to take some discipline!"

"That's a good example, Andre," Obadiah said. "Paul was careful with how and when he disclosed what God had told him. Who has another example?"

"I'm thinking about how Jesus shared more with his disciples than He did with His general followers," Maria said. "Like He often took time after teaching to explain His proverbs to His disciples and to go deeper with the teaching. That means Jesus was careful about what He was disclosing and to whom."

"Good," Obadiah said. "The point of paying attention to disclosure is so you don't cast pearls of wisdom before swine who won't understand, who aren't ready to hear, or worse, who don't want to listen.

"One of the most important things to remember about most revelation you'll receive, especially revelation about how things should be, is that typically it isn't your problem to solve. This tends to be very hard for prophetic people. Just because God tells you something and you know it's going to happen doesn't mean you're responsible to see it through. You need to stay in your realm of authority.

"Your realm of authority is four-fold. The first place you have authority to speak is your immediate family. That said, you still want to use some caution concerning your delivery here because your family won't appreciate constant correction from the 'family' prophet. The second place where you have authority is with your close friends with whom you have a history of mutual trust and dialogue. These are the people who you trust with your deepest secrets, and they trust you with theirs. You also have authority with people who recognize you as their pastor. Take note that these people aren't necessarily the people you want to pastor; they're the ones who see you as their pastor. There should be a mutual recognition that the person has asked you to speak into his or her life. The fourth and final area you have authority is at times when people outright ask you to tell them what the Lord is showing you for them. Again, you want to use caution and wisdom here. Many of these people do not mean what they're saying. What they actually want to communicate is that they have planned to do something and they want to hear that the Lord is in agreement with it. If you come to them with something different, they may not receive it well.

"A good rule for anything you speak prophetically is that it's your responsibility to leave people better than when you found them. If you can't leave people better, don't do anything with the revelation. There are some things you'll never share; some things God wants you to pray about, and some things God just wants to share with you because you're His friend. It says in Amos that the Lord does nothing on the earth without first telling His friends the prophets. When you spend time with God every day, you become His friend, and He'll chat with you. He'll tell you things you don't need to do anything with."

"I've never considered that before," Catherine said. "I love the idea of chatting with God for talking's sake, just to share truths and secrets with one another."

"That's what beholding is all about," Obadiah said. "Now, if no one has any questions, I want to recap a few thoughts on stewarding the mysteries of God."

We all looked expectantly at him, so he continued. "One of the most dangerous things you can do is to believe that every thought that passes through your head is the voice of God. As we discussed earlier, you need to remember to take every thought captive.

"The next way to steward the mystery is to pay attention to your emotions, with God's character in mind. For example, if you feel angry, ask yourself if you're feeling a righteous anger or if you just want revenge? Examine your motives. Another emotion to watch out for is selfish ambition versus regular ambition. If you are selfishly motivated, you'll use "I/me" language and will be concerned with how the bottom line will affect you. Pay attention to what happens in your heart when someone else who is doing a good work gains recognition. Are you pleased for them, or are you critical? If you feel like you want to be the one to bring God glory, that's selfish ambition. Do you remember the first conversation I had with each of you? Do you remember what I said you had been chosen to be?"

The phrase had been on constant repeat in my head for the past several weeks. How could I have forgotten it? I went to say it, but Maria beat me to the punch, reciting word-for-word what Obadiah had spoken to me. "You said I was called to be 'one of the many.'"

"Exactly," Obadiah said. "So if any of you start thinking you're the only one, you're no longer functioning under your calling, which is to be one of many.

"Finally, the last emotion to check is whether you're exhibiting love or just tolerance. Loving people means calling them out if they're doing something wrong, within your realm of authority. It's recognizing what might be destroying them and telling them to stop. While you have to love them through a hard situation, you don't have to be a helper or an enabler."

After taking a moment to ask the Holy Spirit to help me sort through my emotions, I flipped back through my notes and saw all the places I'd grown. As I turned my notebook to read one of my marginal notes, I suddenly realized I had tuned Obadiah out.

When I faded back in, Obadiah was saying, "It's up to you to decide what your future harvest will be. If a farmer decides he wants to sell wheat in the market, he works to build up a good harvest of wheat. He doesn't just wait for God to initiate the sales; he plants the seeds. We have to do the same or, like the farmer, we'll end up with a life of weeds and unfulfilled potential. You get what you plant."

"We know that there's a great spiritual harvest coming. Before we see God's great harvest of souls, we'll see the harvest of what we have sown ourselves. Never stop sowing. And once you define your heart's desire, try to sow it in other people. Bless another person with the thing that you want, and if they get that harvest, you get it too.

"Verses 1 and 6 of Ecclesiastes 11 say, 'Ship your grain across the sea; after many days you may receive a return.... Sow your seed in the morning, and at evening let your hands not be idle, for you do not know which will succeed, whether this or that, or whether both will do equally well.' A harvest is coming of all the good and bad seed we've sown, so we want to bless the good seed and curse the bad. For example, if you are envious, you should repent and you should curse the crop of whatever that envy might have sown. We're tight on time, but this week I want you to write down a crop you want to see wither on the vine in your life, and ask the Lord to spoil the harvest of that seed."

I made note of the activity and then programmed a time to do it into my calendar. I was grateful to have a part of the class extend into my week.

Obadiah paused and looked at the clock. He glanced around the room at each of us, and then said, "I believe you have what you need." With that, he stood up with finality.

Obadiah walked over to Michael who was sitting at one end of our semicircle. As he approached, Michael also stood up. Obadiah placed his right hand on Michael's forehead and rested his left hand lightly on Michael's back to support him. He spoke out loud, "Michael, I proclaim an anointing is upon you to become a prophet who will play a role in the current day transformation."

He then spoke something softly into Michael's ear. Michael looked a little emotional, but he just cleared his throat, shook Obadiah's hand, and sat back down.

Next Obadiah moved to Catherine who stood in turn, and he did the exact same thing—one hand on the forehead and one on the back for support, the audible declaration, and a whispered word just to her. Then Obadiah moved around the room to each of us.

When it was my turn, I could see a glistening in Obadiah's eyes that spoke many thoughts. He was sad to see us depart. I believe he had grown as fond of us as we had of him. He was excited to see that we were about to step into our new adventure, and there was a hopeful fire in his eyes, behind the glistening. But at a deeper level, it felt like Obadiah was looking through us and into our future where he saw the tests we would face and the victories we would achieve. He was simultaneously proud of us and concerned for our wellbeing.

I will never forget the words he whispered into my ears. "You are a true son of Issachar. You will understand the times and know what to do. You will carry the burdens for many brothers and sisters, and you will carry the presence of Jesus everywhere you go. You will draw out the abundance of the seas and the hidden treasure of the sand. You will live in the favor of the Lord and will become a mighty man of valor. You will not rely on your opinions or the opinions of others, but you will seek the truth of God. Transformation will be your harvest."

So many memories, thoughts, and emotions rushed through me. I wondered if he would continue to pray for me. I felt that I had made—and lost—a best friend and trusted confidant. The weight of what it would mean to walk out the door of the cave hit me and a soberness came over me. I looked around the room and could tell everyone was having a similar experience. Catherine was wiping her eyes with a tissue. Maria was openly sobbing. Hayley was quiet and pensive, and I knew she would need alone time for the remainder of the day. Michael was staring off as if watching something playing out in the distant future. Jerry was sitting with his eyes closed and a slight smile on his face. Andre was sitting in his chair, breathing hard, and staring at the ground between his feet. I realized the room was getting blurry, and I wiped the tears from my eyes and took a few deep breaths.

Obadiah spoke again to the group. "It has been an honor getting to know each of you over the past few weeks. I want each of you to know that I am encouraged by what, and who, I see before me now. You have become like sons and daughters to me, and seeing this time come to an end holds a certain degree of sadness. I will miss each of you. I love you, and I really like each one of you." He smiled at his final joke, sighed, and then turned and walked toward the door. Before any of us could say anything or stop him, he disappeared.

The rest of us stayed for a bit to reminisce about the course and talk about Obadiah's abrupt exit. Then we cleaned up the room and, one-by-one as if it was a rite of passage, we walked out the door of the cave. The familiar brightness and darkness made me wonder if I was still being dematerialized as I exited. I walked quietly up the pathway, waved one last goodbye to those who remained, and pulled out of the parking lot, wondering if I would ever see Obadiah again.

EPILOGUE: ONE YEAR LATER...

The past year of training has been incredible. At first we were stunned that Obadiah would walk out so suddenly without giving us a chance to say goodbye, but then we realized that he had stepped into our lives just as abruptly. A couple of us went back to the cave in case he might be there, and not only could we not find him, we couldn't even find the mouth of the cave.

For the first few weeks, we were uncertain as to what to do. Then Mike suggested that we continue to periodically meet as a group. We eventually chose to meet once per month to share our experiences and to encourage each other. Each month we gather and share what we've been doing and how it is going, and then we pray and declare truth on behalf of one another. Scripture says that wherever two or more agree on anything it will be done, and we are seeing that truth on a monthly basis.

Over the months, we have matured. Andre is no longer the dark, closed, skeptical man he was when we first met him. He is now a stable, caring man who desires to see others pulled from darkness. He has been looking up many of his old friends and has been speaking into their lives prophetically. In the past year, he has brought eight of his old crew into the kingdom and has seen another dozen or so decide to follow Jesus while they finish their jail time. As a result, the crime rate in his old area of town has dropped and violent crime is almost non-existent.

Maria, if anything, has become more outgoing and more fun loving. She teamed up with a couple others in her church community to start an afterschool program to help at-risk kids with their homework and more. At first Maria was hesitant to lead in this way, but with the support from our little group, she recognized that this was a part of her calling and her purpose. And what a purpose it has been! Hundreds of kids have discovered God's love for them, and Maria has had the opportunity to speak wonderful things into their futures. One girl who graduated last year has already seen what Maria prophesied come to pass, transitioning from a questionable future into a premed program at one of our country's top universities. Others have discovered hope and are approaching life with a new perspective. The schools in our area have taken notice and have come to examine what makes Maria's program so effective. We're all looking forward to the huge kingdom impact all these kids are going to have because of specific, encouraging truths Maria has spoken into their lives.

Hayley is still a quiet, studious seeker of practical application. But she has learned to embrace new concepts and walk in a peace that releases miracles in and around her. She has been practicing and applying her desire to see people healed and has seen many creative miracles in recent months. She doesn't always visit hospitals. Most of the people she's healed are people she has met on the street and prayed for right away. She has seen people receive hearing, she saw one person throw away his walking cane after having his eyesight restored from total blindness, and she has increased her success in praying for the healing of cancer. She has found that praying for cancer patients outside the hospital seems to work best, but she says she doesn't know why. We tease her that she has found an alternative to government healthcare.

The transformation that began in Mike's workplace during our months in our cave sessions ended up snowballing into something truly amazing. After sealing the deal he had almost lost with that big client, Mike received more work proposals than he could keep up with. His boss was incredibly impressed, so when he retired last winter, he left the company to Mike, naming him as the new CEO. Instead of getting bogged down by work, Mike committed to spending a set amount of time with God and with his family each day and then gave the rest to the office. As a result, he has seen incredible provision. The company has doubled in size in just six short months, and Mike has meetings scheduled with several other organizations to explain how to succeed in business. He keeps saying he can't wait to stand in front of a room of some of the nation's top execs and tell them about a kingdom approach to business and managing a company according to the fruit of the Spirit!

We learned a lot more about Catherine over the past year. She shared how she'd transformed from being an insecure mother and a self-proclaimed starving artist (although Mike pointed out he'd never let her starve) into a person who expresses and releases creativity that transforms herself, her family, and all those who interact with her art. She continued her practice of meeting with the Lord before painting and finding a place of peace before committing anything to the canvas, and she discovered that her work began resonating with others. One couple told her that shortly after they'd purchased one of her pieces and hung it in their living room, their family had found a new calmness in that space. They contacted her and bought pieces for every room in their house! While thankful for the income from all the new orders, Catherine always says that the most important thing to her is that she finally feels like she's using her gift to communicate for the Lord and that it has given her a new confidence as a mom, an artist, and a human.

Jerry continues to show to all of us the power of maturity and wisdom. Not one to accept stereotypes, he is living proof that no one is ever "too old for ministry." Even though Jerry has been touring around the country, preaching and sharing comfort and hope with new generations, he always makes sure to be back for our monthly meetings. Through the power of Jerry's words spoken in the Spirit, relationships have been restored, financial breakthroughs have occurred, people have been healed, and several new people have stepped into a prophetic calling. We joke with Jerry that if he doesn't stop growing in prophetic maturity, he's going to turn into Obadiah. Of course, that wouldn't be a bad thing as the world could certainly use more Obadiahs.

As for me, I am having more fun than I ever did at my old company. Having my own company has allowed me to work as a consultant directly with executives and business owners. I'm still loving my mornings spent talking to Jesus, and as a result, favor has transformed my life. It hasn't always been easy making kingdom decisions and taking up my cross daily, but I've seen miraculous results. My relationship with my wife has improved tenfold, and we've even had other couples approach us to counsel them and share "the secret" of what makes our marriage so great. A few months after I worked through my doubts and fears regarding the prophecy we'd received about having a child, we found out my wife was pregnant. I'm excited to announce that I'm going to be a father this year! In addition to things going well at home, I've also seen more prolific glimpses into the future similar to what I had earlier, and I've been able to speak several prophetic warnings that have transformed many lives for the better. I know God is going to build me in this area as I live in His flow.

I also have a feeling our time with Obadiah hasn't come to an end. I've begun having dreams and visions of a densely wooded, mossy area. Although the visions have come in fragments—short glimpses, really—each time I've been able to identify something new about the place. There is a small creek somewhere nearby. There is a stone path. There is a strong scent of pine. While we haven't talked about it overtly in our group, others have also hinted they think the next level of our training is coming. And last night, a deep, resonating voice in my dream called me a "true son of Issachar" and mentioned a second cave. When I woke up, I immediately identified the voice as Obadiah's. I'm feeling the same way I felt when Obadiah called me to the first cave—intrigued, excited, and a little nervous. But this time, I'm ready for the next level.

ABOUT THE AUTHOR

Joe Shrewsbury is an elder in the gate of the prophetic. He has been instrumental in opening the realm of a practical, hands-on prophetic ministry and lifestyle to thousands of people for over fifteen years through specialized equipping classes and seminars, coaching, mentoring, and teaching. Joe personally applies prophetic insight in the marketplace as a Digital Business Architect and Organizational Consultant, and through Prophetic Mastermind groups. Joe and his wife, Nancy, live in Charlotte, NC, with their three children.

Made in the USA
San Bernardino, CA
16 April 2018